A THEORETICAL APPROACH
TO RURAL LAND-USE PATTERNS

To
Charles L. Hall
my grandfather

A THEORETICAL APPROACH TO RURAL LAND-USE PATTERNS

WILLIAM C FOUND

EDWARD ARNOLD

First published 1971 by
Edward Arnold (Publishers) Ltd
41 Maddox Street, London W1R 0AN

SBN: 0 7131 5599 X

Printed in Great Britain by
Butler & Tanner Ltd
Frome and London

CONTENTS

PREFACE

Rural land-use patterns refer to the geometrical groupings of fields and larger land-use areas at the farm, regional or interregional levels. They are an aspect of the earth's surface which interests geographers, land economists, anthropologists, ecologists, and anyone concerned with the planning of land resource use. They can be seen to reflect an area's natural endowments, such as soil quality or climate; but also some of its less tangible assets, such as the economic structure, culture, and aspirations of its people. Being so complex, land-use patterns are often difficult to analyse and understand, so that the student requires a set of theories and simplifying principles which can help him visualize order out of apparent chaos. Introduction to such a theoretical framework is the function of this volume.

The main point of the book is that land-use patterns reflect the decisions of thousands of individuals and groups, and that an understanding of the patterns can be achieved only by analysing the decision-making process. A considerable body of theory has been developed for this purpose, ranging from the normative models of traditional economics to the more recent attempts to formulate concepts of man's psychological behaviour. These approaches will be examined more or less in historical sequence, beginning with economic theory based on the writings of such contributors as Heinrich von Thünen, David Ricardo, Alfred Marshall, and more recent American agricultural economists, who include R. T. Ely, J. D. Black, E. O. Heady, and E. S. Dunn. Linear programming and other operational research techniques will also be introduced to permit discussion of spatial models which have grown out of earlier economic formulations. Later will come a critical evaluation of the real-world relevance of traditional economic theory, followed by an examination of models which attempt to relax the rigorous, unrealistic assumptions regarding man's behaviour.

This book is not intended to introduce the student to the entire field of rural geography—only to theoretical aspects which centre on land-use decision making. All of the models discussed should improve understanding of certain land-use situations, although they provide, at best, partial explanations of the real world. Attempts to apply the models in real life are not dealt with at length except to discuss the logical implication of such procedures. At the same time, the student will be referred to numerous empirical analyses, some of which should be read to complement this book's approach and to permit the student to reach his own conclusions about the value of alternative theoretical models. The specific purpose of this volume is to help fill a gap which is seen as critical—the gap between descriptive studies, which the student can readily understand, and the more advanced theoretical papers which, although relevant, are often beyond the grasp of undergraduate university students without special training in economics, mathematics or psychology. In preparing the text it has been assumed that the reader will have no special background other than an interest in land use and human behaviour.

The original inspiration to prepare this volume came from David Harvey's 1966 review paper 'Theoretical Concepts and the Analysis of Agricultural Land Use Patterns in Geography'.[1] Later, I received additional encouragement from David Harvey, and I would like to thank him for it. My sincerest appreciation also goes to a number of other people: to David Morley and Dale Dilamarter, who have offered many suggestions, but who are in no way responsible for any shortcomings in the text; to Steven Gribble, who helped prepare the computer programs used in the numerical examples; to my classes at McMaster and York Universities, with whom many of the presentations were formulated; and to Denyse Chapman and Deanna Pearson, who painstakingly saw the manuscript through its entire preparation. Finally, thanks to Karen and Trevor, who have endured an abnormal home life during the past few months.

W. C. F   Toronto, Ontario
November, 1970

General Reading

The following provide useful overviews of the development of theoretical concepts related to rural land-use patterns. Complete publication information for each reference is listed at the conclusion of the book.

CLAWSON, M. 1963: Introduction to *Economics of land use.*
GALBRAITH, J. D. 1963: *John D. Black: a portrait.*
GROVES, H. M. 1969: *Richard T. Ely: an appreciation.*
HARVEY, D. W. 1966: *Theoretical concepts and the analysis of agricultural land-use patterns in geography.*
HENSHALL, Janet D. 1967: *Models of agricultural activity.*
JOHNSON, S. E., and BACHMAN, K. L. 1963: Introduction to *Development of production economics in agriculture.*
MCCARTY, H. H. 1954: *Agricultural geography.*
REEDS, L. G. 1964: *Agricultural geography: progress and prospects.*
SALTER, L. A. JR. 1948: *A critical review of research in land economics.*
SCHULTZ, T. W. 1951: *A framework for land economics—the long view.*
TAYLOR, H. C., and ANNE D. 1952: *The story of agricultural economics in the United States, 1840–1932.*
WIECKING, E. H. 1950: *Land economics research in retrospect and prospect.*

[1] David Harvey, 1966: Theoretical concepts and the analysis of agricultural land use patterns in geography. *Annals of the Association of American Geographers,* **56**(2), 361–74.

1 DEMAND, SUPPLY, AND PRICE

Market transactions—Demand and supply—Price determination—Elasticity—
Price elasticity of demand, total revenue, and acreage—Hypothetical problem—
Further Reading

A basic premise of traditional economic theory is that the motivating force behind men's actions is the attempt to maximize income. To the farmer, then, the way in which a particular land use contributes to his income is vital; and the price he receives for the product associated with the land use is of first importance. This chapter is concerned with the traditional concepts of how prices are determined in a free enterprise system, and how prices interrelate with the actions of producers and consumers.

Market transactions

For any agricultural product to have a price, it must have a market, i.e. someone must be willing to purchase it. The term 'market' is used very broadly in discussions about the saleability of a product, often in a non-spatial sense. But one must remember that all markets or sites where exchanges occur have a location. Whether transactions result from face-to-face bargaining between producer and consumer in a small rural village or from teletype communication through several 'middle men', the location of the exchange is relevant to land-use decision-making. Consequently, 'market' will be used in this book in its more limited, location-orientated sense.

Prices determined at markets depend on the types and numbers of buyers and sellers, among other things. Traditionally, economists have classified the types of competition encountered in the market on the basis of the relative positions of individual buyers and sellers. In the ideal case of *pure competition* there are many producers acting independently, yet all trying to sell the same item with the same quality (i.e. their products are undifferentiated); and they are so numerous that no one seller acting alone can exert a perceptible influence on the price. In the case of *monopolistic competition,* conditions are the same as for pure competition except that the products offered by the sellers differ somewhat in quality. *Perfect competition* is like pure competition with the added feature that all sellers and buyers have complete information about all quantities offered for sale or purchased and the prices involved in any transactions. In *oligopolistic competition* there are relatively few sellers; and, in the case of a *monopoly*, there is only one.

As a very general trend one could hypothesize that the smaller the number of buyers or sellers, the easier it will be for them to cooperate and effect a price favourable to them. In the most exaggerated cases one could allude to a single producer, such as a tea company operating under a monopoly during the Colonial era; or a single buyer, as when all banana farmers must sell their crop to the company which sends the only boat to pick up the crop.

At present, most farmers in countries with some form of free enterprise economy tend to find themselves in markets as pure competitors, at least for some of their products. The reason for this is partly historical, as many past societies tried to distribute farm land in fairly equal quantities to a great many persons. More recently, governments in some of the most highly developed countries have enacted legislation to help preserve 'the small family farm'. Consequently, some of the most relevant theory in understanding present farming practices is concerned with pure competition, and it will be emphasized in the following portions of this book.

Demand and supply

Assume that a number of farms operated by 'pure competitors' surrounds a town X in which buyers purchase all the products sold from the farms, i.e. all demand for the products is located in the town. Under these conditions traditional economic theory suggests that the quantity of a product purchased in the town depends, all other things equal, on its price. Specifically, the higher the price, the lesser the quantity purchased in a given time period, either because fewer buyers will purchase the product or because individual consumers will purchase lesser quantities. This concept, sometimes referred to as the *law of demand*, can be illustrated as in Fig. 1.1. DD is a continuous line which represents the *demand* for a given product (wheat, for example) in town X. It indicates the complete schedule of quantities of wheat which will be purchased at corresponding prices in time T. Movement along the schedule (e.g. from A to B) is called a *change in quantity demanded*. A *change in demand*, on the other hand, would involve movement of the entire demand schedule (e.g. the increase in demand from DD to D'D'). Such a change could result from changes in the population of the town, the average income of the people, the prices of other products which could be used as substitutes for wheat, expectations about the future prices of wheat or substitutes for it, or the personal preferences of the consumers, which could be affected by advertising.

Similar to the concept of demand for a product by consumers is the concept of supply of a product by farmers. It has been theorized that farmers tend to increase the quantity of a product brought to the market as the price rises, all other things being equal. This trend, inverse to that described by the *law of demand*, could be called the *law of supply*. It is derived from the tendency of some farmers, following an increase in the price of a product, to switch to that type of production, or for farmers already engaged in that enterprise to produce larger quantities. The aggregate supply schedule for wheat for our town, for example, could be illustrated as in Fig. 1.1. SS represents all combinations of the prices and quantities

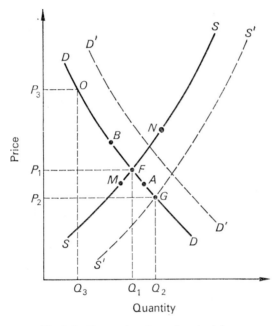

Fig. 1.1 : Demand and supply schedules

supplied for wheat by farmers in the surrounding district during time *T*. Movement from M to N along the schedule would represent a *change in quantity supplied*, while movement of the entire schedule from SS to S'S' would represent a *change in supply*. Such a change could result from changes in the cost of production of wheat (e.g. through technological change) so that the farmers' profit margin was altered, changes in any aspect of other types of farm production (e.g. discovery of more profitable alternative crops), changes in farmers' expectations about future prices and costs, or a change in the number of farmers or the acreage of farm land in the area.

Note that the demand and supply schedules in our hypothetical example are represented by almost continuous straight lines. One should appreciate the enormity of the assumptions required for this highly generalized and simple characterization. These shapes and slopes might vary greatly from reality for a given type of production and given groups of consumers and producers. In many cases it might even be impossible to obtain enough data to determine the general shape of the demand or supply schedules, let alone obtain continuous data with which to construct curves. The curves in Fig. 1.1 describe what classical economists have concluded to be the most general trend, and are purposefully non-specific in shape.

Price determination

If supply and demand schedules occupy a common point on a diagram such as Fig. 1.1, which means that a price and corresponding quantity satisfy both producers and consumers, then that point indicates the market price and the quantity brought to the market and sold during the relevant time period. The market is said to be *cleared* under these conditions. In our hypothetical example, F, the intersection of DD and SS, indicates that Q_1 units of wheat will be brought to town X and sold at price P_1 during time T. One must assume, of course, that somehow farmers respond perfectly to the market conditions to produce just the right amount of wheat, and that no changes occur to upset the market equilibrium. The feasibility and mechanism of such farmer response will be considered further in later chapters.

Diagrams like Fig. 1.1 are useful in analysing changes in price and quantity sold through time. Suppose, for example, that supply changes to S'S'. A new equilibrium point is established at G, and Q_2 units of wheat are produced and sold at price P_2 during time T. Suppose further that in a later time period a natural catastrophe limits the quantity of production to Q_3. The price rises to P_3, and market equilibrium has been destroyed since O does not mark the intersection of the demand and relevant supply schedules.

Elasticity

Elasticity refers to the change in the *quantity demanded* or *quantity supplied* of a product associated with the change in some related variable. Several types of elasticity measures have been defined, the most common of which will be considered here.

One of the most important concepts in understanding rural land-use patterns, farm marketing procedures, rural income, or other related phenomena is *price elasticity of demand*. It refers to the ratio of the percentage change in quantity demanded to the corresponding percentage change in price along a given demand schedule. Perhaps the most common of the several formulas developed to measure price elasticity of demand is

$$E_p = \frac{(Q_1 - Q_2)/(Q_1 + Q_2)}{(P_1 - P_2)/(P_1 + P_2)},$$

where P_1, P_2, Q_1 and Q_2 correspond to prices and quantities at two points on a demand schedule, as illustrated in Fig. 1.2.[1] If the percentage price change is greater than the percentage change on quantity demanded, conditions are said to be *price inelastic*; if the percentage change in quantity exceeds that in price, conditions are *price elastic*; if the percentage changes are equal, the demand schedule has *unit elasticity* between the relevant points. For the formula above, the value of the ratio will be $E_p < -1\cdot0$ if demand is price elastic, $E_p = -1\cdot0$ for unit elasticity, and $0 < E_p < -1\cdot0$ for price inelastic conditions. Note that price elasticity can change between different points on a given schedule. It is possible that one schedule can

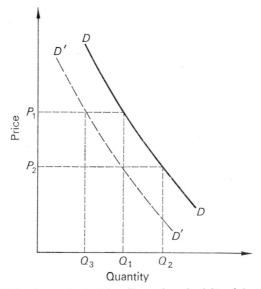

Fig. 1.2: Demand schedules, illustrating elasticity of demand

exhibit price elasticity, inelasticity, or unit elasticity between different pairs of points. This could be true of a schedule which forms a noticeable curve.

A number of elasticity indexes have been defined to measure changes in quantity demanded resulting from shifts in the entire demand schedule. *Cross elasticity of demand* measures the change in quantity demanded of a product whose price remains unchanged as the price of another product changes. Suppose, for example, that the product under consideration is wheat, and the 'other' product is rye. If rye can be used as a substitute for wheat, a decrease in the price of rye can cause a decrease in the

[1] C. E. Bishop and W. D. Toussaint, 1958: *Introduction to agricultural economic analysis* (New York) 189.

quantity demanded of wheat, assuming that the price of wheat remains unchanged. Buyers would probably tend to switch to the cheaper grain. Fig. 1.2 illustrates this situation. DD represents the original demand for wheat, and D'D' shows the new schedule after a drop in the price of rye. If the original quantity demanded of wheat was Q_1 at price P_1, the new quantity will be Q_3 at the same price. In this case the cross elasticity of demand would be positive. Similar indexes of elasticity are *price elasticity of income*, which measures the change in quantity demanded (without a price change) associated with a change in the total income of the consumers; and *price elasticity of expenditure*, which relates changes in quantity demanded (again, without a price change) to changes in the total expenditure of consumers. Formulas of the same type as that indicated for price elasticity of demand can be used to measure the other elasticity indexes.

Just as one can measure changes in quantity demanded along or between demand schedules, one can measure changes in quantity supplied along or between supply schedules. A number of elasticity indexes like those described for demand have been devised for this purpose.

Price elasticity of demand, total revenue, and acreage

If the demand for a product is known, one can easily calculate the total revenue (gross income) that farmers in the aggregate would receive if different quantities were sold. Total revenue is the product of the quantity sold times the respective price per unit. Greater quantities sold do not necessarily lead to greater incomes, a fact which pure competitors often fail to realize. If the demand for the product is price elastic, then larger quantities sold bring prices which show a lesser percentage decrease than the percentage increase in quantity, and larger sale volumes lead to higher total revenue. If demand exhibits unit price elasticity, total revenue remains unchanged with differences in quantity and price. If, however, demand is price inelastic, then greater quantities sold lead to lower prices and lower total revenue. Fig. 1.3 illustrates these trends for a demand schedule with varying price elasticity.

Demand for many agricultural items is price inelastic. Fairly fixed quantities of basic foods, for example, are required by consumers. If excess quantities are marketed, the price falls rapidly. If scarcity of the item occurs consumers will pay very high prices to procure one of life's necessities. Under these conditions, farmers actually gain larger incomes when production is reduced. This relationship seems to be difficult for many farmers to understand. To the individual farmer operating under pure competition, demand for his product seems to be perfectly elastic. No matter how much he markets, he produces such a small portion of the total volume that he can exert no perceptible influence on the price. The best way for him to increase his total revenue is to produce as much as possible. Looking at the aggregate quantity supplied, however, the sum of all farmers' production has a great influence on the price. In some instances, producers' associations or governments have realized that overproduction has led to low farm incomes and product surpluses, and attempts have been made to control production in order to increase total

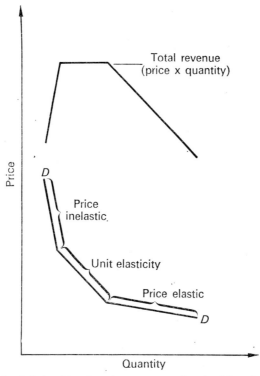

Fig. 1.3: Relationship of total revenue to price elasticity of demand

revenue. Pure competitors are coerced into cooperating and behaving more like a monopoly. Tobacco farmers in Canada and the United States are classic examples. They attempt to maximize their total revenue by restricting output through acreage quotas. Many other examples can be cited where attempts at production control have failed. The attempt to control U.S. wheat production in the early 1960s is one.

Hypothetical problem

Located deep in a mid-latitude desert is the oasis of Shish-ka-pur, an area which includes an important urban centre (Shish-ka-pur City) and a surrounding farming area of 5,000 acres (100 50-acre farms). All of the carrots consumed in Shish-ka-pur City are produced on the oasis, and all of the carrots produced on the oasis are sold in the city for local consumption. Carrot production is split equally among the 100 farms.

Table 1.1 indicates the demand for carrots in Shish-ka-pur City during one year, and Table 1.2 indicates the supply of carrots by oasis farmers during the same time period. The average carrot yield is 760 boxes per acre per year.

Questions

1 Assuming market equilibrium and pure competition among carrot producers, what will be the carrot production and acreage on the oasis farms?

2 Suppose that instead of operating independently, the farmers in the oasis form a Carrot Producers' Association which restricts carrot production to maximize farm income. A decision is made to restrict production through acreage quotas. If all producers share production equally, what will be the size of each farmer's acreage quota?

3 Suppose that the cross elasticity of demand between carrots and celery as measured by a formula of the type described in the section on *elasticity* is +0·405. If the price of celery rises from $2.00 to $3.00 per box, how will this affect the quantity and acreage of carrots produced?

Table 1.1 : Demand for carrots in Shish-ka-pur
City during one year

quantity demanded (*boxes*)	price per box
100,000	$5.00
110,000	4.70
120,000	4.50
130,000	4.20
140,000	3.80
150,000	3.50
160,000	3.20
170,000	2.90
180,000	2.60

Table 1.2 : Aggregate supply schedule for
carrots produced by farmers in the oasis of
Shish-ka-pur during one year

quantity supplied (*boxes*)	price per box
150,000	$2.45
160,000	2.70
170,000	2.90
180,000	3.15
190,000	3.35
200,000	3.65
210,000	4.00
220,000	4.30
230,000	4.55

Solutions:

1 Examination of the demand and supply schedules indicates that market equilibrium is achieved only with 170,000 boxes being sold at a price of $2.90 per box. This is the one combination of price and quantity which satisfies both producers and consumers. On a graph of the schedules, this price and quantity would occur at the point of intersection. Production per farm would be $170,000 \div 100 = 1,700$ boxes, which would require $1,700 \div 760 = 2.24$ acres.

2 The total revenues associated with the quantities indicated on the demand schedule have been calculated and listed in Table 1.3. Maximum income is achieved with the sale of 130,000 boxes of carrots. It appears that demand is price elastic from sales of 100,000 to 130,000 boxes, but inelastic at sales of larger quantities. If 130,000 boxes are to be produced, each farm will produce $130,000 \div 100 = 1,300$ boxes on $1,300 \div 760 = 1.71$ acres.

Table 1.3: Total revenue obtained from sales of quantities of carrots indicated on demand schedule

quantity (*boxes*)	total revenue (*price* × *quantity*)
100,000	$500,000
110,000	517,000
120,000	540,000
130,000	546,000
140,000	532,000
150,000	525,000
160,000	512,000
170,000	493,000
180,000	468,000

3 In the case of pure competition among carrot producers, one can calculate the expected increase in quantity demanded, assuming no change in the price of carrots, by substitution in the formula

$$\text{cross elasticity} = \frac{(Q_1 - Q_2)/(Q_1 + Q_2)}{(P_1 - P_2)/(P_1 + P_2)}$$

where Q_1 = the original quantity of carrots demanded, Q_2 = the quantity demanded after the rise in the price of celery, P_1 = the original price of celery, and P_2 = the increased price.

If cross elasticity $= 0.405 = \dfrac{(170,000 - Q_2)/(170,000 + Q_2)}{(2 - 3)/(2 + 3)}$,

$Q_2 = 20,000$ boxes. If the carrot price remains unchanged, and farmers increase carrot production, per-farm carrot acreage will be $2,000 \div 760 = 2.63$.

If the Carrot Producers' Association anticipates the increase in the price of celery and adopts a new plan to maximize income, it could predict the new quantity of carrots demanded at the old price, and change the quotas respectively. If we assume that the demand schedule for carrots shifts in response to the change in the price of celery but maintains its same shape, then the price should remain the same as formerly to maximize income. The new quantity and old price will still occur at the point on the demand schedule dividing the price elastic and inelastic portions. The new quantity required by the Association is calculated as follows:

$$\text{cross elasticity} = 0.405 = \frac{(130,000 - Q_2)/(130,000 + Q_2)}{(2 - 3)/(2 + 3)},$$

and $Q_2 = 15,291$. The new quota is 2.01 acres per farm

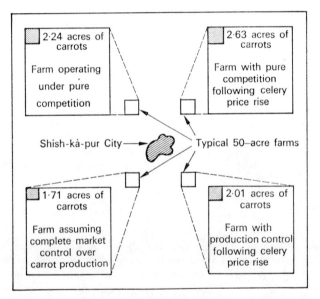

Fig. 1.4: Shish-ka-pur City and typical farms operating under a variety of market conditions

Figure 1.4 is a map illustrating the hypothetical problem described above.

Further reading

The following references provide additional theoretical statements relevant to demand, supply, and price. Most refer specifically to products of agricultural land use.*

BISHOP, C. E., and TOUSSAINT, W. D. 1958: *Introduction to agricultural economic analysis*, chapters 15–18.
BLACK, J. D. 1924: Elasticity of supply of farm products.
CASSELS, J. M. 1933: History of research in prices.
COCHRANE, W. W. 1955: Conceptualizing the supply relation in agriculture.
FOX, K. A. 1951a: Factors affecting farm income, farm prices, and food consumption.
    1951b: Relation between Price, Consumption, and Production.
FRIEDMAN, M. 1949: The Marshallian demand curve.
HEADY, E. O. 1952: *Economics of agricultural production and resource use*, chapter 1.
LEFTWICH, R. H. 1963: *The price system and resource allocation*, chapters 2–7.
MIGHELL, R. L., and ALLEN, R. H. 1940: Supply schedules—'long-time' and 'short-time'.
NERLOVE, M. 1958: *The dynamics of supply*.
NERLOVE, M., and ADDISON, W. W. 1958: Statistical estimation of long run elasticities of supply and demand.
NERLOVE, M., and BACHMAN, K. L. 1960: The analysis of changes in agricultural supply: problems and approaches.
SCHULTZ, H. 1928: *Statistical laws of demand and supply*.
    1925: The statistical law of demand as illustrated by the demand for sugar.
TINTNER, G. 1939: The theory and measurement of demand.
WAITE, W. C., and TRELOGAN, H. C. 1951: *Agricultural market prices*.
WARREN, G. F., and PEARSON, F. A. 1928: *Interrelationships of supply and price*.
WORKING, E. J. 1927: What do 'statistical demand' curves show?

The following describe attempts to relate the theoretical concepts to real-world settings.

BRANDOW, G. E. 1968: A framework for the farm problem.
CASSELS, J. M. 1937: *A study of fluid milk prices*.
ELLIOTT, F. F. 1927: Adjusting hog production to market demand.
ENGLUND, E. 1923: Fallacies of a plan to fix prices of farm products by government control of the exportable surplus.
HEADY, E. O. (Editor) 1961: *Agricultural supply functions*.
MOSER, C. O. 1927: The surplus problem in cooperative cotton marketing.
NERLOVE, M. 1956: Estimates of the elasticities of supply of selected agricultural commodities.
PAULSON, W. E. 1950: Cooperatives, competition, and free enterprise.
WILSON, R. R., and THOMPSON, R. G. 1967: Demand, supply and price relationships for the dairy sector, post-World War II period.
WOLD, H. 1953: *Demand analysis*.
YANKOROSKY, Z. 1968: Agricultural demand and supply projections for 1980.

* Complete reference information listed in bibliography at conclusion of book

2 INPUT–OUTPUT RELATIONSHIPS, ECONOMIC RENT, AND LAND-USE COMPETITION

Inputs, output, and intensity of land use—The production function—Determining the optimim intensity of land use for one input—Cost as a function of output—Time periods, input–output levels, and their relation to demand and supply—Economic rent and land-use Competition—Relevance of direct man–land relationships—land value—Hypothetical problem—Further reading

As an important step in our development of a general spatial model of rural land use, this chapter is concerned with normative economic models of optimum land use at a particular location. It will be assumed that prices are known, supposedly derived according to the concepts discussed in Chapter 1; that the land can be used for only one production process at a time; and that all relevant information for the decision process is readily available. The problem of determining optimum combinations of several inputs simultaneously will not be considered. Only the solution for determining the optimum quantity of one variable input, given fixed quantities of others, will be analysed. These rigid assumptions and restrictions will be relaxed gradually in later chapters.

Inputs, output, and intensity of land use

Optimum land use refers to two characteristics of land use: *type* and *intensity*. 'Type' presents no problem of definition. No matter what land-use classification scheme is being employed, researchers all use the term in the same way. 'Intensity', however, has been used with a variety of meanings. The usual meaning, and one which should be adhered to for the sake of conformity, is *the ratio of inputs to land area*. 'Level of intensity', then, refers to the amount of inputs per unit area. 'Intensive' or 'highly intensive' land use occurs when a large quantitiy of inputs per unit area is used. 'Non-intensive' or 'extensive' land use occurs when small quantities of input per unit area are used. Note that 'intensity' does not refer directly to output, the product of land use.

Inputs are normally subdivided into three types—*land, labour,* and *capital*. To these, *management* is often added in a slightly different category. 'Land' refers to all naturally-occurring phenomena which can be used in the production process. These include size of area, soil quality (unmodified by man), other features of the topography which affect productivity (such as slope or drainage), surface and sub-surface water, precipitation, and

12

air. 'Land' includes so many types of input at a particular location that one could say that it refers to the entire natural ecosystem. 'Labour' refers to the physical input that man himself adds to the production process. 'Capital', which has characteristically been the most difficult input to define, includes all inputs resulting from an earlier combination of land and labour. Included are such inputs as tools, machinery, fences, buildings, domesticated animals, or currency. 'Management' is the decision-making process through which the farmer selects the types and intensities of land use to be carried out, and the types and quantities of inputs to be used. It refers to his ability to operate his farm successfully, given certain production objectives.

Output normally refers to the physical quantities of the products of land use. Sometimes it refers loosely to the value of such output. For clarity, however, the latter characteristic should be clearly designated as the 'value of output' or 'income'.

The production function

One of the most basic concepts in normative economic theory, one on which many others are dependent, is the concept of the production function. The production of output is entirely dependent on—i.e. is a function of—the types and quantities of inputs used; and the production function is the term used to describe the relationship between input and output. The relationship may be described in the form of equations, tables, or other means. In general, non-specific terms it can be represented by the functional form

$$Y = f(X_1, X_2, X_3, \ldots X_n)$$

which states that Y (the quantity of product Y) is dependent on the quantities of n different inputs, namely $X_1, X_2, X_3, \ldots X_n$. Since it is difficult to analyse varying output if the quantities of all or several inputs are varying simultaneously, it is often useful to analyse changes in output as the quantities of only one input vary, with the quantities of all other inputs held constant. Algebraically, this situation can be represented by the form

$$Y = f(X_1, |X_2, X_3, \ldots X_n)$$

where X_1 is the only input varying in quantity.

It has been observed that a particular relationship between output and quantities of a useful input always occurs when the quantities of the input are allowed to vary while quantities of all other inputs are held constant. As the quantity of input is increased, the output or total product will first increase at an increasing rate, then at a constant rate and, after increasing at a diminishing rate, will reach a maximum production and then decline. This relationship is said to follow the *law of diminishing returns*. It is described graphically in Fig. 2.1.

Two useful indexes can be derived from the general input–output relationship, as illustrated in Fig. 2.1. *Average product* is the total product divided by the quantity of inputs (TP $\div$ X_1) at a particular input level. Due to the characteristic shape of the TP curve, average output (AP) first increases, reaches a maximum and declines as the quantity of inputs

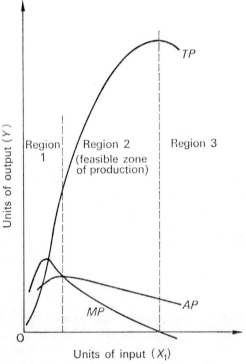

Fig. 2.1 : Production function and related indexes for $Y = f(X_1 \mid X_2, X_3, \ldots X_n)$

increases. *Marginal product* is the change in output resulting from the addition of the last quantity of input (ΔTP $\div$ ΔX_1). It measures the rate of change of total product as the quantity of input increases. Again, due to the basic shape of the production function $Y = f(X_1 \mid X_2, X_3, \ldots X_n)$, marginal product (MP) increases rapidly at first, reaches a maximum, and then declines. Its maximum occurs where output increases at a constant rate, and it becomes negative when maximum output is achieved. Note that it equals AP at the maximum value of the latter.[1] The law of dimin-

[1] For a fuller discussion of the interrelationships of TP, AP, and MP see C. E. Bishop and W. D. Toussaint 1958: *Introduction to agricultural economic analysis* (New York) 36–9.

ishing returns was stated above in terms of the responses of total product to increase in the quantity of input. It could just have easily been stated in terms of the changes in average or marginal product.

Determining the optimum intensity of land use for one input

By the law of diminishing returns, it is obvious that one can use too much of an input in the production process. On the other hand, the encouraging initial response as quantities of input are added suggests that it would often be beneficial to use more than a little. Knowledge of the TP, AP, and MP values alone is not enough to determine the optimum level of input application. But they do enable us to establish some general boundaries for feasible input levels. Firstly, it is obvious that one should not add so many inputs as to cause a decline in total production, causing negative MP values. Secondly, we know that the input level should be at least as high as that giving rise to the maximum average product, since, to the 'left' of this point in Fig. 2.1, it would always be to one's advantage to add more inputs and increase the ratio of output to input units. These two relationships permit us to divide the typical production function into three areas, illustrated in Fig. 2.1 as regions 1, 2, and 3. Regions 1 and 3 are areas of infeasible input application, if one is trying to obtain a maximum return for one's investment in inputs. This leaves region 2 as the zone of 'feasible' production.

The point of optimum input level within region 2 can not be determined unless the value of the output and the price of the inputs are known. This is an economic decision requiring knowledge of the market values of units of input and output. If these are known, the decision-maker should continue to add units of input until the value of the increased output can no longer pay for the cost of the added input. This occurs where the value of the marginal product (VMP) equals the cost of adding the extra input (the price of a unit of X_1 if whole units of X_1 are added at a time). The VMP can be derived directly from Fig. 2.1, as can VTP (value of total product) and VAP (value of average product) just by multiplying the quantities of output by the value of a unit of output (PY). If one assumes that PY remains unchanged at different input–output levels, then the graph of physical output (Fig. 2.1) looks exactly like that for value of output (Fig. 2.2). The level of optimum input application can be derived graphically, as in Fig. 2.2, by adding a line representing the cost of a unit of input. This line is parallel to the X_1 axis if PX_1 remains unchanged for different input–output levels. The point of intersection of VMP and PX_1 (where VMP $= PX_1$) indicates the level of optimum input application (X_{11} units of X_1) if the decision-maker wants to maximize income. At this point income $=$ VTP $= PY \times Y_1$, and costs $= PX_1 \times X_{11}$. The method of analysis whereby marginal returns and costs are calculated and equated to determine an input level is called *marginal analysis*.

Unless the variable input in the analysis is land area, the above method can be used to determine the optimum intensity of land use for one variable input on a given area of land. The method could also be used to determine optimum land area if area were the variable input and all other input quantities were constant.

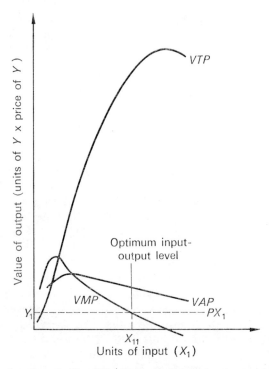

Fig. 2.2 : Value functions for $Y = f(X_1|X_2,X_3, \ldots X_n)$, illustrating graphical determination of optimum input–output level

Cost as a function of output

In the preceding section the various input–output relationships were examined with particular reference to input levels. TP, AP, MP and the associated value indexes were all defined as some value per unit or units of input. It is often useful, however, particularly for cost analysis, to redefine the relationships with particular reference to output.

Costs of production can be classified as either fixed or variable. *Fixed costs* (FC) are those which are the same regardless of output level over a specific time period. Property taxes would be a typical example. *Variable costs* (VC), on the other hand, are those which vary with the quantity of output over the same time period. The cost of hired labour could be such an example. *Total costs* (TC) are the sum of fixed and variable costs; and *average total cost* (ATC), often shortened *to average cost* (AC), is total cost divided by the number of units of output (TC ÷ Y). *Average variable cost* (AVC) is total variable cost divided by the number of units of output

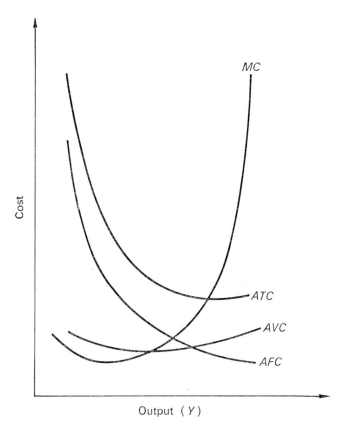

Output (Y)

Fig. 2.3 : Cost–output functions

(VC ÷ Y), and *average fixed cost* (AFC) is total fixed cost divided, again, by the number of output units (FC ÷ Y). *Marginal cost* (MC) is defined as the change in total cost (which is the same as the change in average cost) associated with a change in quantity of output (ΔTC ÷ ΔY or ΔAC ÷ ΔY, since FC never changes). The various cost curves are illustrated graphically in Fig. 2.3. The characteristic shape of the variable cost curve, and all others related to it, is a function of the law of diminishing returns.

An obvious relationship exists between some of the cost indexes and the input–output indexes described above. If there is only one variable input, total variable cost $= PX_1 \times X_1$, where X_1 is the number of input units. Average variable cost is $1/PX_1$ times the reciprocal of the average product, since $\mathrm{AVC} = PX_1 \times X_1/Y = 1/PX_1 \times 1/\mathrm{AP}$. Marginal cost is $1/PX_1$ times the reciprocal of marginal product, since $\mathrm{MC} = PX_1 \times \Delta X_1/\Delta Y = 1/PX_1 \times 1/\mathrm{MP}$.

Just as marginal analysis was used in the preceding section to determine

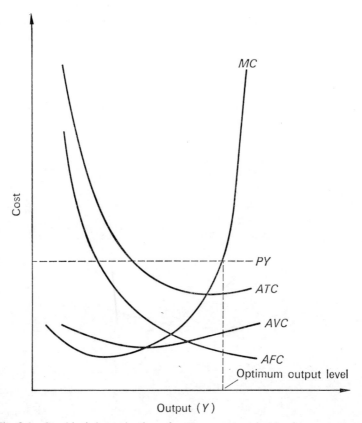

Fig. 2.4: Graphical determination of optimum output level using cost curves

optimum intensity of land use, it can be used with relevant cost indexes to determine the optimum level or quantity of output. In this case, optimum output occurs where the marginal cost is just compensated for by the market value of the increased production. If we are considering output at levels one unit apart, then the optimum level occurs where $\mathrm{MC} = PY$, where PY is the price of a unit of production. The graphic method of determining this optimum level is illustrated in Fig. 2.4.

Time periods, input–output levels, and their relation to demand and supply

Time periods for the production process have been classified into three categories: (1) the market period, (2) the short run, and (3) the long run. The *market period* refers to the time following the production of an item, during which the land-user arranges for its sale. This may be a very short time period, if, for example, a crop is taken directly from the field to the market. If the item is highly perishable and cannot be sorted without deterioration, the farmer should first estimate whether the sale of the item will cover the variable cost of removing it from the field and transporting it to the market. If these costs can be covered leaving any excess income, the item should be marketed, even if the total production costs, including the costs of planting, etc., which can now be regarded as fixed, are not covered. Losses would be less than they would be if the product were left in the field. The supply schedule for such a harvested, perishable product during the market period would be perfectly inelastic for a pure competitor. The same quantity would be available for sale regardless of the price, providing the price at least covers the cost of harvesting and transportation. The aggregate supply for all producers would also be perfectly elastic, and would represent the sum of all individual producers' supply schedules. If conditions of pure competition did not exist, however, and the producers in aggregate could control the quantity marketed, a reduction of the quantity actually sold could be achieved to maximize total revenue. The quantity sold would depend on the nature of the demand schedule. If the product under consideration could be stored on the farm, thus delaying delivery to the market and extending the market period, supply at a given time period would be less than perfectly inelastic for pure competitors, the degree of elasticity depending mainly on the costs of storage and expectations about future prices.

The *short-run* time period refers to time during which all stages of the production process occur and during which the quantities of all imputs except the size of the property can be regarded as variable. For the pure competitor, the short-run demand schedule for a given variable input, assuming fixed quantities of all other inputs, is equivalent to the schedule of prices and quantities indicated by the value of marginal product (VMP) in the rational zone of production (zone 2) of the production function. This relates to the fact that the optimum quantity of input is indicated by the point where the VMP equals the cost of a unit of input. So, as this cost varies, the VMP curve indicates the quantity of input demanded. Of course, quite a different demand for the input could be derived from a different production process. Aggregate demand for the input would be the sum of the demands of all producers.

Short-run supply of a product is indicated by the portion of the marginal cost schedule where MC exceeds average total cost. This relates quantity produced or supplied to the price of the product for the portion of the schedule where production costs are covered. Aggregate supply would be the sum of the supply schedules of individual pure competitors.

The *long-run* refers to the time period during which the quantities of all inputs can be regarded as variable. Even the size of the farm may be altered. Discussion of the derivation of long-run supply and demand will be postponed until later chapters.

Economic rent and land-use competition

Economic rent refers to the net value of the returns generated by production on a given piece of land in a given time period. It is similar to *net income*, in that it represents the residual remaining after all costs of production (except the cost of land) are subtracted from the gross income. But it is different in that all costs of production must be calculated at their full economic value. That is, the cost of an input must represent not only the cash value paid by the operator, but must take into account the value that the input might gain in alternative uses. The highest value that could be achieved in any of the alternative uses is the *opportunity cost* of the input;[1] and in calculating economic rent, each input must be charged with its maximum value, whether that arises in the production process currently undertaken or in some process providing the input with an opportunity cost. All capital and labour inputs must be evaluated, including the time and energy of the operator. Often practical problems arise in attempting to evaluate the full cost of some of the inputs, particularly the labour of self-employed farmers. Even in calculating net income, few farmers seem to differentiate between farm income and personal income. Economic rent is illustrated graphically in Fig. 2.5. It is assumed that average cost represents full, economic cost.[2]

Land-use competition is a principle which recognizes that a given piece of land can normally be put to a number of uses; and that if decision-makers are trying to decide which use or uses to undertake, the situation is somewhat analogous to the various uses 'competing' for the land. It is assumed that the decision-maker can evaluate or rank the uses on the basis of the average returns or economic rent which each can generate in a given time period, and that a decision-maker striving to maximize net income should choose the use or uses yielding the highest economic rent. Uses yielding high incomes are said to be 'high' uses, and the one with the largest economic rent is the 'highest' or 'best' use.[3]

[1] See R. H. Leftwich 1963: *The price system and resource allocation* (New York) 136–7.
[2] For a full discussion of economic rent see R. Barlowe 1958: *Land resource economics* (Englewood Cliffs), chapter 6.
[3] See E. M. Hoover 1948: *The location of economic activity* (New York) 93–7.

In some cases the highest use for a particular operator may be different from the generally-recognized highest use. This situation arises, for example, if the operator lacks the inputs necessary for undertaking the land use generating the largest economic rent. He may lack capital for purchasing important variable inputs. He may be unable to spend much time on the property because he has a higher-than-average opportunity cost for his

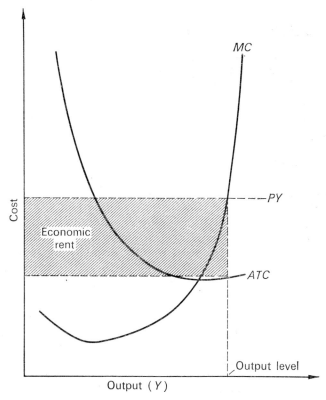

Fig. 2.5: Graphical illustration of economic rent

own labour, due to lucrative employment elsewhere. In some cases, the length of the operator's planning period may affect his decision regarding best use of the land. Suppose, for example, that the use yielding the highest average annual economic rent is the cultivation of fruit trees which take several years to mature. For the first few years the land may yield no income, but high returns after the trees reach maturity will more than compensate for the years with no production. For the total length of the life of the trees, the average income exceeds that produced by any other use. But, if the operator needs an economic return during the early years of land use, or if he has a lease granting him property rights for only a few years, fruit trees are by no means best for him. The distinction between generally recognized highest land use, which assumes a very long planning period and ready availability of inputs, and best use for particular individuals, who are often constrained under less-than-perfect conditions, is highly significant.

Relevance of direct man–land relationships

Social and natural scientists, especially geographers, have a long tradition of examining the direct relationship between natural environment and man's use of the land. The dominant conclusion of this research is that variations in land use, particularly on a large scale, can be 'explained' to a considerable degree by variations in land quality (including climate). Some researchers have even given the impression that this ecological relationship is so important and overwhelming that the role of man as a decision-maker can be largely disregarded. Actually, the existence of such a strong relationship could be regarded as putting the focus on man as a decision-maker who is very sensitive to variations in the land resource base, and who displays a strong rationality by reacting sensibly to them. Man's main purpose for using land is to gain some sort of satisfaction, such as earning an income or providing recreation, rather than 'blending with nature'. Yet it is quite possible, but of secondary consequence, that 'blending with nature' may well help him achieve his primary objective. Such would be the case, for example, if varying environmental conditions led to a spatial variation in the production functions for different crops, and the 'optimum' crop that farmers should grow varied from place to place. If farmers responded to the input–output relationships and chose optimum crops at different locations, they would be providing direct proof of the principle of land-use competition (an economic concept) but not of some environment–land use principle. Yet the two ideas are related, specifically because the nature of any production function is partly dependent on land quality. Viewed in this way, there is no conflict between 'man–land' and 'economic' views of spatial variation in land use.

One should clarify the uses and limitations of attempting to 'explain' land-use patterns solely as a function of natural environment if we accept the verity of traditional economic theory. If farmers are income optimizers operating in a free-enterprise economy and behave like 'economic men', then their land-use decisions regarding type and intensity follow the rules outlined in the preceding portions of this chapter. Their decisions depend ultimately on two things: production functions, and the prices and costs of outputs and inputs. If regional variations in prices and costs are not great compared to variations in production functions due to natural environment, one would expect the variation in 'highest' land use to bear a strong relationship to land quality. In this case, knowledge of land quality would enable one to 'predict' land-use type quite accurately. One must not conclude, however, that such prediction involves an explanation unless the intermediary role of the economic decision is made explicit.

It is possible that part of the confusion over man–land studies has arisen from the similarity between examining man-induced land-use patterns and patterns of natural biosystems. In both cases plants and animals 'compete' for land, and one may identify optimum or 'climax' patterns. The basic nature of the two situations is the same, although the objectives, various alternatives, and control mechanisms are different.

A point often discussed by those engaged in man–land research is that farmers must realize their dependence on land resources, and must avoid destroying them through over-exploitation. This can be interpreted in the language of traditional economics by stating that, in the interest of future resource use, farmers should attempt to maximize their average economic rent over an infinitely long time period—i.e. their planning period should be as long as possible. Some land uses may yield very high returns for a short number of years, but leave the soil exhausted. Conservationists would argue that the land should have been used in such a way as to maximize its use (i.e. economic rent) over a very long time period. This could be achieved, for example, by practising crop rotation or contour ploughing. Recognition of the need and methods of maintaining the natural ecosystem or land quality is not the sole interest of the ecologist. The problem can be stated very precisely in traditional economic terms.

Land value

Land value normally refers to one of two things: (1) the contribution which land makes in the production process, or (2) the price which one receives or would expect to receive from sale of one's land. The two meanings are strongly interdependent, as will be indicated below.

When the costs and returns of production are calculated it is often possible to allocate what portions of the total returns are attributable to the various inputs. The portion attributable to the land input is the economic rent, since it was defined as the net return after the full costs of all factors of production except land had been subtracted. The real value of the land to the producer is the amount of economic rent which it will yield.

The total present value of land from a production standpoint is the present value of the sum of all future incomes (economic rents) which the land will yield. It is important to emphasize that it is the present value of such incomes, since incomes which require the passage of time for collection must have a value today somewhat less than their value at maturity.

The value of an income which will materialize one year hence would normally be a fairly high percentage of the value at maturity. Specifically, the present value would be a sum which would inflate to the value of the income next year on the basis of an acceptable interest rate (say, 6 per cent). By the same process, the present value of the same income 25 years hence would be a very low percentage of that value. Extending this principle, the total present value of land would be the sum of the present values of the expected income for years 0, 1, 2, 3, . . . n where n is infinity. The present values of incomes several tens of years away, however, are so small that eventually it becomes meaningless to calculate them. Mathematically, the process for evaluating the present value of land reduces to the simple equation

$$V = e/r,$$

where V is the present value, e is the expected yearly economic rent (a constant), and r is the interest rate (also a constant). Note that the value increases as the economic rent increases or the interest rate declines.[1]

The interest rate depends primarily on generally accepted rates of return and on the risk involved in obtaining future incomes from the land. Traditionally, farmers have been willing to accept rates of return somewhat less than those which they could obtain through investment of their money in most other enterprises (e.g. the stock market). This may be due to the generally secure outlook for production, or, in some countries, the personal preference for owning land over other investments. Interest rates are affected, however, by the rates available in other investment opportunities. The value of land in highly specialized production which is subject to considerable risk seems to reflect very high interest rates. For example, fruit land in areas of potential frost damage often has values less than one would expect on the basis of 'normal' rates of return.

Although the above method, referred to as the 'income capitalization' approach, theoretically determines the value of land, actual sale values may reflect other factors. Market values could be far below the capitalized values if the market was 'flooded' with farms. In this case the 'capitalized value' could represent the maximum that an individual would pay. If farms were very scarce, some individuals might pay more than the price determined by the capitalization method if they felt capable of obtaining higher-than-average economic rents, or were willing to accept a lower-than average return on their investment. Sometimes persons decide the amount that they will pay on the basis of future, inflated values of the property, which may have nothing to do with production. Such would be the case in areas where changes to higher land uses (e.g. urban-commercial or industrial) were imminent.

It should be apparent that operators who have a mortgage whose

[1] See Barlowe, 1958, 169.

interest rate is as high as the rate used in the capitalization calculation own farms generating no income after land costs are paid. This appears, in many real-life instances, to be the case. Of course, the operator does receive some income which is theoretically considered as the cost of his labour.

Finally, it must be emphasized that the processes and calculations discussed in the theoretical determination of land value can not be assumed to be the conscious realities facing all farmers. It is normally suggested, however, that they are consciously appreciated and used by some operators; and may present 'invisible' forces underlying land price values which develop through time.

Hypothetical problem

Figure 2.6 is a map of Zen County, an agricultural area in the middle of a large, temperate-latitude continent. It is divided into three sections (West,

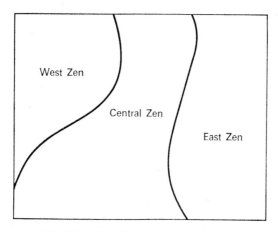

Fig. 2.6: Hypothetical county of Zen

Central and East Zen) which are distinctly different from each other with respect to soil and climate. Farming is highly specialized and commercial, with each farm undertaking only one land use. Conditions of pure competition prevail. All farms are 200 acres in size with all 200 acres under cultivation. West Zen has 100, Central Zen 150, and East Zen 125 farms.

Table 2.1 indicates the average annual economic rents per acre which can be obtained currently for the six leading crops in each section of the country. A new corn fertilizer has just been developed which increases corn yields considerably under certain environmental conditions. The production responses for each section of Zen are indicated in Tables 2.2, 2.3, and 2.4.

Table 2.1 : Average annual economic rent per acre by crop for Zen County with current technology

crop	West Zen (dollars/acre)	Central Zen (dollars/acre)	East Zen (dollars/acre)
wheat	18	18	18
oats	13	15	17
corn (maize)	10	16	25
soybeans	11	14	20
barley	13	13	14
rye	12	13	14

Table 2.2 : Corn production responses to additions of new fertilizer in West Zen

no. of bags of fertilizer (per acre)	increase in per-acre corn yield over current yield (bu.)
0	0
1	1
2	3
3	5
4	6·4
5	7·5
6	8·4
7	8·8
8	9·1
9	9·1

Table 2.3 : Corn production responses to additions of new fertilizer in Central Zen

no. of bags of fertilizer (per acre)	increase in per-acre corn yield over current yield (bu.)
0	0
1	2
2	6
3	10
4	12·7
5	15
6	16·8
7	17·7
8	18·3
9	18·2

Table 2.4 : Corn production responses to additions of new fertilizer in East Zen

no. of bags of fertilizer (per acre)	increase in per-acre corn yield over current yield (bu.)
0	0
1	4
2	12
3	20
4	25·5
5	30
6	33·3
7	35·2
8	36·5
9	36·4

Questions

1 Making the usual assumptions about 'economic man', what will be the land use in each of the three sections of Zen under current technological conditions?
2 When the new corn fertilizer becomes available to farmers in the three areas, will there be any changes in the type or intensity of land use? (Assume a cost of $3.25 per bag for the fertilizer and a price of $1.50 per bushel for corn.)
3 What would be the value of a farm in each section before and after introduction of the fertilizer assuming a capitalization rate of 5 per cent?
4 Derive the aggregate demand for the new fertilizer in East Zen.

Solutions

1 According to the principle of land-use competition operators in each area will grow the crop which yields the highest economic rent. Under current technology, then, farms in West and Central Zen will grow wheat and those in East Zen will grow corn (maize).
2 The impact of the new fertilizer in each area depends, firstly, on whether use of the fertilizer is economically feasible. If use is feasible, then intensity of corn land use will increase to the point where marginal costs equal marginal returns. Increased intensity will lead to higher economic rent, which might enable the rank of corn as a land-use competitor to move upwards. Should corn take over the lead among land uses, a land-use change would occur.

Several approaches to evaluating the impact of the new fertilizer could be taken. One could calculate the complete costs and returns for every level of fertilizer application to determine the optimum input–output level. Or one might calculate variable and marginal costs for different output levels, and determine the optimum level of application by equating marginal costs with marginal returns. Perhaps the simplest method, and the one used here, is to calculate the value of the marginal product associated with each additional bag of fertilizer, and determine the optimum level by equating VMP with the cost of a bag of fertilizer. Each of these methods could be achieved through construction of tables or graphs similar to those in Figures 2.2 and 2.4.

Table 2.5 indicates the value of the marginal product (marginal product × $1.50, price for a bushel of corn) for the different fertilizer input levels in the three areas. Note that in West Zen, use of the fertilizer is infeasible, as the VMP never covers the cost of a bag of fertilizer ($3.25) at any level. In Central Zen, fertilizer use is feasible with an optimum application of 5 bags per acre (assuming that only whole bags can be used). If 6 bags were to be used here the VMP ($2.70) would not cover the cost of the additional bags. In East Zen fertilizer use is feasible with an optimum application of 6 bags per acre.

Table 2.5: Value of marginal product for different fertilizer input levels for each part of Zen

quantity of fertilizer (bags)	value of marginal product		
	West Zen	Central Zen	East Zen
1	$1.50	$3.00	$ 6.00
2	3.00	6.00	12.00
3	3.00	6.00	12.00
4	2.10	4.05	8.25
5	1.65	3.45	6.75
6	1.35	2.70	5.25
7	0.60	1.35	2.55
8	0.45	0.90	1.95
9	0.00	− 0.15	−0.60

Note: VMP = MP × $1.50, where $1.50 is the price per bushel of corn.

The increases in economic rent can be calculated by adding the value of the increased production (15 bushels in Central Zen and 33·5 bushels in East Zen–see Tables 2.3 and 2.4) and subtracting the costs of the fertilizer (5 bags in Central Zen, 6 in East Zen) (see Table 2.6).

Table 2.6: Increases in economic rent at optimum fertilizer input levels

	Central Zen	East Zen
value of increased corn yield	$1.50 × 15 = $22.50	$1.50 × 33.5 = $50.25
cost of fertilizer	$3.25 × 5 = $16.25	$3.25 × 6 = $19.50
net increase in economic rent	$6.25	$30.75
total economic rent from corn-growing with new fertilizer	16 + $6.25 = $22.25	25 + $30.75 = $55.75

Even if the new fertilizer is introduced, wheat will continue to be grown in West Zen. In Central Zen the increased income from using fertilizer for corn enables corn to become the highest land use, and land use will switch from wheat to corn. In East Zen corn remains as the highest use, but intensity, yields and economic rent increase greatly.

Note that the solution to the problem depends entirely on (1) regional response to fertilizer application for corn, which depends on natural environment, (2) the price of corn and other grains, and (3) the price of fertilizer. It is also interesting to note that fertilizer is used most intensively and produces the greatest benefits in the area already experiencing the highest returns from corn cultivation.

3 The capitalization formula $V = n/r$ can be used to calculate the farm values. Table 2.7 indicates this procedure for the three areas before and after the introduction of corn fertilizer.

Table 2.7: Capitalized value of farms in Zen before and after introduction of new corn fertilizer

	West Zen		Central Zen		East Zen	
	before fert.	after fert.	before fert.	after fert.	before fert.	after fert.
'highest' land use	wheat	wheat	wheat	corn	corn	corn
economic rent (dollars/acre)	18	18	18	22.25	25	55.75
capitalized value/acre (dollars) (economic rent/0.05)	360	360	360	450	500	1115
acreage of farm	200	200	200	200	200	200
total farm value (dollars)	72,000	72,000	72,000	90,000	100,000	223,000

4 The aggregate demand for the new fertilizer in East Zen can be derived by calculating the sum of the VMP values at varying levels of fertilizer input within the rational zone of production. Table 2.5 indicates the relevant value for one acre, and Table 2.8 results from a multiplication of the quantity values by 200 to give farm demand, and then by 125 (the number of farms in East Zen) to give the aggregate demand schedule. Note that the schedule begins with a quantity demanded of $4 \times 200 \times 125 = 100{,}000$ bags, since any smaller quantity would occur in region 1 of the production function, within which AP had not achieved a maximum value. Similarly, no value is given for $9 \times 200 \times 125 = 225{,}000$ bags, as this level would occur in region 3, also an irrational 'zone' of production.

Table 2.8: Aggregate demand for new fertilizer in East Zen derived from VMP values (see Table 5)

quantity of fertilizer demanded (bags)	price per bag
100,000	$8.25
125,000	6.75
150,000	5.25
175,000	2.55
200,000	1.95

Further reading

The following are theoretical statements concerning production functions, land quality–production relationships, and land value.*

* Complete references listed in bibliography at conclusion of book.

BARLOWE, R. 1958: *Land resource economics*, chapter 6.
BISHOP, C. E., and TOUSSAINT, W. D. 1958: *Introduction to agricultural economic analysis*, chapters 4–10.
BLACK, J. D. 1931: Statistical measurements of the operation of the law of diminishing returns by Mordecai Ezekiel and others.
1957: A formal proof of the concavity of the production possibility function.
BOX, G. E. P. 1954: The exploration and exploitation of response surfaces: some general considerations and examples.
BRONFENBRENNER, M. 1944: Production functions: Cobb-Douglas, interfirm, intrafirm.
BROWN, E. H. P. 1957: The meaning of the fitted Cobb-Douglas function.
CHANG, J. 1968b: Progress in agricultural climatology.
DAY, R. H. 1962: An approach to production response.
ELY, R. T., and WEHRWEIN, G. S. 1940: *Land economics*.
FELLOWS, I. F. 1949: Developing and applying production functions in farm management.
1955: Production functions in farm management.
GRILICHES, Z. 1957: Specification bias in estimates of production functions.
HARRIS, H. 1947: The development and use of production functions for firms in agriculture.
HEADY, E. O. 1954b: Use and estimation of input–output relationships or productivity coefficients.
1956a: Budgeting and linear programming in estimating resource productivity and cost relationships.
1956b: Integration of physical sciences and agricultural economics.
1956c: Technical considerations in estimating production functions.
1957: An economic investigation of the technology of agricultural production functions.
1958b: Output in relation to input for the agricultural industry.
HEADY E. O., and DILLON, J. L. 1961: *Agricultural production functions*.
HOOVER, E. M. 1948: *The location of economic activity*, pp. 93–7.
JOHNSON, P. R. 1953: Alternative functions for analysing a fertilizer-yield relationship.
KNETSCH, J. L., ROBERTSON, L. S. JR., and SUNDQUIST, W. B. 1956: *Economic considerations in soil fertility research*.
KONIJN, H. S. 1959: Estimation of an average production function from surveys.
LEFTWICH, R. H. 1963: *The price system and resource allocation*, chapters 8–14.
PENN, R. J. 1956: Theoretical concepts relevant to studies in resource productivity and size of business.
REDMAN, J. C., and ALLEN, S. Q. 1954: Some interrelationships of economic and agronomic concepts.
RICARDO, D. 1817: *The principles of political economy and taxation*.
ROBINSON, JOAN 1955: The production function.
SCHMITZ, A. 1967: Production function analysis as a guide to policy in low-income farm areas.
SHEPHARD, R. W. 1953: *Cost and production functions*.
SIMKIN, C. G. F. 1955: Aggregate production functions.
ST. CLAIR, O. 1965: *A key to Ricardo*.
TOLLEY, H. R., and EZEKIEL, M. J. B. 1924: *Input as related to output in farm organization and cost-of-production studies*.
TUCK, R. H. 1961: *An introduction to the principles of agricultural economics*, chapters 7–10.
WATANBE, J. 1945: Theory of production functions.

The following report on attempts to measure production functions or to identify direct land-quality–land-use relationships.

AGRAWAL, G. D., and FOREMAN, W. J. 1959: Farm resource productivity in west Uttar Pradesh.

ANDERSON, R. L. 1956: A comparison of discrete and continuous models in agricultural production analysis.

ANTILL, A. G. 1955: Towards a production function for dairy farms.

BAKER, O. E. 1921: The increasing importance of the physical conditions in determining the utilization of land for agricultural and forest production in the U.S.

BAUM, E. L., HEADY, E. O., PESEK, J. T., and HILDRETH, C. G. (Editors) 1957: *Economic and technical analysis of fertilizer innovations and resource use.*

BAUM, E. L., HEADY, E. O., and BLACKMORE, J. (Editors) 1956: *Methodological procedures in the economic analysis of fertilizer use data.*

BAUM, E. L., and WALKUP, H. G. 1953: Some economic implications of input-output relationships in fryer production.

BHATTACHARJEE, J. P. 1955: Resource use and productivity in world agriculture.

BROWN, W. G., and OVESON, M. M. 1958: Production functions from data over a series of years.

CHANG, J. 1968a: Agricultural potential of the humid tropics.

CLARKE, J. W. 1956: *An analysis of the application of the production function to a sample of farms in southern Saskatchewan.*

DARCOVICH, W. 1958: The use of production functions in the study of resource productivity in some beef producing areas of Alberta.

FOUND, W. C. 1965: The relation of the distribution of citrus to soil type and winter temperature in Orange County, Florida.

FRENCH, B. L. 1956: Functional relationships for irrigated corn response to nitrogen.

GILSON, J. C., and BJARNARSON, V. W. 1958: Effects of fertilizer use on barley in Northern Manitoba.

HANSEN, P. L. 1944: Input–output relationships in egg production.

HEADY, E. O. 1946: Production functions from a random sample of farms.
    1957: A production function and marginal rates of substitution in the utilization of feed resources for dairy cows.

HEADY, E. O., and PESEK, J. 1954: A fertilizer production surface with specification of economic optima for corn grown on calcareous Ida silt loam.

HEADY, E. O., and BROWN, W. G. 1954: *Crop response surfaces and economic optima in fertilizer use.*

HEADY, E. O., DOLL, J. P., and PESEK, J. T. 1958: *Fertilizer production functions for corn and oats; including analysis of irrigated and residual return.*

HEADY, E. O., and OLSON, R. O. 1951: Marginal rates of substitution and uncertainty in the utilization of feed resources with particular emphasis on forage crops.

HEADY, E. O., JACOBSON, N. L., and BLOOM, S. 1956: *Milk production functions, hay/grain substitution rates and economic optima in dairy cow rations.*

HEADY, E. O., MADDEN, J. P., JACOBSON, M. L., and FREEMAN, A. E. 1964: Milk production functions incorporating variables for cow characteristics and environment.

HEADY, E. O., and SHRADER, W. D. 1953: The interrelationships of agronomy and economics in research and recommendations to farmers.

HERRMANN, L. F. 1943: Diminishing returns in feeding commercial dairy herds.

HILDRETH, R. J. 1957: Influence of rainfall on fertilizer profits.

HJELM, L. 1953: *Utbylesrelationer i mjolkproduktionen* (with English summary: input–output relationships in milk production).

JARRETT, F. G. 1959: Estimation of resource productivities as illustrated by a survey of the Lower Murray Valley dairying area.

JAWETZ, M. B. 1957: *Farm size, farming intensity and the input–output relationships of some Welsh and west of England dairy farms.*

JENSEN, E., and SUNDQUIST, W. B. 1955: *Resource productivity and income for a sample of west Kentucky farms.*

LESER, C. E. V. 1958: Statistical production functions and economic development.

LOMAX, K. S. 1949: *An agricultural production function for the United Kingdom, 1924 to 1947.*

PARISH, R. M., and DILLON, J. L. 1955: Recent applications of the production function in farm management research.

PARKS, W. L., and KNETSCH, J. L. 1959: Corn yields as influenced by nitrogen level and drouth intensity.

SCHAPPER, H. P., and MAULDON, R. G. 1957: A production function for farms in the wholemilk region of Western Australia.

SPILLMAN, W. J. 1923: Application of the law of diminishing returns to some fertilizer and feed data.

1924: Law of the diminishing increment in the fattening of steers and hogs.

SURYANARAYANA, K. S. 1958: Resource returns in Telengana farms—a production function study.

TRAMEL, T. E. 1957: Alternative methods for using production functions for making recommendations.

TSUCHIYA, K. 1955: Production functions of agriculture in Japan.

WANG, Y. 1958: *Resource returns and productivity coefficients for selected crop systems in Tainan area.*

WOOD, H. A. 1961: Physical influences on peasant agriculture in northern Haiti.

WRAGG, S. R., and GODSELL, T. E. 1956: Production functions for dairy farming and their application.

YUWATA, Y. 1953: Production functions for rice and barley.

3 OPTIMUM INPUT AND OUTPUT COMBINATIONS

Determining the best combination of inputs for a given level of production—Determining the best combination of inputs for several levels of production—Determining the best combination of land uses with fixed input levels—Determining the optimum combination of inputs and land uses—Linear programming—Non-linear programming—Hypothetical problem —Further reading

In the preceding chapter it was assumed that farmers are restricted to one type of land use in a given time period, and that the optimum intensity of land use can be determined for only one input at a time, while the quantities of the others are held constant. Both of these assumptions will be relaxed in this chapter to consider optimum combinations of any number of land uses and any number of variable inputs. At the same time, the 'economic man' assumptions will be maintained, and pure competition in a market economy will be assumed.

Linear and non-linear programming will also be introduced, as they are methods which fit most conveniently with this stage of the theoretical development. Two main reasons account for this. (1) In many ways the graphical forms of the solutions for linear and non-linear programming are similar to the theoretical arguments for optimum input or output combinations; and (2) these methods have proven so far to be almost indispensable for the practical solution of problems involving optimum input or output combinations.

Determining the best combination of inputs for a given level of production

In accordance with the traditional characteristics of economic man, the objective in deciding what quantities of inputs to use for a given production level is to minimize the costs of production. We will analyse cost-minimization principles for any number of inputs (factors of production), but will begin with the case for two variable inputs, since this situation can be represented easily on a graph.

Figure 3.1 indicates all combinations of the quantities of two variable inputs (X_1, and X_2) in producing a fixed quantity of output (Y_1). Four situations are illustrated: (1) where a given quantity of X_1 must be associated with only one quantity of X_2. This is represented by the point A on the graph, and represents the case of 'fixed proportions'. (2) Where the two inputs can be substituted for each other at a constant rate, giving

33

rise to a straight line of substitution. (3) Where the inputs can be substituted for each other at a varying rate, with the total quantities of inputs required greatest when large portions of each are used. This situation gives rise to a substitution function whose graphical form bulges outwards from the origin. It occurs when the inputs are non-compatible for some reason, and additions of one have a detrimental effect on the production-effectiveness of the other. (4) Where the inputs substitute for each other at

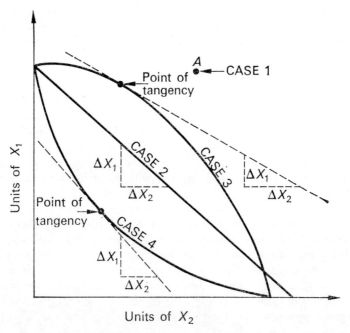

Fig. 3.1 : Types of factor-substitution functions, illustrating measurement of marginal rate of substitution

a varying rate, with the total quantities required less when fairly large proportions of both factors are used. In graphical form this substitution function curves inwards towards the origin. It represents the case where inputs are compatible with each other, and can form a product more effectively combined together than alone.

The extent to which X_1 substitutes for X_2 under each of the four situations can be measured directly from Fig. 3.1. In the first case, a fixed quantity of X_1 is associated with a fixed quantity of X_2, so substitution is not really possible. In case 2, the slope of the substitution line is constant, and its value ($\Delta X_1/\Delta X_2$) measured anywhere along the function indicates the rate of substitution. In cases 3 and 4, the rate of substitution changes at different parts of the functions. A graphical method for determining the rate is to calculate the slopes ($\Delta X_1/\Delta X_2$) of the tangents at whatever parts of the functions are under scrutiny. Fig. 3.1 indicates $\Delta X_1/\Delta X_2$, which is called the *marginal rate of substitution,* for one portion of each case except case 1. In case 1 substitution could hardly be called marginal, as no variation in quantities of X_1 and X_2 occurs for a given production level.

The extent to which each of the four cases occurs in normal agriculture varies greatly. By far the most common case is case 4, which, as will be indicated in the next section, is consistent with the law of diminishing returns. An example would be human labour and land as the two inputs. Neither leads to significant production by itself but, in proper combination, the inputs can be highly productive. Constant rates of substitution (case 2) have been observed in a few cases, particularly when the two inputs are very similar. Certain grains substitute for each other at a constant rate in producing a given quantity of livestock. Case 1, fixed proportions, is occasionally identified when very small numbers of units of the two inputs are required, and the units are not divisible into parts of units. Common examples which are cited are a tractor and a man. For certain functions each requires the other, and the number of tractors must equal the number of men. Case 3 is rarely encountered. In fact, it is not considered a practical possibility by most writers.

The problem of determining the least-cost combination of two inputs can be approached most easily through graphical analysis. Fig. 3.2 will be used to illustrate. The input combinations for producing 75 units of a particular product are indicated for each of the four cases of input substitution described above. The costs per unit of X_1 and X_2 are given as $1.00 and $2.00 respectively. The price of a unit of output is not specified, and need not be if our sole purpose is to determine the minimum-cost combination of inputs.

The first step in the graphical solution is to determine the location of an isocost line—i.e. a line indicating all combinations of the two inputs which can be paid for with a constant amount of money. In our example the isocost line for $6.00 is originally plotted. This value is selected only because it is convenient, in that plenty of space is available for its portrayal in the relevant portion of the graph; and it is easy to calculate the number of units of X_1 and X_2 obtainable with the total sum. The line is constructed by joining the points representing 6 units of X_1 (with zero X_2) and 3 units of X_2 (with zero X_1). The line is straight because the price per unit of either input is assumed to be constant no matter what quantity is purchased. Note that the slope of the isocost line is PX_2/PX_1 if the units used to measure the slope have the same relative spacing on the axes as those used to measure the input units. The slope of the isocost line is the same no matter what original value for the isocost line is selected.

A number of parallel isocost lines can be drawn on Fig. 3.2, each representing a different total production cost. The farther a line is from the origin, the higher is the cost. In order to minimize costs for 75 units of production, one has to use an isocost line which touches a substitution function, yet is as close as possible to the origin. Fig. 3.2 indicates these isocost lines for each of the four types of substitution function. For fixed proportions (case 1), of course, there are no alternatives. For case 3, the optimum solution always requires use of either one or the other of the two factors—never a combination of both. For case 2, constant rate of

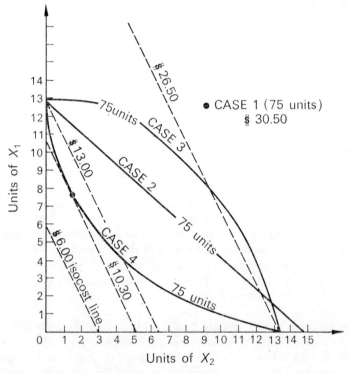

Fig. 3.2: Graphical determination of least-cost input combinations

substitution, the optimum solution always involves one or the other input except in the rare case when the isocost and substitution slopes are equal $(PX_2/PX_1 = \Delta X_1/\Delta X_2)$. In this case any combination of the two inputs will have the same cost. For case 4 (the most usual case) a combination of both inputs always occurs. The optimum point on the substitution function occurs where the slope (i.e. the slope of a tangent at that point) equals the slope of the isocost line. Stated another way, the marginal rate of substitution $(\Delta X_1/\Delta X_2)$ equals the inverse of the price ratio for the two inputs (PX_2/PX_1). The costs of production for the optimum or least-cost combinations for each of the four cases are as follows: case 1—$30.50 ($X_1 = 12\cdot5$ units, $X_2 = 9$); case 2—$13.00 ($X_1 = 13$, $X_2 = 0$);

case 3—$26.50 ($X_1 = 0$, $X_2 = 13 \cdot 25$); and case 4—$10.30 ($X_1 = 7 \cdot 5$, $X_2 = 1 \cdot 4$).

Determination of the optimum combination of more than two inputs for a given level of production is practically impossible using graphical methods. One can use a general rule illustrated above, however, to derive the optimum combination for any number of inputs. For the 'normal' case (case 4) and for constant rates of substitution (probably the 'next-to-normal' one), the optimum combination of two inputs occurs where $\Delta X_1 / \Delta X_2 = PX_2 / PX_1$, or $\Delta X_1 PX_1 = \Delta X_2 PX_2$ (by cross multiplication). Expanding this relationship, the optimum (least-cost) combination of n inputs occurs where

$$\Delta X_1 PX_1 = \Delta X_2 PX_2 = \Delta X_3 PX_3 = \ldots = \Delta X_n PX_n.$$

Practical methods of determining the combination where this rule holds for real-life examples will be discussed below under the sections on linear and non-linear programming.

Determining the best combination of inputs for several levels of production

As in the preceding section, we shall begin the analysis by considering a hypothetical situation with only two variable inputs. Again, this is to facilitate graphical representation. Fig. 3.3 is similar to Figs. 3.1 and 3.2, the main difference being that substitution functions for several fictitious levels of production are indicated. All substitution functions are of the 'normal' (case 4) type. The substitution functions (also called *isoquants* or *isoproduct* curves) are indicated for a large range of production at 10-unit intervals. The intervals are analogous to contour intervals on a topographic map, and the isoquants are analogous to contour lines.

Figure 3.3 has certain characteristics which reveal much about the input-output relationships represented. The basic structure of the isoquants reflects the law of diminishing returns. This can be illustrated by examining the relationship between output and the variation in the quantity of one input. This relationship can be determined by drawing a line such as AB and graphing the output associated with varying quantities of X_1. Such a graph would resemble the typical production function for one variable input (see Fig. 2.1). Similarly, a production function relating output to quantities of X_2 could be derived by plotting the appropriate values along CD. Another feature of Fig. 3.3 which is related to the law of diminishing returns is that the distance between isoquants is variable. The distance decreases as production increases up to about 50 units, beyond which the distance increases.

The points on the isoquants represent the least-cost combinations of inputs for each production level assuming certain prices for X_1 and X_2. The line joining the points is called the *scale line*, and represents the

minimum-cost combinations for all output levels. As greater quantities of
input are added production is, at first, highly responsive. Output levels
increase more rapidly than input levels, the isoquants get closer together,
and we have *increasing returns to scale*. Eventually, increased inputs are
associated with constant increases in output, the isoquants are equally
spaced, and we have *constant returns to scale*. Beyond this point, where

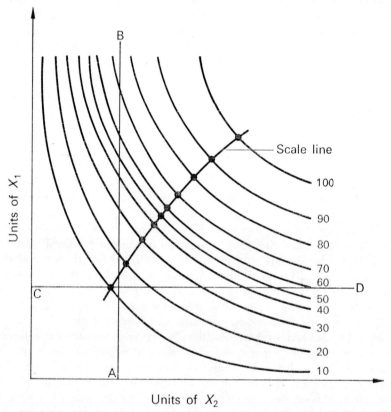

Fig. 3.3 : Factor substitution functions for various levels of production.

greater inputs lead to decreased output responses, *decreasing returns to scale*
are in operation.

   If average total cost is calculated for each least-cost output level along
the scale line, one can derive the *long-run average cost* schedule. Fig. 3.4
is such a schedule, which could have been derived for the situation represented in Fig. 3.3. It is understood, of course, that such data can be
calculated for several variable inputs, not just two as illustrated in the
graphical example. One can recall from Chapter 2 that the long-run is
defined as 'the time period during which the quantities of all inputs can

be regarded as variable'. It was pointed out that even farm size must be variable in this situation.

Note that the long-run average cost curve is U-shaped—i.e. average costs (total cost per unit of output) decline, reach a minimum, and then increase as production levels increase. This reflects increasing, constant, and decreasing returns to scale.

The long-run marginal cost curve can also be derived. It has been plotted in Fig. 3.4. It indicates the change in cost associated with the

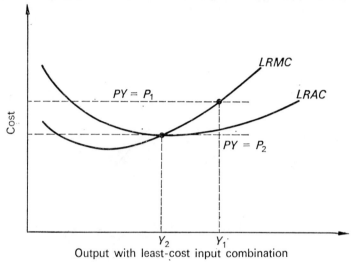

Fig. 3.4 : Long-run average and marginal cost.

increase in output. The optimum long-run level of production and, consequently, optimum size of farm, is determined by equating LRMC with the price of a unit of production. At this point net income is at a maximum. At a price P_1, the optimum size of operation occurs at output Y_1.

Economists have shown that, under pure competition and complete equilibrium of the economy, profits are not generated for the average farm. The profits available with price P_1 would attract other operators into this type of farm production; and, eventually, the price would be reduced, through increased quantity supplied, to P_2. The optimum production would then occur at the minimum output level on the LRAC curve. Farms established at smaller or larger sizes in previous time periods would have to adjust to the new optimum size to prevent financial losses. Assuming pure competition and market equilibrium, then, the optimum farm size occurs at the low point of the LRAC curve. The proof of this derivation goes beyond the scope of this book.[1]

[1] See R. H. Leftwich 1963: *The price system and resource allocation* (New York) 184–93.

Determining the best combination of land uses with fixed input levels

The problem of determining the best combination of product types can be approached in a manner very similar to that used in determining optimum input combinations. Again, for easy graphical representation, we can begin by assuming that only two alternative types (products, in this case) exist. The economic objective in this case is to select a combination of the two products so as to maximize income. It is assumed that the types and quantities of inputs are fixed.

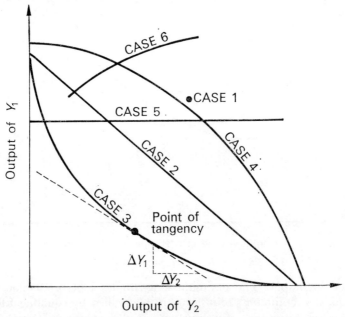

Fig 3.5: Types of product transformation functions

Figure 3.5 illustrates the various combinations of outputs of two products (Y_1 and Y_2) that can be produced with fixed inputs. Six possibilities are illustrated. In case 1, a particular quantity of Y_1 must be associated with a specific quantity of Y_2 (and vice versa). This is the case of 'fixed proportions' or 'joint products' which would apply, for example, to the production of oats and oat-straw. In case 2, a linear function describes the schedule of quantities of Y_1 and Y_2. Such a function is called a *transformation function*, and the linear case occurs with a *constant rate of transformation*. Linear transformation functions are quite common. For example, they have been observed over large sections of functions describing the production of two types of grain which require the same equipment. In the linear case, production is said to be *competitive*, as an increase in the production of one product requires a reduction in the output of the other. Cases 3 and 4 are also competitive, but the marginal rate of transformation is variable. This is indicated by the curved nature of the transformation functions. In case 3, the function curves inwards towards the origin, indicating that greater quantities tend to be obtained when production is concentrated on Y_1 or Y_2, rather than on a combination of both. This would be the case in farming areas where specialization in one of two crops was most profitable. In case 4 the function curves outwards from the origin, indicating that greater quantities tend to be produced with a combination of products rather than with specialization in one. Case 4 is very common, particularly in mixed farming areas. Dairy-cattle and hog raising sometimes form such an example, when excess skim milk is fed to hogs. Case 5 occurs when changes in the production of one product have no effect on the production of the other. The products are said to be *supplementary* under these conditions. This would occur when the inputs required for one product are totally different from those used in the production of the other. Case 6, which is rare, is the case of *complementary* production. With fixed inputs, increases in the production of one product lead to increases in the production of the other. Examples must involve production over several production periods, as agricultural economists claim that complementarity in a given production period is impossible.[1] One example of case 6 is the growing of legumes in combination with grain. Over a long period of time total grain production is increased if, in some seasons, legumes are grown in place of grain. The time lost to legume production is more than compensated for by increased grain yields resulting from the legume-induced improvement of soil fertility and structure.

The degree of substitution of one product for another (*marginal rate of transformation* or MRT) at a given point along a transformation function can be determined in the same way as the marginal rate of substitution is determined for inputs. Geometrically, this value $(\Delta Y_1 / \Delta Y_2)$ is the slope of the tangent at the relevant point on the function. One example is illustrated in Fig. 3.5. For joint products, no substitution is possible, as the ratio of quantities of Y_1 and Y_2 is fixed. For linear transformation, the MRT is always the same, and is the slope of the line. In the case of supplementary production, substitution does not really exist, although one might want to place a value of 0 or ∞ on the MRT, depending on whether the function was horizontal or vertical. In all other cases the MRT is variable along the transformation functions. The MRT is always negative except for the rare case of complementary production.

The graphical method of determining the optimum combination of products is very similar to the method of determining the optimum combination of inputs for a given production level. In this case the objective

[1] C. E. Bishop, and W. D. Toussaint 1958: *Introduction to agricultural economic analysis* (New York) 118–19.

is profit maximization, and the first step is to locate an isoprofit line on the product transformation diagram. The situation depicted in Fig. 3.6 will be used as illustration. Three transformation functions are indicated, representing cases 2, 3, and 4 as described above. Suppose that the prices received per unit of Y_1 and Y_2 are \$2.00 and \$0.30 respectively. Then the \$6.00 isoprofit line, assuming constant prices and linearity, extends from 3 units on the Y_1 axis to 20 units on the Y_2 axis. The slope of the isoprofit

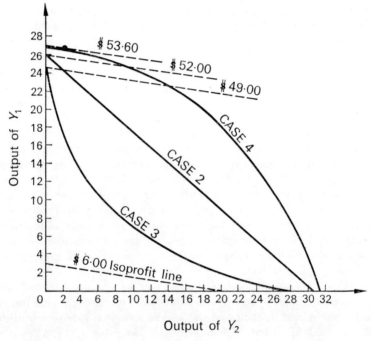

Fig. 3 6 : Graphical determination of optimum output combinations

line is 0·30/2·00 or P_2/P_1, using the units on the Y_1 and Y_2 axes to measure the slope. All isoprofit lines will have the same slopes as that for \$6.00, assuming that no price changes occur.

One can construct a whole series of isoprofit lines, all parallel to the \$6.00 line, which increase in value the farther they extend from the origin. For profit maximization the objective is to select the isoprofit line which is feasible—i.e. which touches a transformation function—but which is as far from the origin as possible. For the example in Fig. 3.6 this leads to different land-use patterns for each type of function. For case 2 (linear function) the optimum plan is to produce 26 units of Y_1; for case 3, 24·5 units of Y_1; and for case 4, a combination of 26·5 units of Y_1 and 2 units of Y_2. The solution for case 4 is determined by selecting the isoprofit line furthest from the origin which touches the transformation function, which has to be at the point on the function whose tangent has a slope equal to that of the isoprofit line. The general rule adhered to is for the marginal rate of transformation to equal the slope of the isoprofit line, or $\Delta Y_1/\Delta Y_2 = PY_2/PY_1$.

The above equation can be expanded to describe the profit-optimizing pattern for any number of possible products. By cross multiplication, $\Delta Y_1 P_1 = \Delta Y_2 P_2$; extending this relationship for n products or land uses, $\Delta Y_1 P_1 = \Delta Y_2 P_2 = \Delta Y_3 P_3 = \ldots = \Delta Y_n P_n$.

Determining the optimum combination of inputs and land uses

The theoretical development so far has been greatly simplified by assuming that either the inputs *or* the products of land use are given. The problem has been to optimize the combination of one, given the other. Over a long period of time, however, an operator is normally free to vary the types and quantities of both inputs and outputs; and, following the motivation of economic man, he would alter his land use so as to maximize net income. If the number of possible inputs or outputs is at all large, the problem becomes exceptionally complicated to solve.

No simple, one-step solution to the problem of determining an optimum multi-input, multi-output land-use pattern exists. Without describing a precise method for attacking the problem, we will just state that some sort of trial-and-error, iterative procedure is required to find a solution. For example, one might assume various combinations of inputs as fixed and calculate the net incomes generated by using the inputs for all feasible combinations of several types of output. By comparing the net incomes, one could then select the 'best' land-use pattern. The volume of data and time required for hand calculations would, of course, be phenomenally large.

Linear programming

Linear programming is a mathematical method of allocating resources so as to maximize or minimize a particular objective. It ties in very closely with this portion of our theoretical development because (1) it has become, to date, the main practical method of solving resource-allocation problems (e.g. selection of optimum input combinations), and (2) its procedure when presented graphically closely parallels the theoretical graphical determination of optimum input or output combinations. It is not the purpose of this book to discuss methods of analysis *per se*; in fact, very little has or will be said about research design or methods of data analysis. But the close interconnection between linear programming and theoretical models warrants at least a cursory discussion of the technique.

Furthermore, a student will be incapable of understanding much of the important literature concerned with rural land-use patterns unless some knowledge of linear programming has been attained.

We shall proceed by describing the method, working through the graphical solution for a sample problem, describing briefly the simplex method of obtaining solutions, and discussing the theoretical relevance of linear programming (LP).

No matter what method of solving an LP problem is used, the initial steps and data requirements are the same. The objective must be to determine which allocation of variables leads to the maximum or minimum value of a specific linear function. For example, the variables could be the inputs labour and capital, and the objective could be to minimize the value of a linear function expressing the costs of production. Such a problem would be meaningless, of course, unless a fixed or minimum level of production were specified. Such a specification, expressed as a functional equality or inequality, is called a *constraint*. One or more constraints, then, set the limits within which the linear function describing the objective—called the *objective function*—is to be minimized or maximized.

As illustration, let us consider a specific problem which we will solve using the graphical method. Suppose that a farmer who owns a 50-acre farm has a choice of growing wheat, corn, or a combination of both. He wants to select the plan, or *programme*, which will maximize his income. He has sufficient capital to undertake the cultivation of the entire 50 acres in either crop at a level of optimum intensity. The only factor which may constrain the operation is a lack of his time. He can gain greater financial returns for his labour from outside employment than from farming; and has taken a part-time job which limits the time available for farm work, particularly in the summer time. He knows the amount of his time remaining for farm work throughout the growing season; the amount of time required per acre for optimum cultivation of each crop for the spring, summer, and autumn; and the average net income per acre which can be gained from growing each crop at optimum input–output levels. All of the information known to him is indicated in Table 3.1.

Table 3.1 : Information known to farmer planning to maximize income

crop	hours per acre labour requirement			net income per acre
	spring	summer	autumn	
wheat	9	7	3	$15.00
corn	9	2.5	10	10.00
Total no. of hours farmer has available	400	80	200	

The variables to be allocated in this case are two: corn and wheat, measured in acres. The problem is to decide how much of each crop to grow. Let us assign C and W as the acreage grown of corn and wheat respectively. The objective is to maximize income, which can be stated algebraically as

$$10C + 15W = \text{max.} \tag{1}$$

since $10C$ is the value of corn grown ($\$10.00 \times$ acreage in corn) and $15W$ is the value of wheat ($\$15.00 \times$ acreage in wheat). Expression (1) is the formal *objective function*. Note that it is linear (i.e. the exponents of the variables are one).

The constraints in this problem are four, one each relating to the availability of labour in spring, summer and autumn, and one relating to the amount of land available. The 'spring' constraint is expressed by the linear inequality

$$9C + 9W \leq 400 \tag{2}$$

which states that the sum of the times spent on cultivating corn and wheat must be equal to or less than 400 hours. Similarly, the 'summer' and 'autumn' constraints are expressed as

$$2 \cdot 5C + 7W \leq 80 \text{ and} \tag{3}$$

$$10C + 3W \leq 200, \text{ respectively.} \tag{4}$$

The last constraint arises from the limited size of the farm (50 acres), and is expressed by the inequality

$$C + W \leq 50. \tag{5}$$

The procedure so far would be followed no matter what LP method was being used to solve the problem. Using the graphical solution, the next step is to draw a graph with one axis for each variable. Each of the constraints is then plotted in its limiting case. Fig. 3.7 is used in this example. The 'limiting case' for each constraint in this problem is the maximum value of each inequality, since all the constraints specify a maximum rather than a minimum figure. For the spring constraint, the maximum is 400 hours, which would permit the production of 44·4 acres of corn if no wheat is produced or 44·4 acres of wheat if no corn is produced. Each of these points is indicated on the appropriate axis on the graph, and a straight line is constructed joining the two points. This line represents, in fact, the equation $9C + 9W = 400$. It is straight because the equation is linear. It represents all possible combinations of acreages of corn and wheat which could be grown by utilizing the full amount of spring labour. Straight lines representing the limiting cases of the summer, autumn, and farm-size constraints are also indicated on Fig. 3.7.

The next step is to identify the *zone of feasible production*—i.e. the area on the graph where production is feasible. The area between each constraint line and the origin is an area of feasible production with respect to that constraint. That is, any combination of corn and wheat acreages specified by a point anywhere in that area could be produced without exceeding the maximum constraint value. Given several constraints, the procedure is to find a portion of the graph that is on the origin side of all constraint lines. In Fig. 3.7 this area is ABCD, which is called the zone of feasible

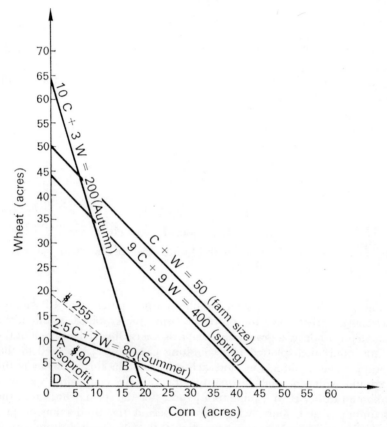

Fig. 3.7 : Graphical solution to linear programming problem

production. Any point outside of this area either involves a negative acreage, which is impossible, or exceeds one or more constraint maxima.

The last step is to find the point in the feasible zone which is best, which means, in this case, the one yielding the highest net income. The technique for finding this point is identical to the graphical method of finding the optimum output combination given fixed inputs which was discussed in a preceding section. An isoprofit line which fits conveniently on the graph must first be constructed. In this case the $90 line is chosen. Its location on the graph is determined by joining the points on the two

axes which represent the acreage of wheat required to net $90 (6 A.)
and the acreage of corn yielding $90 (9 A.). The line is straight, since the
net incomes per acre are assumed to remain constant regardless of total
acreage. The $90 isoprofit line, whose equation is $15W + 10C = 90$,
represents all combinations of wheat and corn which yield $90 profit.
All isoprofit lines will have the same slope as the $90 one, and will
represent larger profits the farther they are from the origin. Graphically,
the way to determine the programme yielding the highest income is to
find the isoprofit line which is farthest from the origin but still touching
the feasible zone. In this case, that isoprofit line is the $255.00 one, and
the programme generating this income is 5 A. of wheat and 18 A. of corn.
Note that only a portion (23) of the total 50 acres is used to maximize
income. One can also see from the graph that it is the summer and autumn
labour constraints which determine the optimum combination of crops.

The graphical linear programming solution can also be used for
minimization problems. For example, a common problem is to determine
a least-cost combination of inputs, subject to a number of constraints.
In these cases the procedure is the same, although the 'limiting cases' of
the objectives normally refer to minimum values, and the zone of feasible
production is on the sides of the constraint lines remote from the origin.
In the final step of the solution, isocost instead of isoprofit lines are drawn;
and the graphical objective is to select the isocost line which touches the
feasible zone but is closest to the origin.

When more than two variables are being considered (e.g. wheat, corn,
and barley) the graphical solution is very impractical. In fact it can not
be used if more than three variables are involved. Even for two variables,
the main use of the graphical method is for illustration and teaching.
The method used for most linear programming problems is the *simplex*
method, which will not be described in detail here.[1] It is not complicated
mathematically, but does involve a great many tabular manipulations of
data. Furthermore, it is iterative, and can require several 'runs' before
an optimum solution is discovered. Most simplex solutions are determined
on electronic computers. Any number of variables and constraints can be
considered providing sufficient computer size and time permit.

The relationship between linear programming and the theory discussed earlier in the chapter is significant. In many ways, linear programming is not just a method of analysis, like map comparison or
statistical inference. If the concepts discussed earlier could be called
theoretical models, then linear programming models are also theoretical.
We have shown graphically that the procedure for determining solutions
to LP problems is just like that used traditionally by economists to solve
theoretical problems. The only difference between LP models and the

[1] A number of good texts are available. See, for example, E. O. Heady and W.
Candler 1958: *Linear programming methods.* Ames, Chapter 3.

traditional theoretical ones is the linear nature of all functions in the former case. Naturally, this inflexibility creates problems in analysing some situations.

Non-linear programming

To allow more realism in the determination of optimum solutions than linear programming will permit, non-linear programming has been developing rapidly in recent years. The objectives are the same as for

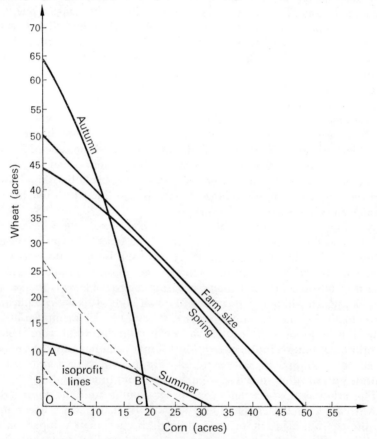

Fig. 3.8: Graphical solution to non-linear programming problem

linear programming, and the procedures similar; but linearity of objective and constraint functions is not required. Consequently, non-linear programming models can be identical to theoretical models, most of which assume non-linear functions in their most general cases.

One of the more common types of non-linear solutions is obtained through *quadratic programming*. A quadratic equation (the largest variable exponent is 2) describes a line with one inflection point—i.e. it bends in one direction. Since these types of lines occur so frequently in theoretical models, it has been useful to describe them with quadratic equations and to use quadratic programming to obtain optimum solutions.

Figure 3.8 is a non-linear, graphical solution to a problem almost identical to that represented in Fig. 3.7. In this case, however, the objective and constraint functions are not linear, and conform to more life-like characteristics. Note the similarity between the constraint lines and some of the isoproduct lines indicated in Fig. 3.2. It appears that crop diversification is preferable to specialization both because of labour shortages at particular times of the year (as in the LP solution) and because of greater production responses to fixed labour inputs when two rather than one crop are grown (as indicated by the curved 'constraint' or 'isoproduct' lines).

The major problem with non-linear programming is that much more information is required than for linear programming. Complete LP data are often very difficult to obtain, and the situation is much worse for non-linear problems, particularly when several variables are involved. For several outputs, for example, one would need to know the substitution functions among all pairs. This problem serves to illustrate the degree of the complexity of real-life situations, and the difference between inventing theoretical models and constructing real empirical ones.

Hypothetical problem

One could discuss a number of examples to illustrate the various concepts introduced in this chapter. Determination of the optimum combination of two inputs or outputs, given fixed output and input levels, respectively, is now possible without special procedures like linear programming. Using linear or non-linear programming, optimum combinations of any number of inputs or outputs can be calculated. The one example chosen, then, is only representative of a number of types of problems which can now be handled.

Figure 3.9 is a map of Agro, a valley located in a sub-humid tropical area. It is divided into a number of 500-acre commercial plantations. Agro has four main sub-regions, each somewhat unique in production capability. Area A has good alluvial soils, and receives reliable rainfall. B has fairly good residual soils, although many of the nutrients have been leached away. Rainfall is somewhat unpredictable, and droughts can occur. Area C is identical to B except that irrigation water is constantly available. D is a hilly area of uncertain precipitation and thin, residual soils.

Seven types of land use are economically possible in Agro—beef pasture, bananas, sugar cane, dairy pasture, rice, sisal, and tobacco. The yields and economic returns at optimum input–output levels vary among the four regions, since physical conditions give rise to different production functions for the same land uses. Similarly, the responses to inputs vary

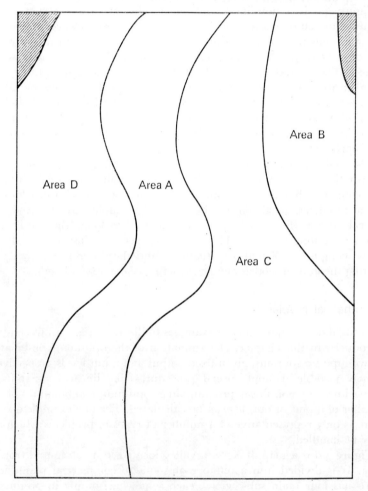

Fig. 3.9: Hypothetical valley of Agro.

among the regions. The average requirements of the inputs labour, fertilizer, and tractors for each land use (assuming optimum intensities of land use) for each region are listed in Table 3.2. The average quantities of available inputs per plantation and the average net annual incomes per acre for each land use are indicated in Tables 3.3 and 3.4.

Table 3.2: Annual per-acre requirements of labour, fertilizer, and tractors by land use and sub-region in Agro

annual per-acre requirements of inputs

land-use	Region A			Region B			Region C			Region D		
	labour*	fert.†	tractors‡	labour*	fert.†	tractors‡	labour*	fert.†	tractors‡	labour*	fert.†	tractors‡
beef pasture	4	100	0.006	4·5	40	0·005	4·5	110	0·005	5	0	0
bananas	16	150	0·020	15	90	0·012	20	180	0·020	26	70	0·006
sugar cane	22	200	0·023	21	160	0·023	22	225	0·023	30	0	0·030
dairy pasture	25	100	0·012	20	80	0·012	30	110	0·012	9	50	0·009
rice	20	150	0·021	20	160	0·020	25	170	0·025	30	0	0·030
sisal	4	20	0·006	4	0	0·006	3	30	0·006	5	0	0·006
tobacco	30	400	0·012	34	300	0·012	35	500	0·012	25	50	0·009

* measured in man-days
† measured in pounds
‡ measured in no. of tractors

Table 3.3: Annual availability of inputs per 500-acre plantation in regions A, B, C, and D

	total quantity of inputs available		
	labour (man-hours)	*fertilizer (pounds)*	*tractors*
Region A	20,000	100,000	10
Region B	10,000	50,000	7
Region C	18,000	100,000	10
Region D	10,000	2,000	5

Table 3.4: Average annual net income per acre by land use for regions A, B, C, and D

land use	*Region A*	*Region B*	*Region C*	*Region D*
beef pasture	$ 5.00	$ 3.00	$ 7.00	$1.00
bananas	$15.00	$12.00	$30.00	$0.50
sugar cane	$21.00	$14.00	$30.00	$0.50
dairy pasture	$17.00	$17.00	$22.00	$0.75
rice	$19.00	$ 9.00	$31.00	$0.75
sisal	$ 2.00	$ 2.00	$13.00	$0.90
tobacco	$30.00	$ 9.00	$29.00	$0.05

Questions

1 Assuming that the operators attempt to maximize profits and possess the full capabilities of 'economic men', what will be the average acreages of each land use, the average net incomes, and the input requirements on plantations in each sub-region?
2 How would these patterns change if the quantity of fertilizer available were (i) halved, and (ii) doubled?

Solutions

1 If we assume that production functions in Agro are linear (e.g. the amount of fertilizer required for optimum land use on 50 acres is exactly five times that required on 10 acres), the problem is a standard profit-maximization one which can be solved by linear programming. Actually, we must assume that production functions are linear, since we have been given insufficient data to assume otherwise.

Transferring the problem to linear-programming terms, we must determine the optimum programs for profit-maximization in each of the four regions. In each case there are seven variables (the seven possible land uses) and four constraints (one each relating to the availability of labour, fertilizer, tractors, and land area). For region A the objective function, which states that profits should be maximized, is

$$5BP + 15B + 21SC + 17DP + 19R + 2S + 30T = \text{maximum}$$

where BP, B, . . . T represent the acreages in beef pasture, bananas, . . . tobacco respectively. The labour constraint is represented by the inequality

$$4BP + 16B + 22SC + 25DP + 20R + 4S + 30T \leq 20,000$$

and the fertilizer, tractor, and land-area constraints are represented respectively by

$$100BP + 150B + 200SC + 100DP + 150R + 20S + 400T \leq 100,000$$

$$0{\cdot}006BP + 0{\cdot}020B + 0{\cdot}023SC + 0{\cdot}012DP + 0{\cdot}021R$$
$$+ 0{\cdot}006S + 0{\cdot}012T \leq 10$$

and $\qquad BP + B + SC + DP + R + S + T \leq 500$

Similar objective functions and constraint inequalities could be listed for regions B, C, and D.

The solutions could be calculated by hand using the simplex method, but long periods of time would be required. In this case, solutions were obtained using a computer.[1] The results are listed in Table 3.5. Note that combinations of land use are indicated in regions A and C, but monoculture is indicated in regions B and D. In all cases all 500 acres on each plantation are used, but portions of other inputs are sometimes left unused.

2 The answers to question 2 are calculated in the same way as indicated above except that the constraint values for fertilizer in the fertilizer inequalities are halved and doubled. The optimum land-use patterns assuming availability of half and double the normal amounts of fertilizer are indicated along with the solutions to question 1 in Table 3.5.

Note that, in most cases, changing the quantity of fertilizer available changes the optimum land-use pattern and the profits greatly. Only region D fails to undergo significant adjustments. This serves to point out that it is impossible to make specific predictions about the impacts of changing the availability of inputs without knowing details about the types of land-use alternatives. It also indicates a restriction of this application of linear programming. One could well ask 'if greater quantities of inputs lead to greater profits, why, over a long period of time should the quantities of those inputs be restricted to sub-optimal levels?' In real life one would expect the plantation owners to continue purchasing inputs until maximum profits were achieved. If unlimited input qualities were available in Agro, plantations in each region would only have one land use—the one yielding the highest profit per acre. Combinations of land uses occur in our example only because of input restrictions, not because of mutual, complementary advantages of sharing inputs among a number of enterprises on each plantation. The latter type of problem can be analysed by linear programming methods, however. One way is to include other categories of land use in our data which are actually combinations of land use—e.g., we could have bananas, sugar, and bananas–sugar. Another way is to

[1] An APL program called LINPRO was written and used on the York University Terminal System (IBM 360–50 computer).

Table 3.5: Linear-programming solutions for optimum acreages of land use, input requirements and income per plantation in the four regions of Agro*

land uses	Region A			Region B			Region C			Region D		
	normal fert.	½ fert.	2×fert.	normal fert.	½ fert.	2×fert.	normal fert.	½ fert.	2×fert.	normal fert.	½ fert.	2×fert.
Beef pasture (acres)	333·3									500	500	500
bananas (acres)							414					
sugar cane (acres)				500								
dairy pasture (acres)		500										
rice (acres)					312	500	53	250	308			
sisal					188			250				
tobacco (acres)	166·7		500				33		192			
Inputs												
labour (man-days)	13,333·5	12,500	15,000	10,000	6,992	10,000	10,760	7,000	14,420	2,500	2,500	2,500
fertilizer (pounds)	100,013	50,000	200,000	40,000	24,960	40,000	100,030	50,000	148,360	0	0	0
tractors (no.)	6·0	6·0	6·0	6·0	4·9	6·0	10·0	7·75	10·0	0	0	0
area (acres)	500	500	500	500	500	500	500	500	500	500	500	500
Profits (dollars)	10,667.	8,500.	15,000.	8,500.	5,688.	8,500.	15,020.	11,000.	15,115.	500	500	500

* Solutions obtained using LINPRO, an APL computer program for performing simplex calculations, on the York University 360–50 computer.

base the data on some real process giving advantages to multiple land use. The distribution of the operator's time on a number of enterprises requiring his labour at different times of the year would be such a process.

Further reading

The following are theoretical references concerning optimum combinations of inputs or outputs, or linear programming.*

BAUMOL, W. J. 1965: *Economic theory and operations analysis*, chapters 5, 7, and 12.
BISHOP, C. E., and TOUSSAINT, W. D. 1958: *Introduction to agricultural economic analysis*, chapters 9–11.
BOLES, J. N. 1955: Linear programming and farm management.
BROWN, W. G., and ARSCOTT, G. H. 1958: A method for dealing with time in determining optimum factor inputs.
CLAWSON, M. 1934: Relationship between farmer's return from an enterprise and changes in the size of the enterprise.
GIAEVER, H., and SEAGRAVES, J. 1960: Linear programming and economies of size.
HEADY, E. O. 1952: *Economics of agricultural production and resource use*, chapters 5–9. 1954a: Simplified presentation and logical aspects of linear programming Technique.
HEADY, E. O., and CANDLER, W. 1958: *Linear programming methods*.
HEADY, E. O., and JENSEN, H. R. 1951: *The economics of crop rotations and land use*.
HUTTON, L. F. 1957: Determining least cost combinations.
JOHNSON, S. E. 1933: The theory of combination of enterprises on individual farms.
LEFTWICH, R. H. 1963: *The price system and resource allocation*, chapters 9–12.
RAEBURN, J. R. 1958: Economies of scale in farming.

The following report on analyses, some using linear programming, to determine optimum combinations of inputs or outputs.

ALLEN, C. W. 1954: *Substitution relationships between forage and grain in milk production*.
ANDERSON, R. L. 1968: A simulation program to establish optimum crop patterns on irrigated farms based on preseason estimates of water supply.
BOWLEN, B., and HEADY, E. O. 1955: Optimum combinations of competitive crops at particular locations.
CALDWELL, H. W. 1956: An application of linear programming to farm planning.
DENT, J. B. 1964: Optimal rations for livestock with special reference to bacon pigs.
HEADY, E. O., and ALEXANDER, R. 1956: *Least-cost rations and optimum marketing weights for broilers*.
HEADY, E. O., BALLOUN, S., and DEAN, G. W. 1956: *Least-cost rations and optimum marketing weights for turkeys*.
HEADY, E. O., and OLSON, R. O. 1952: *Substitution relationships, Resource requirements, and income variability in the utilization of forage crops*.
HOOVER, L. M., et al. 1967: Economic relationships of hay and concentrate consumption to milk production.
HOWES, R. 1967: A test of a linear programming model of agriculture.
KOTZMAN, I. 1956: Solving feed problems through linear programming.

* Complete references in bibliography at conclusion of book.

TALP—C

MCFARQUHAR, M. M., and EVANS, A. 1957: Linear programming and the combination of enterprises in tropical agriculture.
PETERSON, G. A. 1955: Selection of maximum profit combinations of livestock enterprises and crop rotations.
SWANSON, E. R. 1955: Solving minimum-cost feed mix problems.
    1956: Application of programming analysis to cornbelt farms.

4 DISTANCE FUNCTIONS AND LAND USE

Relation between distance from market and economic rent for one land use—relation between distance from market and optimum types of land use—The effects of spatial variations in production functions—The effects of varying transportation routes and costs—Allowing for variation in the number of market centres—Relation to supply, demand, and price—Relation of distance between field and home to land use—Distance-decay functions surrounding urban areas—Hypothetical problem—Further reading

Much of the credit for originally formulating the principles relating distance to rural land use is given to Heinrich von Thünen. On the basis of fairly recent writings about him, one might assume that von Thünen was concerned exclusively with the effects of distance on land use, particularly distance between farm and market. One might even conclude that he was only interested in land-use rings surrounding a central market! On reading his original work[1] and its English translation,[2] however, one realizes that von Thünen's concern was far more comprehensive than is generally recognized. 'Distance' factors were analysed, but no more so than others, such as soil fertility, long-run crop rotation systems, changes in technology, or marginal analysis. The remarkable fact is not that von Thünen considered distance in depth, but that so many writers following him failed to do likewise. His other significant contribution was a method of analysis—the technique of postulating a simpler-than-reality model based on specific assumptions and deduced relationships to clarify some aspect of a real-life situation.

Relation between distance from market and economic rent for one land use

Von Thünen pointed out the tendency for economic rent to decline for a given land use as the distance to the market increased. The decline was due to rising costs of transportation since longer distances to the market had to be covered. Most writers have simplified von Thünen's concept somewhat by treating the decline as linear, even though von Thünen obviously envisaged a more complicated relationship. The theoretical

---

[1] J. H. Von Thünen 1826: *Der Isolierte Staat in Beziehung auf Landwirtschaft und Nationalokonomie* (Rostock).
[2] P. Hall 1966: *Von Thünen's isolated state* (London).

argument below will illustrate why a curvilinear relationship is more probable, at the same time indicating that an assumed linear one may be sufficiently accurate for much practical research.

Suppose that a single market is located in the middle of an agricultural area, every part of which has identical environmental quality and direct, 'straight-line' access to the market. All products of land use are sold at the one location. Uniform land quality occurs so that the same production functions occur at every location. If economic costs and returns are the same everywhere, one would expect the highest land use and optimum intensity of use to be the same in all locations.

In our hypothetical case, however, let us assume that all prices, yields, etc. are constant except the cost of transporting the products of land use to the market. The effect is that the price received for any product after transportation costs are covered declines with increasing distance from the market. If one assumes that transportation costs increase linearly as distance to the market increases, then the price received declines linearly with distance. This could also lead one to conclude that economic rent declines linearly with distance if it was assumed that land-use intensity remained constant everywhere. Several writers have described this assumed relationship in the form of an equation

$$E = (p - c - td)y,$$

where E = economic rent per unit area,
p = price per unit of production,
c = costs (excluding transportation) per unit of production,
t = transportation cost per mile per unit of production,
d = distance (miles) to the market, and
y = yield (units of production) per unit area.

When plotted on a graph (Fig. 4.1), the relationship takes the form of a straight line with a negative slope, indicating a linear decline in economic rent with distance. The steepness of the slope depends on the transportation rate. Rent declines with distance from the market until a *no-rent* distance is reached. Beyond this point, called the *extensive margin of production*, production is economically infeasible. A map of the area depicted in Fig. 4.1 would indicate a circular area (radius = MR) of uniform land-use type and intensity with the market located in the middle.

E. S. Dunn has shown that the rent–distance relationship should normally not be linear because (1) optimum intensity of land-use changes in response to changes in the 'effective' price of the product, and (2) transportation rates per-unit distance often decline as the distance increases.[1] With respect to the first point, one would expect a decline in land-use intensity and, consequently, output with distance from the market since

[1] E. S. Dunn 1954: *The location of agricultural production* (Gainesville) 6–55.

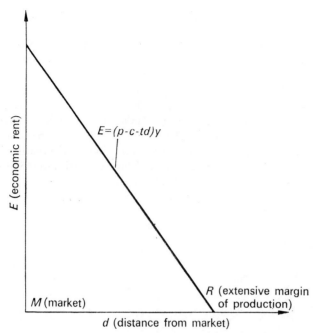

Fig. 4.1 : Linear rent–distance function.

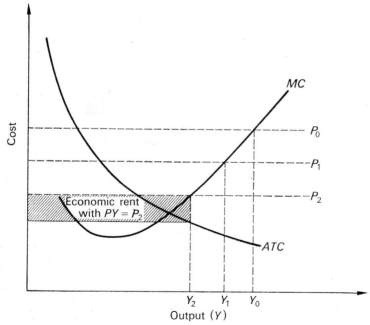

Fig. 4.2 : Optimum output level with varying price of output due to distance from market

the price per unit of output (after subtracting transportation costs) declines with distance. If a farmer operates where marginal costs equal marginal revenue (price of output), one would expect a decline in output, as illustrated in Fig. 4.2. Optimum output at distance 0, 1, and 2 units are indicated (Y_0, Y_1, and Y_2 respectively). Economic rent is also illustrated, since it can be represented by the areas of rectangles with height MC–ATC and length Y for each level of production. When economic rent is plotted against 'distance from market' allowing for decreasing intensity of use as illustrated in Fig. 4.2, a curvilinear relationship with an increasing rate of decline is revealed (Fig. 4.3). The exact shape depends, of course, on the specific production process under consideration.

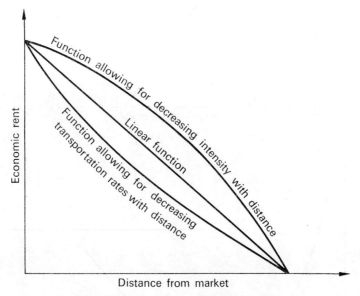

Fig. 4.3 : Alternative rent–distance functions

As for Dunn's second point, it is common for transportation costs per unit distance to decline as the total distance travelled increases. This would cause a rent–distance function to become curvilinear with a decreasing rate of decline (Fig. 4.3). This shape is contradictory to that derived for the situation allowing changes in land-use intensity. It appears to be relatively easy to predict distance–rent functions with most factors fixed, but difficult to derive a function for a general case where factors such as transportation rates change. Perhaps all that can be said as a completely general hypothesis is that economic rent declines with distance from the market with the general rate of decline depending on the transportation rate. The specific shape of the rent–distance function depends on the production functions involved and on any variations in

per-unit distance transportation rates. Whenever insufficient information
is available to predict the shape of a rent–distance curve, one might be
advised in the first instance to hypothesize the simplest possible relationship—i.e. a linear one.

Relation between distance from market and optimum type of land use

If a number of land uses are feasible, each will give rise to a characteristic
rent–distance function. Under certain conditions the land use yielding
the highest rent can change with distance from the market, and the
optimum land-use pattern in the area surrounding the market will
include a number of uses. If environmental quality and accessibility are
the same in all locations, the land-use zones will appear on a map as
portions of concentric circles surrounding the central market.

As illustration, consider the following situation. Suppose that four
land uses (vegetables, dairying, beef cattle, and wheat) are economically
possible in our area of uniform natural environment and uniform accessibility to the central market. Assume further that the transportation
rates per mile are constant for the products of each land use and that the
intensity of each land use does not vary with distance from the market.
The latter assumption is, of course, inconsistent with our theory; but it does
permit us to assume linear rent–distance functions which can be calculated
with a minimum of data. The relevant data for each land use are listed in
Table 4.1. The distance to the extensive (no rent) margin of production
for each land use has also been calculated and included in Table 4.1.

Table 4.1 : Production and transportation data for four land uses in
hypothetical area

land use	(1) price per acre of production	(2) production costs per acre of production	(3) economic rent without transportation cost
vegetable	$55.00	$25.00	$30.00
dairying	30.00	13.00	17.00
beef cattle	20.00	10.00	10.00
wheat	13.00	5.00	8.00

land use	(4) transportation cost per acre of production per mile	(5) distance to exten- sive margin of production (3 ÷ 4)	
vegetable	$3.00	10	miles
dairying	0.80	21·25	''
beef cattle	0.25	40	''
wheat	0.50	16	''

When a graph is made of the four rent–distance functions it is evident that the land use yielding the highest economic rent is different for different distances (Fig. 4.4). If the principle of land-use competition applies, vegetables are grown from 0 to 6 miles from the market, dairying takes place from 6 to 13 miles, and beef cattle are produced from 13 to 40 miles. Beyond 40 miles no land use is economically feasible. Note that wheat is not produced, as it is never the highest land use at any distance from the market.

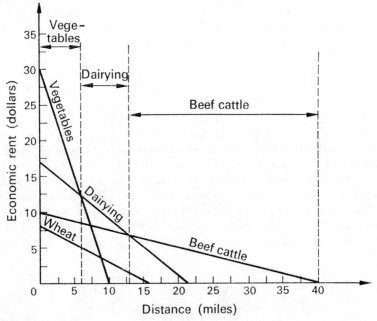

Fig. 4.4 : Rent–distance functions for various crops, and determination of optimum land uses

Figure 4.5 is a map of the hypothetical area illustrating the characteristic 'von Thünen rings'. One must emphasize the great many assumptions (which one would never expect to find in real life) lying behind the construction of such a map. These include the homogeneous nature of the hypothetical area, the linear rent–distance functions, the complete disregard for possible land-use variations relating to complementary production or economies of scale, and failure to relate price to supply and demand schedules. The only purpose of such a map is to illustrate in its very simplest (therefore unrealistic) case the effects of variable transportation costs and distance from market on optimum land use. That is not to say, of course, that real-life land-use patterns never bear any similarity to such a map.

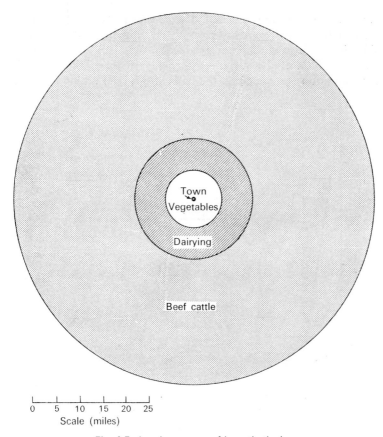

Fig. 4.5: Land-use map of hypothetical area

The effects of spatial variations in production functions

Spatial variation in land use has been attributed in Chapters 1 to 3 to only three factors: (1) spatial variation in production functions, which is related to natural environment, (2) spatial variation in the prices of inputs and outputs, and (3) regional constraints or limitations on factors of production. In chapter 4 the transportation-cost rent–distance factor, which is really a special case of (2), has been introduced. The purpose of this section is to show how it can be incorporated with the notion of locational variation in production functions to form a more comprehensive model of land use.

Suppose that the hypothetical area considered above is changed so that the east half is 'twice as productive' as the west half—i.e. physical yields of all products in the east half are twice as great as those obtainable for the same land uses in the west half. The greater productivity relates to a superior natural environment, particularly climate and soils, and is manifest in the form of different production functions for the same products. The effects of the variation in yields on the optimum land-use pattern can not be predicted on the basis of this information alone, since

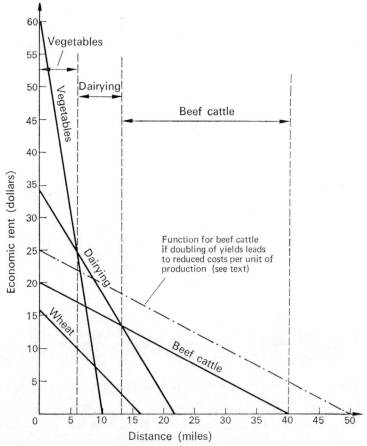

Fig. 4.6: Rent–distance functions for area 'twice as productive' when doubling of yields leads to doubling of economic rents for all land uses

economic rent, which is the variable of ultimate concern in land-use competition, can not be predicted solely on the basis of yields and product prices. Costs of production per acre must also be known. A doubling of yields will lead to a doubling of the gross value of an acre of production (yields × price per unit of production), but will lead to a doubling of economic rent only if the costs of production per acre also double. This would be unlikely, as one normally expects increased yields to lead to reduced costs per unit of production. Doubling of production costs would be possible only in situations where costs are closely related to yields— e.g. where most costs are those of harvesting, calculated on a per-unit-of-production basis. In the unlikely event that a doubling of yields leads to a doubling of economic rent in our example, the 'new' economic rent for vegetables in the east half, transportation costs excluded, is $60.00 per acre; but the distance to the extensive margin is 10 miles, if the costs for transporting a unit of vegetables remains the same as before (i.e. transport costs per acre of production double). The distance to the extensive margin is the same as in the west half. Similar changes occur in the rent–distance functions for the other land-uses (Fig. 6), while the radii of the land-use rings remain the same as in the west half. One concludes that, as a general rule, the distances to the extensive margins of production and the widths of the land-use 'rings' in different environmental regions are independent of inter-regional variations in yield. This assumes that the changes in natural environment affect all land uses equally (e.g. both vegetables and wheat *double* their economic rents in the east half of our area). If different land uses are affected unequally, the situation becomes much more complicated, and must be analysed separately for each region and land use.

It is much more likely that increased yields resulting from variations in production functions will lead to decreased costs per unit of production, since the costs of inputs such as fertilizer, fences, etc. will be much the same for all areas. So a doubling of yields will be accompanied by increases in economic rents which are more than double the 'old' ones. Under these conditions, the distances to the extensive margins of production and the widths of the land-use zones are greater than they were with lower yields. Suppose, for example, that the price per acre of production of beef cattle doubles to $40.00 per acre in the east half, and the costs per acre increase from $10.00 to $15.00 per acre. The 'new' economic rent is $25.00 per acre, and the distance to the extensive margin is 50 miles (Fig. 6) assuming that the transportation costs per unit of production are the same as in the west half (i.e. transport costs per acre of production double to 50 cents). This illustrates the often-reported phenomena of better environmental conditions (or production functions) leading to increased radii and sizes of land-use zones.[1]

The effects of varying transportation routes and costs

Since the basic cause of rent–distance decay functions is the increase in transportation costs with distance, it follows that any change in transportation cost or in accessibility to routes will have a profound effect on land use. It has been stated that the slope of the decay function depends

[1] E.g. see R. Barlowe 1958: *Land Resource Economics* (Englewood Cliffs), 253–5.

on the transportation rate—the greater the rate, the greater the slope. The exact slope can be calculated by determining the distance to the extensive margin, and observing the decline in rent over that distance (e.g. $30.00 over 15 miles, or $2.00 per mile, assuming a linear function). The distance to the extensive margin is calculated by dividing the economic rent obtainable before transportation costs by the transportation rate per unit distance. It is inversely proportional, then, to the transportation rate.

If transportation rates were not uniform throughout our hypothetical

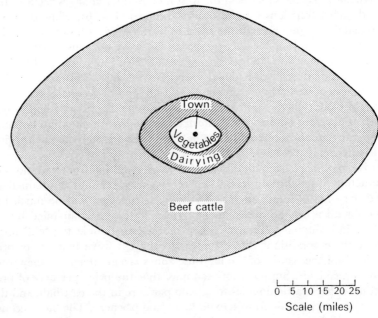

Scale (miles)

0 5 10 15 20 25

Fig. 4.7: Hypothetical area with altered transportation routes

area, but were reduced by one-third in the northern half, then the distances to the extensive margins of land use and the distances between land-use zones would increase by one-third (all other factors remaining the same). As a general rule, these distances vary inversely with the transportation rate. If the rates for the different products changed in different ways, however, one would have to complete detailed calculations for each land use before being able to predict precisely the changes in land-use zones.

The assumption of uniform accessibility to the market is quite unrealistic, as products are almost always transported along specific routes (roads, rivers, etc.). So straight-line distance to the market is less important than proximity to a route and distance along the route to the market. It is a common occurrence for farmers to transport products in a series of steps by a variety of facilities. For example, wheat may be carried from the field to the barn by tractor and wagon; from the barn to a grain terminal by truck; and from the terminal to the market by a combination of train and boat. Almost never is any of the routes a perfectly straight line. So land-use zones shaped like portions of perfect circles with uniform radii would be unexpected in real life.

Figure 4.7 is a map of our hypothetical area assuming uniform soil fertility, etc., but not assuming uniform transportation costs or accessibility of farms to the market. The transportation system includes a main east–west road where haulage rates are one-third cheaper than those on a main north–south route. A series of 'feeder' roads connects all farms to one of the two main routes. It is assumed that each farm uses the cheapest (not necessarily the closest) route to the city. Note the distortion of the land-use pattern from the perfect-circle type illustrated earlier.

Allowing for variation in the number of market centres

Our model can be modified very simply to allow for a number of market centres in the hypothetical area. If a number of markets are introduced each farm's land-competitive position is determined by calculating the economic rents (after subtracting for transportation costs) obtainable from each land use, repeating the calculations for each market centre; and the combination of land use and market yielding the highest rent is assigned to the farm. The total number of calculations per farm is the number of land uses times the number of markets.

Figure 4.8 represents the hypothetical area, now with three market centres. Physical environment, transportation costs, accessibility to the markets, linearity of rent–distance functions, and land-use intensity are assumed to be uniform. It is also assumed that no trade occurs among the centres, and that all products are sold to the three centres.

Relation to supply, demand, and price

The determination of optimum land-use patterns discussed so far in this chapter has taken no direct consideration for the types and quantities of agricultural products required in the market centre. We have assumed that certain unchanging prices will be paid for specific items regardless of the quantity supplied. This, of course, is inconsistent with the concept of price determination as a function of supply and demand. If transportation costs are lowered so that the distances to the extensive margins of production increase, larger areas will be devoted to the various land uses. An increase in quantity supplied will occur which will 'flood the market' and cause a decrease in price. Then economic rents will decline, the area under cultivation will shrink, which will cause shortages of goods in the markets. Prices will rise again, and so on. The entire concept of land-use equilibrium, which the reader should now recognize as a problem posed by situations such as that just described, will be discussed in the next

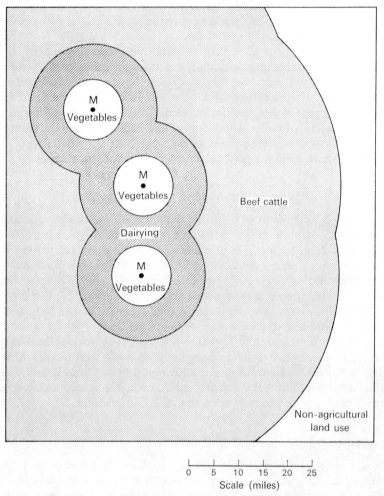

Fig. 4.8: Hypothetical area with three market centres (m)

chapter; but the part of that concept relating supply, demand, and price to 'von Thünen' land-use zones is best introduced here.

Let us refer to the situation represented in Fig. 4.4 and Table 4.1, and assume that the prices paid for the three products in the optimum land-use pattern (vegetables, dairy products, and beef cattle) represent a real outcome of the interaction of demand in the market and supply in the

countryside. The quantity supplied of each product is directly proportional to the area of each land-use zone, which can be calculated with some
simple geometry. If r_1, r_2, and r_3 are the radii of the circles demarcating
the outer boundaries of each zone, then the area of vegetable production
is

$$Av = \pi r_1{}^2 = \pi \times 6^2 = 122 \cdot 82 \text{ square miles.}$$

The area of dairying is

$$A_d = \pi r_2{}^2 - \pi r_1{}^2 = \pi(13^2 - 6^2) = 453 \cdot 74 \text{ square miles.}$$

And the area of beef cattle production is

$$A_b = \pi r_3{}^2 - \pi r_2{}^2 = \pi(40^2 - 13^2) = 4,882 \cdot 0 \text{ square miles.}$$

Now, if one knows the production yield per square mile of land use, the
quantity supplied of each product can be determined. This determination
is quite easy if a uniform intensity of land use is assumed, as it has been
in most of the examples. If the more realistic decrease in intensity with
distance is assumed, however, the calculation of the quantity supplied is
much more difficult using simple mathematics.

If the demand schedule for a particular product is known, and one has
calculated a change in quantity supplied resulting from a change in the
size of a land-use zone by the method described above, the new price
can be predicted by finding the price on the demand schedule associated
with the new quantity. As a further step one could determine the rent–
distance function based on the new price for the product, and calculate
the new, diminished area devoted to cultivation of the product. Such
calculations could continue almost indefinitely, however, since changes
in the area of one land use affect changes in the areas of surrounding
land uses, which, in turn, affect the prices of those products. Appreciation
of this fact serves to illustrate the interdependence of the area of a land-
use zone and the price of the land-use product, and, consequently, the
dependence of the price of a product on its transportation cost.

It is worth noting that the von Thünen type of model indicates that,
initially, changes in quantity supplied need not be related to changes in
the price of the product since changes in the transportation rate have the
same effect. One could formulate a supply schedule relating quantity
supplied to the rate of transporting the product. Such a schedule would be
unique for each land use, since the response of production to a change in
transportation rate would be dependent on the rent–distance functions of
other products in the area. This occurs because the boundaries of a land-
use zone coincide with areas where rent–distance functions of different
land uses intersect.[1] One could determine a number of indexes for the
transportation-rate versus quantity-supplied schedule similar to those

[1] It helps to understand this phenomenon if one envisages three-dimensional
distance–rent surfaces declining from the market rather than simple two-dimen-
sional lines on a graph.

defined for 'normal' supply schedules. For example, transportation elasticity of supply could relate a percentage change in quantity supplied to a percentage change in transportation rate. Or an index of cross elasticity could relate a percentage change in quantity supplied to a percentage change in the transportation rate of another product. Several spatial indexes of this sort could be formulated, but few have been.

Relation of distance between field and home to land use

The effects of the distances between a farmer's home and his fields on the land uses in those fields were of considerable interest to von Thünen, and have been discussed by a number of writers more recently.[1] Several instances of changes in land-use type and intensity which can be related to increasing distance from the home have been described. Many of the suggested explanations relate to characteristics of the social groups involved in agriculture, which offer little possibility of general applicability. Edwards, for example, has noted that fields far from homes in Jamaica tend to be used for types of production which do not require careful protection from thieves.[2] But certain other observations do appear to recur on a world-wide scale. It is for these observations that the economic type of model described below seems to offer some explanation.

The model developed to date is very similar to that relating land use to distance from market. It shows that, subject to particular assumptions, land-use intensity, gross income and net income decrease with distance from the home; and that net income diminishes more rapidly than gross income. It also indicates that optimum type of land use may change with distance from the home. Beyond these general statements, specific conclusions vary somewhat according to who formulated the models. Our purpose is to describe generally-accepted formulations, indicating only briefly areas of contention.

The simplest way to begin the development of a model relating land use to distance from home is to assume that a farmer, fulfilling all the qualities of 'economic man', lives in a house located a varying distance from a number of field sites of equal area. Let us also assume that he can only be engaged in one particular land use, and that the optimum output and combination of inputs for production in a field located at the home site are known. The problem is to determine how the input–output level will change for fields at varying distances from the home.

As distance from the home increases the time taken to commute between the field and the home increases. The effect is to increase the difficulty of providing standard amounts of human labour. This can be

[1] Chisholm, for example, has provided an excellent summary of much empirical research on the topic. See M. Chisholm 1962: *Rural settlement and land use* (London).
[2] D. Edwards 1961: *An economic study of small farming in Jamaica* (Kingston) 120.

interpreted as increasing the cost of labour, since the time consumed in commuting gives rise to an added cost of production. If one assumes that the cost of labour increases linearly with distance, then one expects a decline in land-use intensity as optimum inputs of labour decline with distance. The optimum input levels are determined, of course, by equating marginal costs with marginal returns at each location. Figure 4.9 illustrates the changes in output level associated with linear changes in the price of labour. Optimum levels in Fig. 4.9 occur where the VMP equals the price of a unit of labour. The author has argued elsewhere that the ultimate

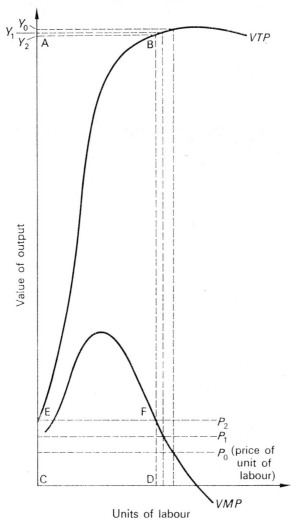

Fig. 4.9: Optimum input–output levels for various prices of labour

conclusion of this line of argument is a decline in output with distance
which tends to be concave away from the origin (Fig. 4.10).[1] This assumes,
however, that the input levels of other factors of production remain
constant, which is unlikely. One would expect some substitution of other
factors of production for labour as the price of labour rises. So the actual
shape of the output–distance decay function depends on the specific type
of land use and production functions under consideration. Chisholm
reports that decay functions with shapes convex towards the origin have
been described in many areas.[2] This can reflect factor substitution for

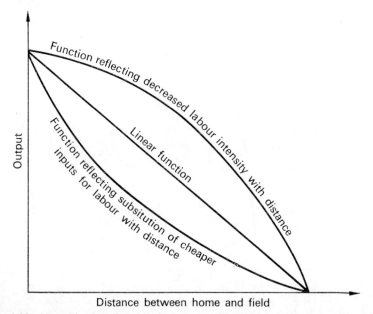

Fig. 4.10: Alternative functions relating output with distance between home and field

labour with increasing distance or, possibly, faster forms of transportation
for longer distances (Fig. 4.10). As for the economic-rent versus distance-
to-market functions, it is probably safest to begin by hypothesizing the
simplest relationship for unknown situations (i.e. linear) until more
specific information is obtained (Fig. 4.10).

The slope of the decay function depends on the type of land use—
specifically the extent to which production is dependent on labour. It
also depends on the time required for commuting standard distances,
which is closely dependent on types of transportation. In areas where
persons walk on foot to dispersed fields, one expects significant distance

[1] W. C. Found 1970: Towards a general theory relating distance between farm
and home to agricultural production. *Geographical Analysis* **2**, 165–76.
[2] M. Chisholm, 1962, 54–9.

effects on land use. If fast transportation is used, however, one expects little distance effect unless very long distances are involved.

The production-cost diagram illustrated in Fig. 4.9 can be used to indicate how gross output (or income) declines less quickly than net output (or income) with increasing distance from the home. Let us assume in this case that net income and economic rent are the same. The large rectangle ABCD represents gross income, and the smaller rectangle ABEF net income at an optimum input–output level. As distance to the home and the price of labour rise, ABCD diminishes in area, but not as

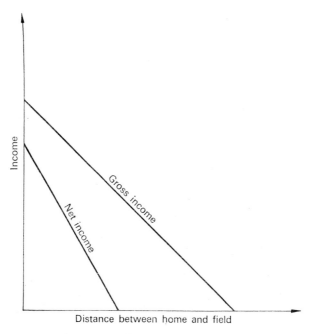

Fig. 4.11 : Decline in gross and net income with distance between home and field

rapidly as ABEF (compare, for example, these areas at prices of labour P_1 and P_2). From this relationship one can derive complete decay functions for gross and net output, as indicated in Fig. 4.11. The functions in Fig. 4.11 are assumed to be linear for simplicity.

If we drop the assumption that only one type of land use is possible it becomes apparent that the optimum land use—the one yielding the highest economic rent—may change with distance from a given homestead. Consider the situation represented in Fig. 4.12. Here three land uses are possible (vegetables, fruit trees, and beef grazing), each yielding different economic rents at zero distance from the home, and each having a different rent–distance function. It is probable that the different labour requirements give rise to the different slopes of the decay functions; and that a fairly primitive form of transportation (e.g. donkey) is used since separation from the home has an erosive effect on land use over very short distances. Linear decay functions have been assumed. Note that the highest land use changes with distance. Fields located from 0 to 2·5 miles grow vegetables; those from 2·5 to 4·5 miles grow fruit trees, and those from 4·5 to 10 miles are used for grazing beef cattle.

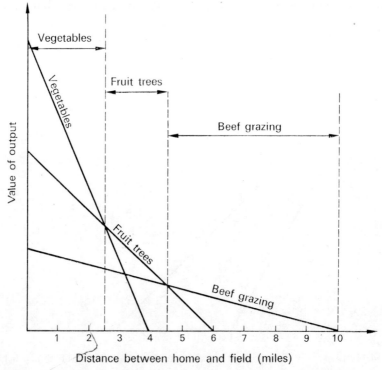

Fig. 4.12: Derivation of optimum land uses at varying distances between home and field

The discussion above has assumed that the operator has only one location for farming, and that all of his labour is used at that location. The situation changes considerably if the operator is using fields at a number of locations simultaneously, which is a fairly common occurrence. Obviously, distance-decay functions are important in determining optimum land-use patterns under these circumstances, whether the fields are dispersed or contained in one contiguous property. Other concepts not considered so far are involved, however; a more complete discussion of multi-field land-use patterns will be presented in the next chapter.

Distance-decay functions surrounding urban areas

Regular changes in rural land use which have nothing to do with the market-distance relationship discussed in the first section of this chapter can be observed surrounding many large cities. The phenomenon occurs particularly in areas with a relatively free land market and with a minimum of government control over land-use regions. It relates to a demand for rural land by various urban interests. Since cities are growing rapidly throughout most of the world, and since their effects are often widespread throughout the countryside, an understanding of the process is important.

It is impossible now to present one model relating rural land use to proximity to urban areas which, by itself, could explain the complicated patterns encountered in real life. A number of concepts have been formulated, however, each of which helps us to understand reality more clearly. The three discussed here relate land use and value to (1) the land's potential for urban development; (2) its value as a rural residence or playground for urban dwellers; and (3) the effects of urban employment on farm output.

If rural land surrounds an urban area which is growing in size, rural land uses normally switch to urban ones along the periphery of the city. This occurs because the land prices paid by urban users far exceed those which farmers can pay. This is an example of the principle of land-use competition, although the land under urban use may not generate any economic rent from a production process. In the case of residential use land value is unrelated to the capitalized value of any rent-producing process, unless one considers the possibility of an owner renting residential space to another user. The prices paid by residential land users reflect, mainly, a demand for space proximous to many urban functions. Commercial or industrial uses, on the other hand, generate an economic rent attributable to location, which is reflected in land price. Agricultural uses can practically never compete with urban ones within city areas. Occasionally, a very profitable or intensive land use (e.g. mushroom or citrus-tree growing) may survive against urban pressure for a long time; but capitulation to urban uses is almost universal, particularly in areas of free land markets and land-use selection.

Unless government controls over land value and use are in force, one expects the future possibility of rural land attaining a very high urban value to affect current land value and use in the broad area thought to have urban potential. If the area of future urban development and the timing of such development are known, the present value of the future price of rural land in the area can be calculated. This value is the future price discounted over the intervening time period at an acceptable rate of return. For land liable to become urban in a very short time period, the present value will be very high. Land to be developed further in the future will have a lower present value. One can envisage that this process, which can be called the *speculative process*, gives rise to a schedule of present land values which declines from the periphery of the city. The variables affecting the shape and steepness of the slope include the future urban values, the timing of future development, and acceptable rates of return on investment. The last variable, of course, reflects the degree of certainty of future urban development. A theoretical urban-speculative-value decay function is illustrated in Fig. 4.13.

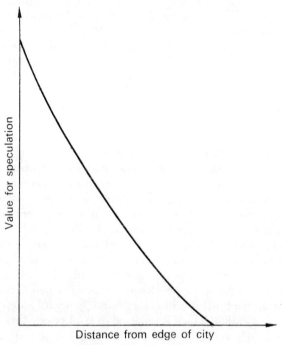

Fig. **4.13**: Speculative value–distance from city function

Expected urban development can affect present land use as well as value, as Sinclair,[1] particularly, has pointed out. For operators still farming the land, the land-use planning period can be much shorter than for farms beyond the speculative zone. So they are reluctant to undertake long-term investments, which may lower output levels. Sinclair argues, in fact, that agricultural land-use intensity generally declines as one approaches North American cities. The situation could be the reverse, however, if farmers, realizing that an early switch to urban use was probable, decided to abandon conservation practices and deplete the

[1] R. Sinclair 1967: Von Thünen and urban sprawl. *Annals of Association of American Geographers* **47**, 72–87.

land resources through very intensive use over a short period of time. Declining or increasing agricultural use with distance from the city would depend on the nature of the land use under consideration. Another reason for declining intensity of use with proximity to the city would be the tendency for some farmers to forgo optimum profits at the present in light of high future profits from urban development. It could be argued that such farmers would subconsciously place a much higher price on their own labour than formerly, thus reducing the current labour input on their farms. Another factor leading to low intensity of use could result

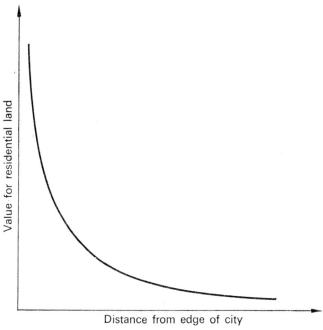

Fig. 4.14 : Function relating residential value of rural land to distance from city

from the sale of rural land to non-farmer speculators. Such persons might lack the necessary skill or capital to undertake agriculture, and would be satisfied to let the land remain idle until urban development occurred. They would defer all income from the land until the future.

The second quality of rural land surrounding an urban area which could provide for a distance-decay function is its value as a residence or playground for persons employed in the city. Certain persons or groups of people employed in urban areas often prefer to live out of the city, either because of the particular amenities provided in the rural countryside or because of relatively inexpensive living costs. If the demand for such land is great enough, urban buyers may be able to out-bid the value of land for agricultural purposes, and commercial agriculture will disappear.

Since proximity to the city is vitally important for this land, one would expect the values paid by urban employees to decrease with distance, producing a decay function like that indicated in Fig. 4.14. Since the area of rural land increases with the square of the distance from the city (the area of a circle is πr^2), the demand for land should increase with proximity to the city much more rapidly than in a linear fashion. For this reason the decay function in Fig. 4.14 increases exponentially with proximity to the urban centre.

The third factor which could affect agricultural land use surrounding an urban area is the possibility of farmers obtaining full- or part-time

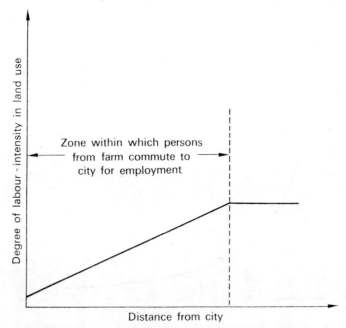

Fig. 4.15 : Function relating land-use intensity with distance to city

employment in the city. If city wages are higher than the returns obtainable from their labour on the farm, the opportunity cost of their labour should lead to a reduction of labour inputs in agricultural production. If one assumes that the availability of urban employment increases with proximity to the city, a distance-decay function for land-use intensity like that indicated in Fig. 4.15 could occur.

This section has presented three possible models relating rural land value and use to proximity to an urban area. All or none of them might have some application in a given situation, or totally different models might have more relevance. Up to this time no one has formulated a well-tested, combined model of general application. Much theoretical and empirical research remains to be done in rural–urban fringe areas as well as much broader rural areas surrounding urban centres. Furthermore, more accessible and faster transportation facilities seem to be constantly increasing the interaction between rural and urban areas, and having numerous effects on the rural land economy. In addition to the effects of urban areas on rural land use, other phenomena located within reach of agricultural regions could well give rise to other types of distance-decay functions. Decentralized industries could have a city-like effect by creating opportunity costs for farmers' labour, local demands for residential property, or speculative values for farm land. Proximity to electric power centres or telephone lines which could be accessed by farmers are other examples of phenomena which one might expect to create land-use distance-decay functions.

Hypothetical problem

Figure 4.16 illustrates a 400-square-mile area surrounding a central city. Three agricultural land uses are possible in the area: dairying (D), fruit-tree cultivation (F), and vegetable growing (V). The area contains

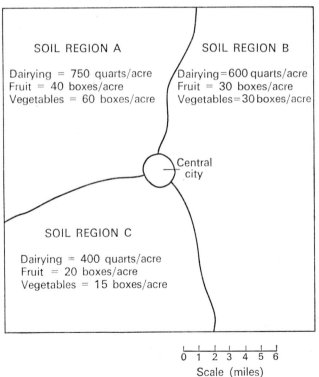

Fig. 4.16: Hypothetical agricultural area indicating soil regions and production levels

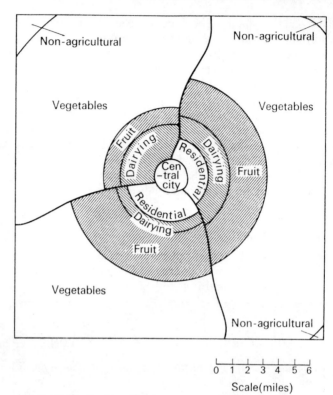

Scale(miles)

Fig. 4.17 : Optimum land-use pattern surrounding town

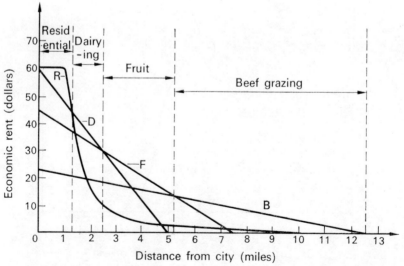

Fig. 4.18 : Graphical determination of optimum land uses for soil region B

three soil regions, each giving rise to different yields for the three land uses (see Fig. 4.16). Prices for the three products and their transportation rates are indicated in Table 4.2.

All agricultural products are sold in the central city, and uniform accessibility to the market and constant transportation rates are maintained.

In addition to the demands for agricultural products, persons living in the central city have some preference for rural land as a place to live. They will pay $1000.00 per acre for land within one mile of the edge of the city, but this value declines rapidly with distance from the city. In fact, the value declines inversely with the square of the distance beyond the one-mile zone, and becomes zero at 10 miles.

The current rate of return acceptable for investment in agricultural land is 6 per cent.

Table 4.2: Prices available at the market (edge of the city) and transportation rates for the three products of land use

	dairy product (fluid milk)	fruit	vegetables
Price at market	$0.10 per quart	$1.50 per box	$0.75 per box
Transportation cost per mile	$0.02 per quart	$0.20 per box	$0.06 per box

Question

Construct a map of optimum land use surrounding the city.

Solution

Figure 4.17 is a map representing optimum land use under the conditions described in the question. Its construction could be achieved in a number of ways,[1] but is easiest, in this case, using the graphical method outlined earlier in the chapter. Figure 4.18 indicates the graph used to determine the radii of the land-use zones in soil region B. Note the curvilinear distance-decay function for rural residential land. Its relative position in the 0–1 mile range was determined by calculating the economic rent which would give a value of $1000.00 capitalized at 6 per cent ($60.00). The value at two miles was $60 \div 3^2$ (10), and so on.

Further reading

The following concern distance relations and land use, particularly of the 'Von Thünen' type.*

BARNES, C. P. 1935: Economics of the long-lot farm.
BENEDICT, E. T. (Editor) 1935: *Theodor Brinkmann's economics of the farm business.*

[1] For example, computer programs are available to produce such maps directly. See G. Rushton 1969: A computer model for the study of agricultural land-use patterns, in *Computer-assisted instruction in geography* (Washington) 141–50.
* Complete references in bibliography at conclusion of book.

BIRCH, J. W. 1963: Rural land use and location theory: a review
BROWN, R. C. 1968: The use and mis-use of distance variables in landuse analysis.
CHISHOLM, M. 1962: *Rural settlement and land use.*
DUNN, E. S. 1954: *The location of agricultural production.*
     1955: The equilibrium of land-use patterns in agriculture.
FOUND, W. C. 1970: Towards a general theory relating distance between farm and home to agricultural production.
GARRISON, W. L. 1959: The spatial structure of the economy.
GARRISON, W. L., and MARBLE, D. F. 1957: The spatial structure of agricultural activities.
GROTEWALD, A. 1959: Von Thünen in retrospect.
HALL, P. (Editor) 1966: *Von Thünen's isolated state.*
HANSEN, W. G. 1959: How accessibility shapes land use.
HARVEY, D. W. 1963: Locational change in the Kentish hop industry and the analysis of land use patterns.
HARVEY, R. O., and CLARKE, W. A. V. 1965: The nature and economics of urban sprawl.
ISARD, W. 1956: *Location and space economy.*
JOHNSON, H. B. 1962: A note on Thünen's circles.
KRYMOWSKI, R. 1928: Graphical presentation of Thünen's theory of intensity.
LEWTHWAITE, G. R. 1964: Wisconsin cheese and farm type; a locational hypothesis.
LÖSCH, A. 1954: *The economics of location.*
SINCLAIR, R. 1967: Von Thünen and urban sprawl.
STEWART, C. L. 1936: Land values as affected by roads and distance.
VON BOVENTER, E. 1967: Land values and spatial structure: a comparative presentation of agricultural, urban and tourist location theory.
WEHRWEIN, G. S. 1942: The rural urban fringe.
WEINSCHENK, G., HENRICHSMEYER, W., and ALDINGER, F. 1969: The theory of spatial equilibrium and optimal location in agriculture: a survey.

5 COMPARATIVE ADVANTAGE AND GENERAL SPATIAL EQUILIBRIUM

Land-use regions—The principle of comparative advantage—Applications to the individual farm—Interregional competition—Spatial applications of linear programming—General spatial equilibrium—Dynamic models and recursive programming—Hypothetical problem—References and Suggested Readings

The theory discussed so far has two major weaknesses in accounting for real-life situations, aside from the problems arising from the specific assumptions regarding human behaviour: (1) it fails to allow for the trading of goods among areas with specialized land use, and (2) it fails to specifically interrelate the various concepts considered in time and space. This chapter will attempt to overcome these weaknesses with an introduction to the relevant theoretical arguments.

Land-use regions

Land-use regions have been referred to indirectly in a number of places in preceding chapters, but have not been explicitly discussed or defined. From the beginning, regional variations in land use have been emphasized and it has been assumed that such variations can be identified. Often such descriptive procedures are complicated, however, and the land-use region is a concept which has been developed to help in the descriptive process.

Due to variations in the scale and complexity of spatial land-use variation, the definition and identification of *land-use regions* or *type-of-farming areas* have often presented difficulties. Geographers particularly have groped with and advanced the theory and technique of establishing 'regional' characteristics and boundaries.[1] Without going into the complexities of these developments, we can provide a definition which will serve our general purpose and which represents the commonly-held meaning of a land-use region. It can be defined as *a spatially contiguous grouping of aerial units which exhibits a degree of uniformity in land-use type and/or intensity.* Land-use regions, then, are idealized models or concepts developed to characterize and simplify some aspect of the real world. Sometimes, when regional boundaries are abrupt and easy to identify on the earth's surface, the validity of the concept is commonly accepted, and agreement regarding

---

[1] See, for example, P. E. James, C. F. Jones, and J. K. Wright (Editors) 1954: *American geography, inventory and prospect* (Syracuse) chapters 2 and 10.

the location of boundaries is attained. Even persons not concerned with
the academic or theoretical aspects of land use recognize boundaries of
this type. Persons in many countries are familiar with local 'corn belts',
'tobacco areas', or other such regions. Problems often arise, though,
when broad, transitional areas of land-use change occur, when the
'degree of uniformity' is difficult to specify, or when the presence of several
land uses complicates classification procedures.

The degree of land-use specialization and the size of commonly
recognized land-use regions vary greatly. Throughout much of the U.S.
'Cotton Belt', for example, cotton acreage seldom exceeds five per cent of
the available cropland; yet in the western 'Wheat Belt' of Canada, wheat
acreage occupies much higher percentages of the cultivatable land. With
respect to size, land-use regions can be very large—perhaps half of a
country—or very small—e.g. three or four contiguous farms. It is even
possible to envisage groupings of fields as composing land-use regions
within single farms. A concept which may prove useful, but which has not
been well developed to date, is that of a hierarchy of land-use regions.
Groups of fields could be seen as mini-regions within local land-use sub-
regions composed of groupings of farms, which in turn could form parts of
larger land-use regions, and so on.

Explanation in standard economic terms for the occurrence of areas of
land-use specialization is more complex than one might first assume. In
the final analysis, land-use competition at the farm level is the explanatory
principle; but this principle is dependent on costs and returns which relate
to other concepts. One might be tempted to relate regional variations in
land use just to regional variations in resource base (production functions
therefore). The numerical examples at the conclusions of Chapters 2, 3,
and 4 involve this sort of explanation; and hundreds of articles, particularly
in geographic or agronomic journals, can be listed where the same basic
argument is emphasized. Even the traditional explanations of general,
world-wide agricultural regions relate strongly to world-wide variation in
land resources. No one can legitimately criticize the validity of these claims
as long as it is recognized that other factors are also involved in many
situations. The second major explanation discussed in preceding chapters
is a spatial variation in the prices of inputs and outputs which is not
necessarily related to the natural resource base. 'Von Thünen' land-use
zones surrounding a central market represent land-use regions related to
this principle. Regional constraints on the availability of inputs is the
third factor affecting the type of land use in a region which we considered.
The numerical example at the conclusion of Chapter 3 illustrates this
principle. In this section a fourth principle—that relating to comparative
advantage—will be considered.

The principle of comparative advantage

A feature common to almost every society is some regional specialization in types of land use, accompanied by trade of agricultural items among the regions. The Cotton Belt of the southern United States, the Wheat Belt of the Ukraine, or the coffee-producing zones of south-eastern Brazil are examples of areas where a degree of specialization has developed, and where the products are distributed widely throughout national or international markets. Persons throughout the more 'developed' nations have diets which are remarkably similar; but this is not achieved by local similarities in land-use patterns. In fact, areas of agricultural self-sufficiency are practically non-existent.

Whenever the trade of agricultural products among land-use regions occurs, it is highly improbable that the concepts introduced so far are capable of providing a thorough explanation of regional variations in land use. For example, one might try to relate land use in the Corn and the Winter Wheat Belts of the U.S.A. to resource base alone and be moderately successful until it was discovered that wheat yields in the Corn Belt exceed those obtainable in the Wheat Belt. The simple view of each region always representing the optimum resource environment for the dominant crop is soon destroyed, although individual cases exist where this holds true. This does not deny, however, that the resource base has a direct bearing on the dominant land use.

Suppose that two unlike areas can produce a particular crop—say potatoes. Usually the returns (physical quantity of potatoes) obtainable per input unit are different in the two areas. This could reflect differences in soil fertility, labour productivity, or other factors relating to land, labour or capital. If the returns to a particular input in one area are greater than those in the other, then we say that that area has a comparative advantage *with respect to that input* for the type of production under consideration. For example, for rice production southern India has a comparative advantage over northern India with respect to land productivity—i.e. rice yields are greater in the south under similar applications of labour and capital. Usually writers do not specify the particular input under consideration, and treat all inputs in aggregate. It is normally inferred that land is the input of concern. When it is stated that the Ukraine has a comparative advantage over Germany in the production of wheat or that Florida has a comparative advantage over Tennessee in citrus cultivation, it is assumed that the advantage is due to differences in land resources. Such assumptions are probably stated less often than they should be.

One should distinguish between a comparative advantage related to physical input units or to the value of such inputs. Two areas may obtain identical potato yields under identical applications of capital and labour. No comparative advantage with respect to quantity of output per quantity of input will exist. But if labour costs are cheaper in one of the areas, then it will have an economic comparative advantage. It is important, therefore, to distinguish between *physical* and *economic comparative advantage*.

Comparative advantage thus far has referred to the quality of one area relative to another. It is also the name of an important principle which states that, *where trade among areas is possible, each area will tend to produce those products for which it has the greatest ratio of advantage or least ratio of disadvantage relative to other areas.* If one assumes that the inputs have prices determined already, then the principle refers to economic comparative advantage. Otherwise, it refers to physical comparative advantage. The principle indicates that regional specialization will occur, and that each region's requirements will be obtained with the aid of interregional trade. It is not proposed that producers decide to specialize by recognizing the explicit functioning of the principle. Rather, the principle may be in operation without any producer being conscious of it. It may be seen not so much as a cause, but as the indirect result of each producer seeking to maximize net income within a free-trade economy. It is a condition which will be met if income is to be maximized within each region.

As an example, suppose that areas A and B both require and can produce rye and potatoes. The yields obtainable with identical inputs are indicated in Table 5.1. Area A has a physical comparative advantage over area B in the production of both potatoes and rye; and if the costs of inputs are the same in the two areas it also has an identical economic comparative advantage. Its *ratios of advantage* for rye and potato production are, respectively, 4 : 3 (60 : 45) and 3 : 2 (7,500 : 5,000). According to the principle of comparative advantage, area A should specialize in the production of potatoes (the product for which it has the greatest ratio of advantage) and B should grow rye (the product for which it has the least ratio of disadvantage). A simple calculation shows that maximum returns can be obtained for each region if the principle is followed. Suppose that each area has two input units available. If each area invests its two inputs equally in the two crops, the total production will be as indicated in Table 5.1. If A and B specialize according to the principle, A will produce 15,000 lb. of potatoes and B will produce 90 bu. of rye. The value of total production under specialization is greater if the value of the 2,500 (15,000−12,500) lb. of potatoes gained over the non-specialized production is greater than the 15 (105−90) bu. of rye lost. In area A the production of 2,500 lb. of potatoes would 'cost' or have to be accompanied by a reduction in rye production. 2,500 lb. require $\frac{1}{3}$ unit of input, so the reduction in rye output would be $\frac{1}{3} \times 60 = 20$ bu. In B the 'cost' of producing 2,500 lb. of potatoes would be $\frac{1}{2} \times 45 = 22 \cdot 5$ bu. of rye. In both A and B the cost of producing 2,500 lb. of potatoes exceeds the 15 bu. of rye lost through specialization, so regional specialization pays off. Specialization is only useful, though, if each area can obtain necessary products through trade.

Suppose that A requires 50 bu. of rye from B. The most that it will pay will be the amount of potatoes that it would have to give up to produce its own rye (125 lb. per bu.). On the other hand, the least that B will accept for rye is the amount that it would have to give up to produce its own potatoes (1 lb. for 111·1 lb.). After negotiation, suppose that a price of 118 lb. of potatoes per bu. of rye is established. Then A will obtain 50 bu. of rye and have 9,100 lb. of potatoes remaining; B will have 40 bu. of rye and 5,900 lb. of potatoes. If A requires more rye but B can not spare it, A would have to either produce some of its own rye by giving up some potato production or obtain rye from another region.

Table 5.1 : Yields obtainable for potatoes and rye in areas A and B

area	rye yield (from one unit aggregate inputs)	potato yield (from one unit aggregate inputs)
A	60 bu.	7,500 lb.
B	45 bu.	5,000 lb.
total	105 bu.	12,500 lb.

The case discussed refers to only two crops and two regions. The same concept can be applied, though, to any number of products and regions. Many suspect that such a principle is at work at many scales in such a complex manner. Rigorous proof of this has yet to be attained, partially because of the enormous data, mathematical, and computer-time requirements to predict land-use patterns on the basis of such a complex model.

Applications to the individual farm

The concept of comparative advantage has certain applications in analysing land-use patterns of individual farms. Often a tendency exists to think of farms as units of homogeneous nature, where field-to-field variations in land use reflect long-term rotations or, perhaps, proximity to the farmer's base of operations. Considerable variation in field-to-field productivity often occurs, however, because of variations in land-resource base. These variations may be man-induced, as when years of dumping of barnyard manure on fields near the barn create soil of above-average fertility; or they may be naturally-occurring, as when an historical geomorphic process has given rise to soils of varying structure, texture, drainage, or fertility. Fields or combinations of fields may be thought of as regions of varying productivity, and land-use specialization within these 'regions' can be expected. Admittedly, trade among regions of this type does not occur. But trade among other regions only occurs to maximize total productivity, and the maximization of total income can be seen as a rational objective for an individual farm. Adherence to the principle of comparative advantage and resulting specialization, whether among regions of fields, farms, or political units, reflects a basic maximization process common to individual operators, large societies or groups of nations.

TALP—D

The theoretical concepts developed so far suggest that land-use patterns of individual farms are very complex if economic-man assumptions are maintained. To begin with, attempts to maximize average yearly income over a long period of time (probably the safest general assumption regarding objectives discussed so far) normally involve annual changes in specific elements of the geometric pattern. For example, many agricultural systems require that crop rotations by field and/or year occur in order to obtain highest sustained yields from the soil. Secondly, production costs arising from the distance between individual fields and relevant points, such as the farmer's home, must be taken into account in predicting optimum land-use type and intensity. Thirdly, variations in the land-resource base within the farm make it impossible to consider the farm as a single resource unit. Complementarity of different types of output must be examined from the standpoint of regional complementarity as well as complementarity resulting from the use of common inputs. The determination of optimum inputs and outputs requires the consideration of an enormous number of possibilities. The problem is complicated in a computational as well as a conceptual sense.

Interregional competition

One way of envisaging an agricultural land-use pattern is to consider that land-use regions compete for the production of goods required at specific market centres. Demand can be considered to be concentrated at the market centres, with production being allocated to the agricultural regions on the basis of their comparative advantages. The allocation can be made on the basis on a number of criteria, such as the minimization of production costs. The criterion most in keeping with our usual assumptions is the maximization of net income for individual farmers within each region. If the demand at each market centre reflects the requirements of consumers in each region, one would expect the resultant land-use pattern to reflect operation of the principle of comparative advantage.

Note that if the allocation is made on the basis of maximum net income per farm, if there is only one market centre, and if differences in income are related solely to transportation costs, we could have a land-use pattern very similar to the standard von Thünen one, complete with land-use rings. The only difference is that the limitations placed on production at the market can cause discrepancies in the pattern from the normal von Thünen case, where no such limits exist.

Spatial applications of linear programming

As the reader may have suspected, linear programming has been useful in attempting to solve empirical problems related to the concepts discussed in this chapter. This is not to suggest that simulations of the complete, real-life processes associated with comparative advantage have been achieved; in fact, attempts at such model-building have begun with rather crude, limited examples. But progress in the form of better mathematical formulations, refinements of theoretical concepts, and increased computer capacity is constantly occurring; and Government as well as private land-use planning is relying increasingly on such models. The purpose of this section is to outline briefly, within the limits of concepts presented earlier in the book, a few ways in which linear programming can be used in the analysis of spatial problems.

Two applications of LP have already been discussed in Chapter 3. The determinations of optimum input combinations, given outputs, and of optimum output combinations, given inputs, for farms at specific locations were discussed. If one repeats these calculations at several locations (e.g. see example at conclusion of Chapter 3) the method acquires spatial connotations. Spatial LP normally refers, however, to problems where calculations for a given location depend in part on calculations derived from other locations. Space or location, then, become much more 'active' variables.

One of the simplest uses of LP is to allocate production to land-use regions, given market demand, on the basis of comparative advantage.[1] In such analysis regions and market centres are treated as units or points in space. Regions are considered as variables which are allocated values within specified production limits. Market demand, in simple problems, is not a schedule of prices and quantities, but rather a specific quantity demanded which is assumed to remain constant. Allocation is made on the basis of regional maximization of net income, minimization of cost, or other criteria. Following is a two-region, graphical example to illustrate the method.

Figure 5.1 is a map indicating a market centre and two land-use regions, A and B. The market requires 60,000 bushels of corn, and the problem is to allocate production of the 60,000 bushels between the two regions. Cost and production data for each region are listed in Table 5.2. The higher price received for corn from region B is due to its superior quality.

Table 5.2 : Cost and production data for land-use regions A and B

	region A	region B
maximum production	40,000 bu.	35,000 bu.
on-farm cost per bu.	$0.30	$0.32
transportation cost to market per bu.	$0.07	$0.02
price received at market per bu.	$0.80	$0.85

[1] A standard reference on this technique is A. C. Egbert, E. O. Heady, and R. F. Brokken 1964: *Regional changes in grain production: an application of spatial linear programming* (Ames).

Stating the problem in LP format, we have the following two inequalities and one equality. A represents the number of bushels produced in region A, and B represents production in region B.

$$A \leq 40,000$$
$$B \leq 35,000$$
$$A + B = 60,000$$

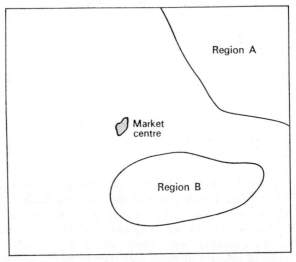

Fig. 5.1 : Hypothetical area with one market centre and two land-use regions

A number of objective functions can be used, depending on the criterion for optimization. If the objective is to maximize total gross farm income, the following function is appropriate:

$$0 \cdot 80A + 0 \cdot 85B = \text{max.} \tag{1}$$

For maximization of net income, excluding transportation costs, we have

$$0 \cdot 50A + 0 \cdot 53B = \text{max.} \tag{2}$$

If transportation costs, which are at least partly a function of distance from market, are included in total production costs, the maximization of net income requires the following function:

$$0 \cdot 43A + 0 \cdot 51B = \text{max.} \tag{3}$$

Included among other possible objective functions are those to minimize on-farm production costs (4), to minimize transportation costs (5), and to minimize total production costs (6).

$$0 \cdot 30A + 0 \cdot 32B = \text{min.} \tag{4}$$
$$0 \cdot 07A + 0 \cdot 02B = \text{min.} \tag{5}$$
$$0 \cdot 37A + 0 \cdot 34B = \text{min.} \tag{6}$$

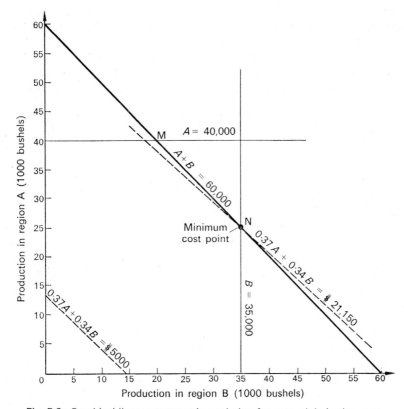

Fig. 5.2: Graphical linear programming solution for cost minimization case

The graphical solution to the problem is illustrated in Fig. 5.2. The two inequalities in their limiting cases and the one equality are plotted. Only the solution for objective function (6) (minimization of total production costs) is illustrated. The solutions for all of the objective functions are listed in Table 5.3. In this case there is not really a 'feasible zone' of production so much as a 'feasible line', since the equality A + B = 60,000 specifies a particular quantity of production. All feasible programs fall along the line MN.

Table 5.3: Optimum LP solutions for six objective functions

objective function	production in A	production in B
1	25,000 bu.	35,000 bu.
2	25,000 bu.	35,000 bu.
3	25,000 bu.	35,000 bu.
4	40,000 bu.	20,000 bu.
5	25,000 bu.	35,000 bu.
6	25,000 bu.	35,000 bu.

The problem discussed above is presented in simple, skeleton form to indicate a method which can be used to handle cases with many regions and market centres. The optimum solutions above can be determined easily without formal LP, but this is normally untrue if more regions or market centres are introduced. In the latter situation, researchers have found it necessary to use electronic computers and the simplex method.

Although the procedure offers intriguing possibilities, serious problems are evident, and much recent research has been concerned with overcoming them. One problem arises from choosing the proper objective function. Is it theoretically meaningful to assume that total production costs are minimized? Do *regions* maximize their net incomes? Is there any market mechanism by which transportation costs are minimized? Is the maximization of gross income ever an objective? There may not be a general answer to all of these questions except to point out that, in a purely-competitive society, regions as such do not decide anything; and the ultimate mechanism by which land use is determined must emphasize the individual farm operator. He may be subject, though, to regional or market processes beyond his immediate comprehension. The need for very clear theoretical thinking should be obvious.

A second major problem arises from the specification of a constant quantity demanded at the market, which is inconsistent with the general theory of demand. In reality we would expect the quantity demanded to be variable, depending on the price of the item and its price elasticity of demand. One might argue that the price specified for the crop would be accompanied by the stated quantity demanded; but this leads one to question the derivation of the crop price without considering demand. The search for justification rapidly probes into many unspecified areas, and many of the arguments become circular. For example, price is dependent on quantity demanded, but this is dependent on price. Examining the problem of price further, with particular reference to our example, one notes a basic inconsistency with respect to the corn prices in each area. If the prices are as stated, rational operators in each region could expect to grow corn and sell it. But if everyone follows this practice, the quantity demanded will be exceeded, and some corn will have to be unpurchased. So its price is not really 80c or 85c, but 0c.

A third problem concerns the lack of consideration in the procedure for alternative land uses which might affect production decisions. Individual farmers may not make decisions regarding corn cultivation without considering other possibilities. Operators in region A might find it more profitable to grow soybeans than corn, and any LP solutions might be meaningless in real life if this possibility was not considered. Furthermore, acreage may not be available for corn for other reasons, such as the necessity to keep some land fallow in rotation systems. In attempts to overcome these problems, two techniques have been particularly useful. In one case, regional allocations of production have been preceded by analyses of all land uses in each region to determine the types of land use that would be optimum and, consequently, undertaken at different price levels. Secondly, the area available for particular land uses within regions has been calculated to leave sufficient areas remaining for other uses, such as those involved with rotation systems or those yielding higher returns.[1]

The last problem concerns the assumption of linearity required in LP methods. Does, for example, the doubling of acreage mean a doubling of production? This problem may well be less bothersome than that indicated for individual farm analyses (see Chapter 3). It is normally feasible to envisage a number of linear relationships in large-scale situations. One example would be the assumption that aggregate farm production levels at the regional level are independent of land-use intensity.

In summary, two facts should be emphasized in this brief consideration of spatial applications of LP: (1) in analysing regional situations the particular LP format can create a number of serious problems, but careful manipulations following rigorous theoretical reasoning can overcome many of the apparent restrictions; (2) the usefulness and interpretation of any spatial LP model depends very much on a clear statement of all assumptions in the model.

General spatial equilibrium

A technique which has made possible much of the theoretical development discussed so far has been to assume that many variables involved in a given land-use situation are constant or given so that the inter-relationships among a few remaining variables can be examined. Examples of such assumptions are those concerned with market demand or the constant nature of prices and transportation rates. The models developed under these assumptions may be logically consistent within themselves, but, due to their artificially 'closed' nature, only represent *partial equilibria*. Such models are unrepresentative of much of real life, even in an abstract, simplified manner, because they fail to specify the inter-relationships of all of the major factors influencing the spatial distribution of land uses. This failure has been pointed out in preceding sections, particularly those concerning von Thünen land-use patterns and spatial applications of linear programming. The purpose of this section is to introduce the concept of general spatial equilibrium, to indicate some ways in which such equilibrium models can be formulated, and to outline their usefulness.

General equilibrium is said to occur in a land-use pattern when none of the elements or variables concerned with it is under any 'pressure' to

[1] See B. Bowlen and E. O. Heady 1955: *Optimum combinations of competitive crops at particular locations* (Ames).

change its status or value, i.e. the values of all elements within the whole system are compatible with each other. By definition, such an equilibrium is static in nature. As an example, if the land uses yielding the highest economic rent occur in circular zones surrounding a central town in concurrence with 'von Thünen' principles, no reason exists for the land-use pattern to change, and at least a partial equilibrium has been achieved. But suppose that the quantity demanded in the town for each product is suddenly specified, rather than being assumed to accommodate the current production pattern, and that an attempt is made to match up quantity demanded with quantity supplied. Chances are that the apparent equilibrium will be upset, as was illustrated in Chapter 4. The equilibrium established without consideration for demand is a partial equilibrium, then, in that consistency occurs within only part of the system. For consistency to occur with respect to demand as well, a *more general equilibrium* is required. One could continue to expand this argument, gradually doing away with assumptions regarding trade between regions, the prices of 'other' products, and every other assumed situation until a *completely general equilibrium* was envisaged. Such a model would have to interrelate every major component of the land-use pattern or 'system'.

A number of attempts have been made to devise models of general equilibrium for land-use patterns, even for non-market orientated economies. We will reserve our discussion of non-market economies until later chapters, and concentrate here on classical economic statements of equilibria. These are based on the usual assumptions of perfect competition, complete divisibility of all inputs and outputs, and total rationality. Typically, such models are concerned with equilibrium at the regional or 'industry' level, without specific reference to the individual farm. They are described, for simplicity and conciseness, by mathematical equations specifying functional relationships between variables.

A model described by Dunn[1] follows conveniently our discussion of the relation between von Thünen land-use models and the concepts of price, supply, and demand. We noted that the supply of a product in a typical land-use 'ring' surrounding a central market is proportional to the area of the ring, assuming a constant yield throughout its area. The equation by which the area is calculated is $A = \pi (r_0^2 - r_i^2)$, where r_0 and r_i are, respectively, the radii of the outer and inner circles bounding the ring. The two radii, of course, are a function of the graphical positions of the rent–distance lines for the various land uses, since they always coincide with the intersection points between pairs of these lines. And the rent–distance lines for each product are functions of yield per unit of land (y), market price per unit of production (p), costs (excluding transportation) per unit of production (c), transportation costs per unit distance per unit

[1] E. S. Dunn 1955: The equilibrium of land-use patterns in agriculture. *Southern Economic Journal* **21**, 173–87.

of production (t), and distance to the market (d). For any one product, the relationship was summarized by the equation

$$E = (p - c - td)y$$

where E is economic rent per unit of land. Building on this, Dunn has devised a series of equations which describe a state of general spatial equilibrium surrounding a single market. He postulates two conditions for such equilibrium, the first called the subjective condition, the second the objective condition: (1) all individuals and groups of individuals assume that prices are constant parameters, independent of their influence; and they base their maximizing decisions on these prices, which are derived from an equilibrium situation. (2) The equilibrium prices are determined by the condition that the quantity demanded for each product must equal the quantity supplied.

There are two aspects of the subjective condition, one referring to quantity demanded and the other to quantity supplied. As for demand, Dunn assumes that, for each of n different products, quantity demanded (D) is a function of the incomes (I) of the S different consumers in the market and the prices (b) of all n products. The set of equations describing quantity demanded for the n products is as follows:

$$D_1 = f_1 (I_1, I_2, \ldots I_s; b_1, b_2, \ldots b_n)$$
$$D_n = f_n (I_1, I_2, \ldots I_s; b_1, b_2, \ldots b_n)$$

With respect to quantity supplied, the quantity of each commodity produced is a function of the area devoted to that land use, assuming that yields are constant. In the simple von Thünen model, the quantities supplied of the n products are represented by the following set of equations (S is quantity supplied, r_i and r_o are the radii of the inner and outer bounding rings, and y is the yield per unit area):

$$S_1 = y_1 \pi (r_{1o}^2 - r_{1i}^2)$$
$$S_n = y_n \pi (r_{no}^2 - r_{ni}^2)$$

The radii, of course are related to the rent–distance functions for all land-use types, and can be related to the variables upon which those functions are dependent in another series of equations. The equations for the radii of the outer circles for the n land-use types are as follows (key to letters listed above):

$$r_{1o} = \Phi_1 (y_1, p_1, c_1, t_1; y_2, p_2, c_2, t_2; \ldots y_n, p_n, c_n, t_n)$$
$$r_{no} = \Phi_n (y_1, p_1, c_1, t_1; y_2, p_2, c_2, t_2; \ldots y_n, p_n, c_n, t_n)$$

So much for the subjective conditions. The objective conditions are that the quantity demanded for each product equals the quantity supplied. The equations representing this condition are as follows:

$$D_1 = S_1$$
$$D_n = S_n$$

It is appropriate to summarize the postulated conditions underlying this formulation of equilibrium. It is assumed that (1) perfect mobility and divisibility of all inputs other than land exist (returns to scale are constant); (2) intensity of land use and yield for each product are the same in all locations; (3) the supply of inputs is adequate for optimum production levels, and is available at constant prices; (4) only agricultural commodities are included in the system; (5) the incomes of all consumers are known and constant; (6) transport rates are constant over time and space; and (7) land uses are ordered around a single market.

The reader will realize that the equilibrium model described above is not completely general, particularly since multiple markets and interregional trade are not considered. It only represents one attempt at describing equilibrium. Different approaches to developing general equilibrium models have been attempted, and models of more general nature have been formulated. The important point to be made here is not to review all such models but to illustrate the type of procedure and the theoretical requirements involved in these formulations.

One might well question the usefulness of such general theoretical models, particularly the type described above where specific functional relationships are not measured. All that the equations do, in fact, is indicate in a very general way the types of relations which must be fulfilled if a certain level of equilibrium is to be achieved. It is mathematically possible to solve the equations listed above, and supply them with correct coefficients; but this represents an awesome task, even if proper field conditions and data could be discovered. This type of research has been undertaken, but it probably does not represent the real value of such models, at least for us. To this author, the most important contribution of such formulations is to specify the variables which are interrelated in conditions of spatial equilibrium, which is of great value in examining real-world situations. Spatial equilibrium may not exist, as will be discussed in the next section; but it is a very useful and logical concept in attempting to visualize and understand land-use patterns. Without it one runs the risk of failing to connect separate models of partial equilibrium, and of forgetting how limited and unrealistic such models can be.

Dynamic models and recursive programming

Several writers have pointed out that static spatial equilibrium can never be completely achieved, although it may be approached. They note that a change in any of the components of land-use equilibrium can change the other components, and that change is one of the most permanent aspects of life. For example, a change in the price of a commodity, or the prices of competing products, or of any costs of production or transportation can upset equilibrium and set off a 'chain reaction' of events. That no part of an economic system is independent of any other part is becoming increasingly obvious. Since the probability of change is so high, the best that one could expect would be for land-use patterns to reflect a constant attempt to achieve equilibrium, without ever reaching it. The process is complicated enormously by the interrelation of the land-use system with other systems, such as rural settlement or industrial sectors of the economy.

One can classify changes within components of land-use systems as those generated externally or internally. The external changes are the easiest to envisage, as they are seen as originating outside of the land-use economy, yet having important effects on it. Examples are the invention of synthetic foods which compete with farm products, the invention of new types of farm machinery which affect production costs, and the availability of industrial employment which increases farmers' opportunity costs. Changes generated within the land-use system are often much more difficult to perceive, but may be important. The most obvious example concerns the common occurrence of price variation and resultant oscillations in production and acreage as an equilibrium position is regained. For example, cold weather in a certain year might kill tomato plants and reduce production considerably. Prices would rise, particularly if demand was price inelastic, and farmers who did have crops to sell would obtain large profits. Seeing the above-average prices, farmers in the next crop period might overplant in order to share expected above-average profits; but the overproduction would lead to below-average prices and profits, which would lead farmers in the next crop period to underplant, and so on.[1]

Less obvious examples of changes in land-use components generated within the land-use system relate to reciprocal relationships between components. In the models discussed so far some variable is always assumed to be independent or given, and other variables are affected by it. But this simple relationship rarely occurs. For example, the personal tastes of consumers affect demand schedules and prices of agricultural products; but it appears that, through time, prices can affect personal tastes. Caviar may appeal to consumers as much for its price as its flavour. As another example, production techniques affect net profits; but, in the long run, profit margins also affect production techniques. Wheat was a product of proven worth before improved varieties were developed to increase the reliability and profits of production. Recent studies suggest that almost all relationships in economic and some other systems are reciprocal; and that such *feed-back* effects reduce even further the probability of equilibrium being established. This realization places the economic models discussed above on even more tenuous ground, as they

[1] See the discussion of the Cobweb Theorem in E. O. Heady 1952: *Economics of agricultural production and resource use* (Englewood Cliffs) 482–8.

were developed on the assumption of one-way relationships and given constant variables.

What types of dynamic land-use models are available, then? Some writers have been very quick to point out that the traditional economic models offer little in terms of dynamic processes. Although this is true in a general way, particularly with respect to the models of general equilibrium, dynamic aspects are present in a number of traditional concepts. Demand, for example, is defined for a specific time period; yet it is recognized that the shape of demand schedules is partially dependent on schedules expected in the future. Many traditional models can also be useful in dynamic situations if one assumes that relationships apparent in one time period will also hold in others. One could devise a type of dynamic model of land use which is composed of a number of static models strung together, with each 'new' model based on the same relationships as the others, yet with changed variable values. The example at the conclusion of Chapter 3 is a dynamic model of this type in that land-use patterns are predicted assuming various availabilities of fertilizer which could be correlated with time periods. It is probable that many theoretical dynamic models of this type could be devised on the basis of existing static theory. The general equilibrium model discussed above assumes that quantity demanded depends solely on the incomes of consumers and the prices of all commodities. But one could add interesting dynamic qualities to this model by making quantity demanded also a function of expected future prices for all products.

What most land-use theories have been incapable of providing are models to predict genetic or evolutionary changes through time. And such models are exceptionally important, particularly in regional or national planning situations. Much effort is being spent on such theoretical problems, but it is too soon to conclude the extent to which these efforts will be successful. The problem is formidable, perhaps as formidable as that faced by an historian trying to develop a model of historical change.

Linear programming and similar methods have been applied to provide empirical models with certain dynamic qualities. Normally they are called recursive or dynamic programming models. In the simplest type, land-use patterns are generated in accordance with some static theoretical model during a number of successive time periods. Each 'run' of the model is independent of others except for the definition of functional relationships among the variables, and the model achieves its dynamic quality by allowing the values of some variable or variables to change from one time period to another. The value changes may be assumed, predicted from some other concept, or observed in real life. The models may be designed to optimize some objective in each time period (in recursive programming models), or to optimize an objective at the completion of the entire run (in dynamic programming models). In some models land-use patterns in a given time period are not completely independent o preceding ones. Limits are set on the amount of change permissible between time periods in an attempt to replicate lag or inertial effects in real life. In many cases these inertial effects are built in to simulate postulated slow human response to changed situations. In the extreme case of this type of model land-use patterns are entirely dependent on the specified functional relationships and on the outcome of the preceding pattern. Attempts are made to replicate oscillating or constantly changing patterns by forcing the model to generate its own changes without given variable changes.

Hypothetical problem

Figure 5.3 is a map of Luro, a central market surrounded by seven land-use regions. Each of the regions can produce a number of crops, but oats is the crop yielding highest economic rents. Transportation and other production costs vary among the seven regions, yet producers in each area receive 80 cents per bushel for oats at the market. All oats are of the same quality, and all can be marketed only in the central location. Table 5.4 indicates the maximum production, the costs and the profits for oats production in each region.

Questions

1 Determine the optimum distribution of oats production among the seven regions so as (a) to maximize net farm income, and (b) to minimize transportation costs. Assume that the quantity of oats demanded at Luro is 10,000 bushels.

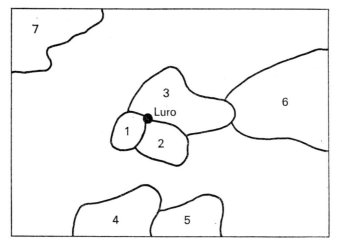

Fig. 5.3 : The seven land-use regions surrounding Luro

Table 5.4 : Costs, returns and limits for oats production in the seven regions surrounding Luro

region	prod. costs (cents per bu.)	transportation costs (cents per bu.)	net returns, exclusive of transportation costs (cents per bu.)	net returns after transp. cost (cents per bu.)	maximum production (bushels)
1	35	4	45	41	1,000
2	37	4	43	39	1,500
3	33	5	47	42	2,500
4	26	7	54	47	2,000
5	25	8	55	47	2,000
6	30	10	50	40	3,000
7	32	10	48	38	3,000

Table 5.5: Optimum allocations of oats production among the seven regions surrounding Luro*

criterion	region 1	region 2	region 3	region 4	region 5	region 6	region 7
1. (a) maximize net farm income (farmers pay transportation)	1,000	0	2,500	2,000	2,000	2,500	0
Total prod. = 10,000 bu.							
1. (b) minimize transportation costs	1,000	1,500	2,500	2,000	2,000	1,000 ⤳ OR ⤳	1,000
Total prod. = 10,000 bu.							
2. maximize net farm income (gov't pays transportation)	0	0	0	2,000	2,000	3,000	3,000
Total prod. = 10,000 bu.							
3. maximize net farm income (farmers pay transportation)	0	0	2,000	2,000	2,000	0	0
Total prod. = 6,000 bu.							

* Simplex calculations made using LINPRO, an APL computer program at York University (I.B.M. 360–50 computer).

2 Determine the optimum distribution if the government decides to subsidize oats production by paying for all transportation costs. Assume that net farm income is maximized.

3 If the quantity demanded is decreased to 6,000 bushels, how will this affect the distribution of production? Assume that transportation costs are paid by farmers, and that net farm income is maximized.

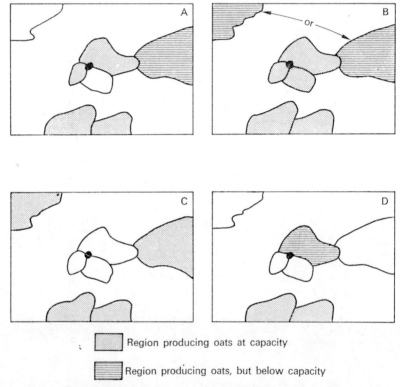

☐ Region producing oats at capacity

▤ Region producing oats, but below capacity

Fig. 5.4: Optimum spatial allocation of oats production according to 4 different criteria: **A**: Maximization of net farm income (farmers pay transportation). Production = 10,000 bu. **B**: Minimization of transportation costs. Production = 10,000 bu. **C**: Maximization of net farm income (govt. pays transportation). Production = 10,000 bu. **D**: Maximization of net farm income (farmers pay transportation). Production = 6,000 bu.

Solutions

The problems can be solved most easily by using spatial linear programming, as discussed earlier in the chapter. To state the problem in LP format, let X_1, X_2, X_3, . . . X_7 represent the number of bushels of oats produced in regions 1, 2, 3, . . . 7. Then the constraints arising from the production limits of each region are as follows:

$$X_1 \leqslant 1,000$$
$$X_2 = 1,500$$
$$X_3 = 2,500$$
$$X_5 = 2,000$$
$$X_6 = 2,000$$
$$X_7 = 3,000$$

For question 1(a), a further constraint, specifying total production, is

$$X_1 + X_2 + X_3 + X_4 + X_5 + X_6 + X_7 = 10,000.$$

The objective function is

$$41X_1 + 39X_2 + 42X_3 + 47X_4 + 47X_5 + 40X_6 + 38X_7 = \text{max.}$$

The problem can then be solved using the simplex method, as can the other problems, using similar procedures. In the case of question 3, the quantity-demanded constraint specifies 6,000 rather than 10,000 bushels. Table 5.5 indicates the optimum solutions for each problem, and Figs. 5.4 A–D illustrate the results in map form.

Further reading

The following are theoretical and methodological references concerning comparative advantage, interregional competition, dynamic models, and agricultural regions.*

BELLMAN, R. 1957: *Dynamic programming.*
BELLMAN, R., and DREYFUS, S. F. 1962: *Applied dynamic programming.*
CANDLER, W. 1960: Reflections on dynamic programming models.
DAY, R. H. 1963a: On aggregating linear programming models of production. 1963b: *Recursive programming and production response.*
DAY, R. H., and TINNEY, E. H. 1969: A dynamic von Thünen model.
DAY, R. H., and KENNEDY, P. E. 1970: On a dynamic location model of production.
GARRISON, W. L., and MARBLE, D. F. 1957: The spatial structure of agricultural activities.
HADLEY, G. 1964: *Nonlinear and dynamic programming.*
HASSLER, J. B. 1959: Interregional competition in agriculture: principal forces, normative models and reality.
HEADY, E. O., and HALL, H. H. 1968: Linear and non-linear spatial models in agricultural competition, land use and production potential.
HEADY, E. O., and EGBERT, A. C. 1964: Regional programming of efficient agricultural production patterns.
HENDERSON, J. M. 1959: The utilization of agricultural land: a theoretical and empirical enquiry.
HORVATH, R. J., and SPENCER, J. E. 1963: How does an agricultural region originate?
JOHNSON, S. E. 1937: Interregional competition and comparative advantage in agriculture.

* Complete references given in bibliography at conclusion of book.

JUDGE, G. T., and WALLACE, T. D. 1958: Estimation of spatial price equilibrium models.

MCARTY, H. H. 1946: The Theoretical nature of land use regions.

MCLOUGHLIN, P. F. M. 1966: Development policy-making and the geographer's regions: comments by an economist.

MIGHELL, R. L., and BLACK, J. D. 1951: *Interregional competition in agriculture.*

MINDEN, A. J. 1968: Dynamic programming: a tool for farm firm growth research.

NEWSHAUSER, G. L. 1966: *Introduction to dynamic programming.*

SCHALLER, W. N., and DEAN, G. W. 1965: *Predicting regional crop production: an application of recursive programming.*

THROSBY, C. D. 1964: Some dynamic programming models for farm management research.

YARON, D., PLESSNER, Y., and HEADY, E. O. 1965: Competitive equilibrium.

The following represent attempts to apply regional and dynamic concepts in real-world settings.

BAKER, O. E. 1926: Agricultural regions of North America.

BLACK, J. D., and MIGHELL, R. L. 1957: *Interregional competition in agriculture with special reference to dairy farming in the Lake States and New England.*

BREDO, W., and ROJKO, A. S. 1952: *Prices and milksheds of northeastern markets.*

CARTER, H. A., and HEADY, E. O. 1959: An input–output analysis emphasizing regional and commodity sectors of agriculture.

CRADDOCK, W. J. 1970: *Interregional competition in Canadian cereal production.*

EGBERT, A. C., and RENTLINGER, S. 1965: A dynamic model of the livestock feed sector.

EGBERT, A. C., BROKKEN, R. F., and HEADY, E. O. 1964: *Regional changes in grain production.*

EGBERT, A. C., and HEADY, E. O. 1961: *Regional adjustments in grain production: a linear programming analysis.*

FOX, K. 1958: A spatial equilibrium model of the livestock-feed economy in the United States.

FOX, K., and TAEUBER, R. 1955: Spatial equilibrium models of the livestock-feed economy.

HALL, H. H., HEADY, E. O., and PLESSNER, Y. 1968: Quadratic programming solution of competition equilibrium for U.S. agriculture.

HAMMERBERG, D. O. 1940: Allocation of milk supplies among contiguous markets.

HEADY, E. O., and SKOLD, M. 1965: *Projections of U.S. agricultural capacity and interregional adjustments in production and land use with spatial programming models.*

HERTSGAARD, T. A. 1962: *Interregional Analysis of the corn sector.*

1963: *Interregional analysis of the soybean sector.*

1964: *Optimum patterns of production and distribution of livestock and poultry products.*

HILL, L. D. 1965: *Agricultural market planning in resource development.*

JONASSON, O. 1926: Agricultural regions of Europe.

KOTTKE, M. 1970: Spatial, temporal and product-use allocation of milk in an imperfectly competitive dairy industry.

LOFTSGARD, L. D., and HEADY, E. O. 1959: Application of dynamic programming models for optimum farm and home plans.

MACLEOD, A. 1937: *The milksheds of New Hampshire.*

MCDONALD, G. T. 1970: *Background to constructing a synthetic predictive model of agricultural land use in Ontario.*

MEYER, C. F., and NEWETT, R. J. 1970: Dynamic programming for feedlot optimization.

MORRILL, R. L., and GARRISON, W. L. 1960: Projections of interregional patterns of trade in wheat and flour.

RANDHAWA, N. S., and HEADY, E. O. 1964: An interregional programming model for agricultural planning in India.

SCHNITTKAR, J. A., and HEADY, E. O. 1958: *Application of input–output analysis to a regional model stressing agriculture.*

SNODGRASS, M. M. 1956: Linear programming—a new approach to interregional competition in dairying.

WHITTLESEY, D. 1936: Major agricultural regions of the earth.

WOOD, A. W. 1965: The implications of interregional competition in Canadian agriculture for government programs aimed at direct support of farm incomes.

6 DECISION MAKING UNDER RISK AND UNCERTAINTY AND THE THEORY OF GAMES

Decision making under risk—Decision making under imputed risk—The regret criterion—Mixed strategies—Hypothetical problem—Further reading

One of the most permanent aspects of land-use decision making is that many events cannot be predicted with 100 per cent accuracy. Prices at the time of harvest, availability of hired labour, machinery breakdown, technological change, government action, and weather conditions are all examples of factors which affect land-use productivity and income, but which are seldom known precisely before they occur. Yet all of the theory discussed so far assumes that future events are known in advance, which is a serious weakness in attempting to account for real-life conditions. In response to this realization, many advances have been made, particularly in the last twenty years, in the development of theoretical models which take into account man's inability to predict future events with accuracy. Many of these models, and all of those discussed in this chapter, still assume that man optimizes some objective, although it need not be to maximize net annual income.

Decision making under risk

In social science, use of the term *risk* assumes that decision makers have an estimate of some future value or event, but that their estimate is subject to some error. If the probable error is small, we say that the risk is slight; if the probable error is large, the situation is said to be quite 'risky'. It may be highly unlikely that a farmer's crops and barns will be destroyed by a tornado, so little risk from this possibility is incurred. Yet a great deal of risk may be incurred by a farmer planting a citrus grove in an area subject to frequent frosts. In both of these cases the farmer has a fairly good idea of the probability of disaster, so a situation of risk occurs. This is in direct contrast to the situation where a farmer has no estimate of the probability of a future event, which is referred to as a condition of *uncertainty*.

Suppose that a farmer has four crops which can be grown (rice, wheat, soybeans, and oats) and that, on the basis of many years of climate records, he knows the probabilities of five types of weather occurring in a single year. The five weather types are very dry, dry, average, wet, and very wet, and it is assumed that a given year fits entirely into one of the five categories. The five probabilities add up to 1·0 since the five categories include all possible weather types. The farmer knows the average income per acre obtainable under optimum input–output conditions for each of the four crops in each of the five weather types. The four-by-five matrix summarizing all the information known to the farmer is indicated in Table 6.1.

Table 6.1 : Average per-acre income, by crop and weather type, and probability of weather type in a given year

weather type	very dry	dry	average	wet	very wet
probability of occurrence	0·10	0·20	0·30	0·20	0·20
crop	average per-acre income ($)				
rice	10	13	18	20	22
wheat	25	21	17	12	8
soybeans	12	17	23	17	11
oats	12	13	17	19	21

What land use should the farmer undertake? Let us assume in the first instance that a state of competitive production exists such that only one land use is feasible in a given year (i.e. crop combinations are not economically feasible). A simple solution would be to note that 'average' weather conditions occur more regularly (30 per cent of the time) than any others, and to select the crop which yields the highest income in an 'average' year (soybeans). But note that 'average' weather doesn't really occur very often, even though it occurs more often than any other single type; and that under very dry and very wet conditions soybeans yield very low incomes. So perhaps another crop would be a safer 'bet'.

A more complicated but better decision can be made by using an elementary probability technique of discovering which crop would have the highest 'expected' income, taking into account the probabilities of all possible weather conditions. The overall expected value for each crop is calculated by adding together the products of weather-type probability and average income for the relevant weather type. The expected income for rice, for example, is

$$0·10(10) + 0·20(13) + 0·30(18) + 0·20(20) + 0·20(22) = \$17.40$$

The similar expected incomes for wheat, soybeans, and oats are, respectively, $15.80, $17.10 and $16.90. So the best crop to grow on the basis of the 'expected value' criterion is rice.

It is possible that other criteria might be used to decide on other crops as being the best. Suppose that the farmer is a gambler and wants to try for the highest possible income—$25.00 per acre, obtainable with wheat. He might plant wheat on the chance of obtaining this income, even though the chances are only one in ten that he will succeed. At the opposite extreme is the pessimist or conservative who wants to get away with the least damage in case of a weather disaster. He would select the crop which yields the highest income under the worst possible conditions. In this case oats, which brings $12.00 under very dry conditions, would be selected.

Farm operators should consider the consequences of using crop combinations. Let us assume that optimum per-acre incomes can still be obtained if combinations of land uses are employed—i.e. product transformation functions are linear. The optimum combination is that which yields the highest 'expected' value, as defined above. In this case we do not know the relative proportions of the four crops, which makes the calculations more complicated. Linear programming can be used to solve the problem. Let R = the proportion of land in rice, W = proportion in wheat, S = proportion in soybeans and O = proportion in oats. Then the total 'expected' income is:

$$
\begin{aligned}
I = {} & R\,[(0{\cdot}1)(10) + (0{\cdot}2)(13) + (0{\cdot}3)(18) + (12)(20) + (0{\cdot}2)(22)] \\
& + W\,[(0{\cdot}1)(25) + (0{\cdot}2)(21) + (0{\cdot}3)(17) + (0{\cdot}2)(12) + (0{\cdot}2)(8)] \\
& + S\,[(0{\cdot}1)(12) + (0{\cdot}2)(17) + (0{\cdot}3)(23) + (0{\cdot}2)(17) + (0{\cdot}2)(11)] \\
& + O\,[(0{\cdot}1)(12) + (0{\cdot}2)(13) + (0{\cdot}3)(17) + (0{\cdot}2)(19) + (0{\cdot}2)(21)] \\
= {} & 17{\cdot}4R + 15{\cdot}8W + 17{\cdot}1S + 16{\cdot}9O. \qquad\qquad (1)
\end{aligned}
$$

To obtain the optimum crop combination we maximize statement (1) subject to just one constraint: $R + W + S + O = 1{\cdot}0$. Solving by the simplex solution (or visually) we obtain $R = 1{\cdot}0$, $W = 0$, $S = 0$ and $O = 0$. So the farmer should plant 100 per cent of his acreage in rice. Using this system, the total expected income is $17.40. Many other combinations of crops could be selected in accordance with a variety of individual criteria; but the cultivation of 100 per cent rice is the best procedure to maximize income taking risk into account.

Many real-life examples of attempts to maximize land-use returns under conditions of risk have been documented. Enterprise diversification is probably the most common example. Some land-use programs are much more complicated than those analysed here, such as those designed to combat a number of risks simultaneously. One procedure observed on 'peasant' farms, where the operators do not have substantial cash reserves, is to diversify crops to 'spread the risks' of poor weather; but also to maintain a commodity or commodities which, although not yielding a steady annual income, can be sold for cash in the event of a household emergency. Commercially valuable trees or large livestock are examples of the latter. Examples of the transference of risk to non-land-use agencies can also be cited. The use of crop insurance, whereby risk is passed on to an insurance company, or crop contracts with food companies who guarantee prices, are two instances.

Problems can arise in analysing land-use patterns when risk-reducing procedures are similar to those related to other concepts. Diversification, for example, may represent an attempt to reduce risk, an example of complementary production, or a long-run rotation system. Or it may represent all three. This overlap makes the problem of identifying a land-use pattern as related to one specific motive very difficult. The situation is complicated further if production costs per acre per crop are partially dependent on the degree of diversification. If costs increase with diversification a farmer might have to decide between the risk benefits of diversification and the cost benefit of monoculture.

Decision making under imputed risk

Suppose that in the example cited above the farmer does not know, and cannot find out, the probabilities for the five weather types. The example then becomes one of decision making under *uncertainty*, since there is no way of estimating the risks involved. We must assume, however, that whatever weather does occur, it will be one of the five classified types; otherwise, any attempts at decision making break down. It is felt that farm operators are often forced into situations of decision making under uncertainty, with the uncertainty referring to weather, prices or a host of other variables. The theory discussed below, then, should be of considerable relevance in attempts to understand land-use patterns.

Several researchers have advanced the idea that decision makers faced with uncertainty may estimate or impute risk probabilities in accordance with their own psychological characteristics in the absence of empirical evidence. One of the simplest methods, and one discussed for many years, is to assume that each of the unknown 'states' has an equal probability of occurrence.[1] In our example, one would assume that the probability of occurrence for each of the five weather types is 0·2. The 'expected' incomes for each land use on the basis of this assumption are as follows:

rice $16.60 (0·2(10) + 0·2(13) + 0·2(18) + 0·2(20) + 0·2(22))
wheat   16.60
soybeans $16.00
oats   16.40

A farmer using an equal-likelihood criterion for assigning probabilities would grow either rice or wheat if he is restricted to one crop. If diversification is permitted and economically feasible, the optimum combination is 40 per cent wheat, 20 per cent soybeans and 40 per cent rice. The expected income is:

$$0·2(25) + 0·2(21) + 0·2(23) + 0·2(20) + 0·2(22) = \$22.20.$$

Starr notes that the equal likelihood criterion is particularly relevant for decision-making under uncertainty, not so much because of its simplicity as its implied assumption that the operator is totally incapable of

[1] This is the Laplace or equal-likelihood criterion. See M. K. Starr 1963: *Product design and Decision theory* (Englewood Cliffs) 59–60.

estimating—or even ranking—the risk probabilities.[1] If a person is truly uncertain, the only rational course of action he can take is to assign equal probabilities to all 'states of nature'.

A second method of imputing risk is to take a pessimistic attitude and 'assume the worst'. Some mention of this procedure was made in the above section, and it will be discussed in detail below. It fits most conveniently in a consideration of game theory.

Hurwicz has devised the concept of decision making on the basis of the *partial optimist criterion*.[2] He argues that most people are neither optimists

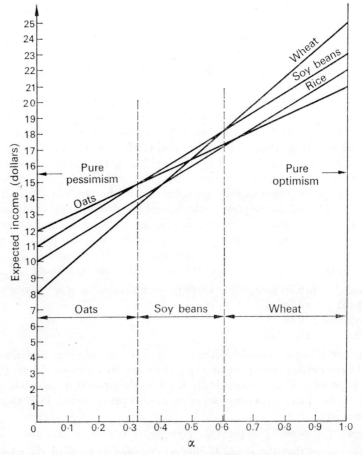

Fig. 6.1 : Graphs of expected values of land use based on the Hurwicz partial-optimist criterion, $\alpha = 0 - 1$

[1] M. K. Starr 1963, 64–5.
[2] L. Hurwicz 1950: *Optimality criteria for decision making under ignorance.*

nor pessimists, but that their degree of optimism can be described by a coefficient called alpha (α). Alpha ranges from zero to one, with a higher value representing a greater degree of optimism. It is used to obtain an 'expected' value in the following way: multiply the best value by alpha and the worst by $1 - \alpha$, and add them together. Let us assume an alpha value of 0·7. Then the expected values in our hypothetical case calculated by the Hurwicz method are:

rice	$0·7(22) + 0·3(10) =$	$18.40
wheat	$0·7(25) + 0·3(8) =$	19.90
soybeans	$17(23) + 0·3(11) =$	19.40
oats	$0·7(19) + 0·3(12) =$	16.90

The decision maker using the partial optimist criterion with an optimism rating of $\alpha = 0·7$ would grow wheat, assuming that combinations of land uses are not feasible.

A useful graph can be drawn on the basis of the partial optimist criterion representing the complete range of expected values as alpha ranges from zero to one. Fig. 6.1 illustrates our hypothetical example in this way. It indicates that persons with an alpha rating of 0 to 3·2 will grow oats assuming that diversification is not feasible; they could be called 'pessimists'. Those with ratings of $\alpha = 3·2$ to 6·1 will grow soybeans; they are 'partial optimists' or 'partial pessimists'. The 'optimists', with $\alpha = 6·1$ to 1·0 will grow wheat. Note that rice, the crop chosen on the basis of the expected value criterion taking into account the known probabilities of all five weather types, is never chosen. The reason, of course, is that only the maximum and minimum values are considered in Hurwicz's formula. All of the valuable information about yields in the other three weather conditions is not used.

The regret criterion

A special case of imputed risk is decision making on the basis of the *regret criterion*, as originally formulated by Savage.[1] He has suggested that to some operators the most attractive objective is to minimize the losses that would be incurred if an unfavourable state of nature occurred. Persons using this criterion are less concerned about actual gains as the gains which they stand to lose in case of disaster. For each selection, say a crop type, which a farmer chooses, he can calculate opportunity costs for each state of nature. Such costs, or measures of regret, are the differences between actual outcomes and the best possible outcome for that crop. In our hypothetical example, if the decision maker selects rice and the weather is very dry, the opportunity cost, which measures his regret, is $22 - 10 = $12.00. The regrets for all possible crops and weather conditions,

[1] L. J. Savage 1951: The theory of statistical decisions. *Journal of American Statistical Association* **46**, 55–67.

calculated in the same manner, are indicated in Table 6.2. The maximum
regret for each crop is also listed. In order to minimize the maximum
regret the decision maker would grow oats.

Table 6.2 : Matrix of regrets (Opportunity Costs) for all crops and weather
conditions

crop	very dry	dry	average	wet	very wet	maximum
rice	12	9	4	2	0	12
wheat	0	4	8	13	17	17
soybeans	11	6	0	6	12	12
oats	4	8	4	2	0	9

The Wald criterion in strictly determined games

Formal game theory, set out in detail in 1944 by Von Neumann and
Morgenstern, is a mathematically oriented framework for decision making
under conditions of uncertainty.[1] It should not be confused with informal
gaming, which is a general technique of simulating real-life processes in
the form of games with individuals playing the roles of real-life participants.
As the reader will soon realize game theoretical models are very similar
to those discussed for decision making under conditions of risk. Decision
making under imputed risk can, in fact, be seen as transitionary between
risk and game theoretical models.

Game theory envisages a number of opponents or competitors, each
trying to obtain certain objectives, usually at the expense of others, in the
absence of any knowledge about the actions of their opponents. Thus the
analogy to a gaming situation. It was originally devised to analyse
economic decision making among small groups of 'opponents', but can be
applied in a variety of circumstances. The various opponents are seen to
formulate *strategies* which yield differing *pay-offs*, depending on the strategies of the others in the game. The strategies and resultant pay-offs are
normally indicated in a *pay-off matrix*.

In land-use planning one can envisage a number of game theoretical
situations. The farmer can be seen as an opponent against 'nature', which
determines future weather patterns, or against the invisible opponents
who manipulate prices, technology, subsidies and so on. The simplest
situation is the two-person, zero-sum game—two-person because there
are two opponents, and zero-sum because one person can only gain
exactly what the other loses. Table 6.1 can represent the pay-off matrix in
a two-person, zero-sum game, with the farmer and the weather as the two
opponents. The four crops and five weather types are the strategies of the
farmer and the weather, respectively; and the average incomes are the

[1] J. Von Neumann and O. Morgenstern 1953: *Theory of games and economic behaviour*
(Princeton).

pay-offs. A high income is a good pay-off for the farmer, and a low income a good pay-off for the opponent—weather.

Table 6.3 is the pay-off matrix for another two-person, zero-sum game, this time between two regional farm-marketing boards who are competing for the same consumer market. Together they account for all of the food sales to consumers in the specified market, and each has a specific proportion of the business. But each board would like to increase its percentage share of the consumer's expenditure, and has devised a number of strategies to achieve this objective. Region 1 has decided to advertise its products, and has developed four different plans or strategies of advertising. Region 2 is going to change its land-use pattern so that new types of products can be introduced; five specific plans or strategies have been formulated. Both regional boards know what the complete pay-off matrix looks like—i.e. they are fully aware of the strategies of their opponents and of the pay-offs that will be incurred for every pair of strategies. But neither knows which strategy the other will employ.

Table 6.3 : Pay-off matrix for strategies of Region 1 and Region 2

Region 1's advertising strategies	Region 2's land-use strategies				
	1	2	3	4	5
	%	%	%	%	%
1	+9	−4	−2	+0	−2
2	+6	+2	+11	+1	+4
3	−2	−12	+2	−4	−4
4	−7	+3	+6	−1	−3

Note: the percentage changes in consumer expenditure indicated in the matrix refer to Region 1. E.g., '5' means a 5 per cent gain for Region 1, which necessarily means a 5 per cent gain or 5 per cent loss for Region 2)

The two regional boards can make their decisions according to a large number of criteria, including all of those discussed previously in the chapter. If one were to know the other's strategy, of course, one's decision would be easy. If Region 2 discovered that Region 1 was going to employ strategy 4, it would employ strategy 1 and gain 7 per cent of the market. But this would not be a typical game theoretic situation since a strategy was known by the other opponent. Each region could estimate the probabilities of the opponent using his various strategies according to one of the risk-imputing criteria, but this could be very dangerous since the opponent is rational and could behave in a manner designed to trap the other player. Under these conditions Wald has formulated the *maximin* or *minimax* criterion, which can be regarded as the 'best' or 'safest' criterion for each opponent to use.[1]

[1] A. Wald 1950: *Statistical decision functions* (New York).

According to Wald's procedure, each opponent chooses the strategy which will yield him the minimum possible disadvantage. The assumptions are that the 'worst' will happen, which is a pessimistic or conservative point of view, and that the player wants to suffer the least damage. In our example, Region 1's board will select strategy 2; then the worst that can befall the region is a one per cent gain in consumer expenditure. Region 2 will use strategy 4, since the worst possible outcome is a one per cent loss in market to Region 1. Region 1's strategy is called a *maximin* strategy, since it is the strategy with the maximum minimum outcome (+1 per cent). The minimum pay-offs for strategies 1, 3 and 4 are −4 per cent, −12 per cent, and −7 per cent respectively, all of which are less than the 1 per cent of strategy 2. Region 2's strategy is a *minimax* strategy, as it is the one with the minimum maximum loss.

Note that Region 1's minimum pay-off and Region 2's maximum loss are both the same (1 per cent). The value occurs at the intersection of the two strategies in the pay-off matrix, and is called the *saddle point*. Since this situation need not arise, saddle points are not present in all pay-off matrices. When one does occur, however, the game is said to be *strictly determined*. When this happens each player can do no better than to select his maximin or minimax strategy and use it repeatedly. If he selects another he will, inevitably, be worse off. In our example, Region 1 will eventually have to decide on strategy 2 and Region 2 on strategy 4. This means that Region 1 will gain 1 per cent of the market from Region 2, and Region 2 can do nothing to stop it. One per cent to Region 1 is said to be the *value* of the game played according to Wald's criterion.

Mixed strategies

Many two-person, zero-sum games are not strictly determined and have no saddle point in the pay-off matrix. Our earlier example (Table 6.1) is such a case. Under this condition there are optimum maximin or minimax strategies which the opponents can use in accordance with Wald's criterion, but they involve using combinations of strategies rather than repeated single or *pure* strategies. A player may lose badly during a given 'play' of the game, but in the long run his use of the right *mixed strategies* will guarantee a minimum average loss.

By simplifying our earlier example somewhat we can illustrate the determination of optimum strategies through a simple use of graphs and algebra. For graphic analysis we must limit one of the opponents to two strategies, so we will reduce the number of weather conditions to two— very dry and very wet. This also permits us to delete one of the crop types. Soybeans can be dropped as a strategy since oats would always be superior. Both oats and soybeans yield $12.00 under very dry conditions, but oats yields a much higher value than soybeans when the weather is very wet.

So there would never be an advantage in cultivating soybeans. Examination of Table 6.1 indicates that no other crops can be deleted. Each one remaining is superior to the others in some respect. The pay-off matrix can now be reduced to Table 6.4.

Table 6.4: Reduced pay-off matrix for crops and weather conditions

crop	very dry weather	very wet weather
rice	10	22
wheat	25	8
oats	12	21

The first step is to determine the relative proportions of strategies for the two-strategy opponent—weather. Let X represent the probability of very dry weather, and $Y = 1 - X$ the probability of very wet weather. If rice is grown as a pure strategy, the expected income (or loss, in this case) to the weather is $-10(X) + (-22)(1 - X) = 12X - 22$. Note that the pay-offs to weather are negative numbers, since the values in Table 6.4 are pay-offs in terms of gains to the farmer; and one opponent's gain is the other's loss in a zero-sum game. If wheat is grown, weather's expected pay-off is $-25(X) + (-8)(1 - X) = -17X - 8$. Similarly the expected pay-off for oats is $-12(X) + (-21)(1 - X) = 9X - 21$.

Figure 6.2 is a graph relating values of X to the pay-offs to weather for each of the three crop strategies. It is constructed by plotting the lines represented by the three X equations derived above. It permits us to determine the value of X which will guarantee the minimum maximum loss for the weather—i.e. the minimum loss that will be incurred if the farmer adopts the strategy best for him. The lines indicating the maximum losses for all values of X are emphasized with shading. For low values of X the weather loses most if rice is grown. For X values of about 0·4 to 0·5, oats brings the greatest loss. From about 0·5 to 1·0, wheat yields the greatest loss. The minimax point, where the maximum loss is least, occurs at the intersection of the oats and wheat lines. One can observe the corresponding X value directly, or determine the value precisely by equating $9X - 21$ with $-17X - 8$, and solving for X. The value is $X = 0·5$. So very dry and very wet years would have to occur in equal numbers to keep the farmer's gain at a minimum. The farmer's gain can be determined by direct observation of the graph or by substitution of $X = 0·5$ in either the oats or wheat equation. The calculation reveals the farmer's gain to be $16.50, assuming, of course, that he adopts his best mixed strategy. $16.50 is the mixed-strategy saddle point, and represents the value of the game.

The problem remains of determining the optimum proportions for the farmer's crop strategies. An important clue to the solution is revealed in

Fig, 6.2, where it is observed that the farmer's best mixed strategy—the one yielding the greatest loss to the weather—involves use of two crops, oats and wheat. Rice, then, will not be used. Let p_1 = the probability of planting wheat and p_2 = the probability of planting oats. Then optimum

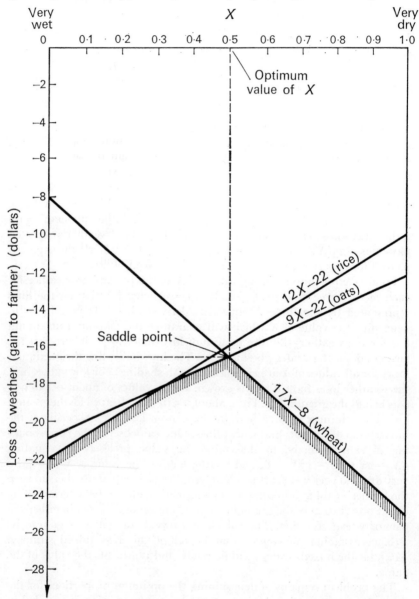

Fig. 6.2: Graphical solution to game-theoretic problem using Wald's criterion

values for p_1 and p_2 can be calculated by using the fact that the value of the game when played in maximin fashion by the farmer is $16.50. In very dry weather

$$25p_1 + 12p_2 = 16\cdot5,$$

and in very wet weather

$$8p_1 + 21p_2 = 16\cdot5.$$

Solving the simultaneous equations we obtain $p_1 = 0\cdot35$ and $p_2 = 0\cdot65$.

The question remains of how the opponents play their mixed strategies. If we assume that the weather in a given year can be wet or dry but not both, then the weather must oscillate between very wet and very dry years so that each occurs 50 per cent of the time. But the oscillation must be in random fashion so that the farmer has no way of estimating the correct strategy ahead of time. The farmer, however, has two ways of using his strategy mix. He can alternate randomly years of wheat and oats cultivation so that wheat is grown in 35 per cent of the years and oats 65 per cent of the years; or he can devote 35 per cent of his acreage to wheat and the remainder to oats year after year. The latter plan has the advantage that his income will be regular—$16.50 per acre per year. The former plan is riskier, but he does have the chance of making a very large income (up to $25.00 per acre) in a lucky year.

One could cite many other game theoretical situations involving any number of opponents and a large number of different decision criteria. It is interesting to note that as the number of players increases the economic framework approximates that of oligopoly and, eventually, pure competition, where no one decision maker can, by his strategies, affect the outcomes of others. One can envisage a continuum of economic environments ranging from that of two-opponent competition to pure competition. Viewed in this general way, game theory assumes very wide-ranging applications, of which the traditional competition environments are specific cases. On the other hand, game theory, as narrowly defined, assumes the complete inability of opponents to foresee the strategies of each other, which is not really the case in perfect competition. Another important continuum in economic decision making is the ability of opponents to know or estimate the risks (probabilities) of various counter strategies.

To what extent are the game theoretical situations discussed so far applicable to land-use decision making? What we have done primarily is to describe a variety of ways in which individuals might make land-use decisions when faced with uncertainty or risk, within the limits of the availability of pay-off matrices. We have not argued for the particular validity of any one decision criterion but have, hopefully, opened the door to a quite different way of evaluating or hypothesizing decisions.

Some emphasis has been placed on the minimax (Wald) criterion, as this reflects a trend in much of the literature. But one could question the emphasis given this approach. The Wald criterion assumes ultra-defensive tactics by all opponents, a situation which may not apply in many cases. The weather is not a highly intelligent opponent, carefully calculating its strategies to effect minimum land output. In many areas climatic conditions are fairly predictable, and farmers might be expected to base decisions on known risks rather than on a minimax principle, which would lead to low, although dependable incomes. The minimax principle would be more applicable among poor farmers who could not survive a 'bad' year and who would be forced to adopt highly conservative tactics. Gould has discussed this possibility for peasant farmers in parts of Africa.[1]

Special mention should be made of the assumptions lying behind the use of pay-off matrices. To construct the types of matrices discussed above one must assume linear production functions (e.g. doubling the land area doubles production), constant intensity of land use, and the ability to classify pure strategies as finite occurrences. The first two assumptions, which are closely related, certainly oversimplify the economic relationships which we have theorized in earlier chapters. The third assumption raises problems in real life if we have opponents with strategies which form a continuous series. Weather conditions, for example, do not occur in a few, homogeneous types. A given year may be unlike any other, possessing a unique combination of wet, dry and other characteristics. If the researcher is aware of these assumptions, however, and can compensate for them with appropriate modelling or interpretation, game theory can be a powerful concept in land-use analysis.

Game theoretic and related risk problems can become mathematically complex as the matrices become large. Fortunately, linearity is a feature of the formal solutions to such problems, and linear programming is normally adapted to solve them.

Hypothetical problem

Theoretical solutions to problems of decision making under risk and uncertainty have particular spatial applicability if the strategies of an opponent refer to action in specific locations. This numerical example is one such application.

A plantation owner has the capital and labour to grow 100 acres of pumpkins, and he has to decide where on his 5,000-acre property to locate them. There are four areas in the plantation which are available—steep hills, low hills, plain and valley bottom—each of which has soils of different productivity. Pumpkin yields vary considerably among the sites due to soil fertility. They also vary from year to year since weather conditions are somewhat unpredictable. In dry weather the best yields are

[1] P. R. Gould 1963: Man against his environment: a game-theoretic framework. *Annals of Association of American Geographers* **53**, 290–7.

obtained in the rich alluvial soils of the valley bottom, where some irrigation is possible. But in wet weather the valley is subject to flooding, which
destroys some of the plants; and fairly good yields are obtained in the hills
where orographic precipitation can drain off the land easily. The yields
for all four parts of the plantation for wet and dry years are listed in
Table 6.5. The probabilities for wet and dry years are also indicated.

Table 6.5 : Pumpkin yields in four locations for wet
and dry years

	wet year	dry year
probability of occurrence	0·6	0·4
location	*yield (tons per acre)*	
steep hills	27	9
low hills	31	8
plain	24	7
valley bottom	6	50

Question

The plantation owner wants to maximize his income, and would like to
distribute production among the four locations to achieve this objective.
Assuming that production costs per acre are the same in all locations
and that all transformation functions are linear, how many acres
should be planted in each location if the probabilities of wet and dry
weather are (1) unknown and (2) known?

Solution

1 Just knowing that the plantation owner wants to 'maximize income' is
not enough to predict exactly how he will distribute production among
the four locations. What spatial pattern he 'should' use depends entirely
on the conditions under which he is willing to attempt income maximization. We do not know whether he requires a minimum annual
yield, whether or not he has estimated or guessed what weather conditions will be like, or anything about his personal risk-taking characteristics. All we can do is determine some optimum land-use patterns based
on assumptions about these unknowns.

We have a game theoretical situation, with Table 6.5 indicating the
strategies and pay-offs of the two opponents—the plantation owner and
the weather. The owner's strategies can be pure or mixed, since transformation functions among areas are linear and per-acre costs are
independent of field size or location.

The various programs usable by the operator vary with his require-
ment for a minimum annual yield and his characteristics of conservatism. If he tends to be a 'gambler' and will risk a very low yield on the
chance of getting the highest possible production, he should plant all
100 acres of pumpkins in the valley bottom. Then he will obtain either

6 tons per acre (the least possible) in a wet year or 50 tons if the weather is dry.

The next degree of 'gambler' characteristic would be for the plantation owner to recognize that risk was involved in 'putting all his eggs into one basket' (the valley bottom), and to compensate for this somewhat by planting some pumpkins in another location in case the weather was wet. But he could still be optimistic about having dry weather, and plant most of his acreage in the valley. Depending on his degree of optimism he could be assigned a Hurwicz alpha value; and his optimum plan could then be determined. Suppose that alpha is 0·8. Then he would plant 80 acres in the valley and 20 acres in the location giving the highest yields in wet weather—the low hills.

A less optimistic individual might use the 'equal-likelihood' criterion, and assume that wet and dry years will come in equal numbers. Such a person should plant 50 acres in the valley and 50 acres in the low hills. A more pessimistic operator could, again, use the partial optimist criterion. Assuming alpha = 0·3, he should plant 30 acres in the valley and 70 acres in the low hills.

If the plantation owner wants to guarantee that his production will be a maximum, assuming that the worst possible combination of weather conditions prevails, he should determine his location pattern on the basis of the maximin or Wald criterion. We can already eliminate the plain as a possible production site since both the steep and low hills are superior to it in wet or dry years. The next step in the pure-pessimist solution is to discover if a saddle point exists in the reduced pay-off matrix. In this case it does not, so we know that the operator should use a mixed strategy. We can determine the optimum mix using geometry and algebra, as discussed in the preceding section. Fig. 6.3 illustrates the graphical determination of the optimum or 'worst' combination of weather types (X = probability of wet weather), the saddle point value of the game, and the optimum strategies (locations) usable by the plantation owner. It appears that the worst possible weather combination is 62·7 per cent wet years and 37·3 per cent dry years, in which case the value of the game is 22·4 tons per acre to the plantation owner if he uses his optimum mixed combination of acreage in the valley bottom and the low hills. Solving the simultaneous equations (p_1 = probability of low hills location, p_2 = probability of valley location):

$$31p_1 + 6p_2 = 22\cdot4$$
$$8p_1 + 50p_2 = 22\cdot4$$

we obtain $p_1 = 0\cdot656$, and $p_2 = 0\cdot344$. So the operator should plant 65·6 acres of pumpkins in the low hills and 34·4 acres in the valley bottoms.

If the plantation owner is particularly concerned about losing out on potential yields, he might base his distribution decision on Savage's

minimum regret criterion. The maximum regrets for the four locations
are as follows: steep hills–18, low hills–23, plain–17, valley bottom–44.
So, to minimize the maximum regret, the operator should plant all of
his pumpkins on the plain.

2 If the plantation owner wants to obtain the highest average production
over several years and is not particularly concerned about production
in a given year, he should use the distribution plan which has the highest

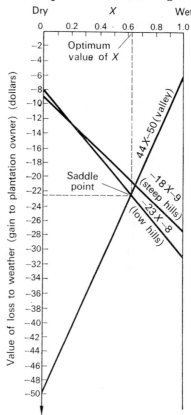

Fig. 6.3: Graphical solution to game theoretic problem facing plantation owner

'expected' value, based on the known weather probabilities. Our
analysis in part (1) indicates that his optimum plan will involve some
combination of low hills and valley bottom, so we need not consider
other strategies. If h = the acreage in the low hills and $100 - h$ = the
valley acreage, the equation by which 'expected' total production can
be calculated is

prod. $= h((0.6 \times 31) + (0.4 \times 8)) + (100 - h)((0.4 \times 50) + (0.6 \times 6))$,
which reduces to

$$\text{prod.} = 2360 - 1.8h.$$

The equation simply states that expected production is the sum of the expected outputs from each location. For the low hills expected output per acre is 0·6 (probability of wet weather) times the wet-weather yield (31) plus 0·4 (probability of dry weather) times the dry-weather yield (8). The expected production for the valley bottom is calculated in the same manner. One can see that the equation above is maximized if $h = 0$, so the plantation owner should plant all 100 acres in the valley. Actually, one can observe this solution directly from Fig. 6.3 by observing that, for a value of $X = 0·6$, the strategy yielding weather the greatest loss is the valley bottom. For $X = 0·6$, the valley 'line' has a value of 23·6 (per acre).

If the operator has particular concern for a given year (e.g. wants to maximize minimum gains or minimize regret) he should use the appropriate plan outlined in (1) even though he knows the weather probabilities. If, by chance, he achieves the ultimate in knowledge about his opponent and knows what each year's weather will be in advance, he should plant in the low hills in a wet year and in the valley in a dry one. Using this procedure he would obtain a total production through the year much higher than by any other plan. Of course, this would not represent decision making under risk or uncertainty.

It might be interesting for the reader to compare the average or 'expected' production under the different spatial patterns discussed, calculated on the basis of the known weather probabilities (Table 6.6). In this particular case any decision involving a combination of low hills and valley bottom, even based on the maximin solution, yields good production, with the more optimistic decision bringing slightly better results.

Table 6.6: 'Expected' pumpkin production according to a variety of distribution decisions, based on known weather probabilities (p (wet) = 0·6, p (dry) = 0·4)

	acreage				'expected'
criterion	steep hills	low hills	plain	valley bottom	producton (100 tons)
gambler	0	0	0	100	23·6
optimist ($\alpha = 0·8$)	0	20	0	80	23·2
equal-likelihood	0	50	0	50	22·7
pessimist ($\alpha = 0·3$)	0	70	0	30	22·3
maximin	0	65·6	0	34·4	22·4
minimum regret	0	0	100	0	19·2
knowledge of weather probabilities	0	0	0	100	23·6
prior knowledge of each year's weather	0	100, 60% of time	0	100, 40% of time	38·6

Further reading

The following are theoretical and empirical analyses of decision making under risk or uncertainty, many within farm management settings.*

BELLMAN, R. 1954: Decision making in the face of uncertainty.

BERKMAN, H. G. 1965: The game theory of land use determination.

BOUSSARD, J. M., and PETIT, M. 1967: Representation of farmers' behaviour under uncertainty with a focus on loss constraint.

DILLON, J. L., and HEADY, E. O. 1960: *Theories of choice in relation to farmer decisions.*

GOULD, P. 1963: Man against his environment: a game theoretic framework.
   1965: Wheat on Kilimanjaro: the perception of choice within game and learning model frameworks.

HEADY, E. O. 1958a: Application of game theory in agricultural economics.

HURWICZ, L. 1950: *Optimality criteria for decision making under risk.*

KAUFMANN, A. 1968: *The science of decision making,* chapters 4 and 5.

LANGHAM, M. R. 1963: Game theory applied to a policy problem of rice farmers.

LUCE, R. D., and RAIFFA, H. 1957: *Games and decisions.*

MALYA, M. M., and RAJAGOPALAN, R. 1964: Nature of risk associated with rainfall and its effect on farming—a case study of Kumoal district, Andra Pradesh.

MCFARQUHAR, A. M. M. 1961: Rational decision making and risk in farm planning.

MCINERNEY, J. P. 1967: Maximum programming—an approach to farm planning under uncertainty.

MERRILL, W. C. 1965: Alternative programming models involving uncertainty.

OFFICER, R. R., and ANDERSON, J. R. 1968: Risk, uncertainty and farm management decisions.

SAVAGE, L. J. 1951: The theory of statistical decision.

SCHLAIFER, R. 1970: *Analysis of decisions under uncertainty.*

STARR, M. 1963: *Product design and decision theory,* chapters 2, 3, and 5.

VON NEUMANN, J., and MORGENSTERN, O. 1944: *Theory of games and economic behaviour.*

WALD, A. 1950: *Statistical decision functions.*

WALKER, O. L., HEADY, E. O., TWEETEN, L. G., and PESEK, J. T. 1960: *Application of game theory models to decisions on farm practices and resource use.*

* Complete references listed in bibliography at conclusion of book.

7 INTRODUCTION TO BEHAVIOURAL CONCEPTS

The limitations of normative economic theory—utility, transitivity, and subjective probability—Problem-solving versus routine behaviour—Information and the decision environment—Multiple objectives and Simon's satisficer—Stochastic decision making—Adaptive decision making—Group versus individual behaviour—Further reading

For the past twenty years certain social scientists have been concerned with decision-making theory which emphasizes man's behavioural characteristics. Such concern is probably derived from two sources: (1) a reaction to the unrealistic assumptions regarding man's behaviour on which normative economic theory is constructed, and (2) enquiry into human behaviour by those unconcerned with economic theory, but who are interested in man's physiological, ecological, and psychological characteristics. The result of this concern has been the development of behavioural concepts, some of which have been related to land-use decision making. No single highly integrated theory, similar to economic theory, has evolved as yet; but, increasingly, certain concepts have re-appeared in the literature, and have gained common interest. It is felt by many that further developments may lead to a significantly better understanding of the way man uses land.

The purposes of this chapter are to introduce major behavioural terms and concepts, some of which will be considered in greater detail in Chapters 8 and 9; and to relate these to the economic theory discussed in earlier chapters by raising the common criticisms about the relevance of such theory.

The limitations of normative economic theory

Traditional economic theory relating to land use is based on very specific assumptions regarding the behaviour of the decision maker and the conditions under which he operates. Man is assumed to have complete information related to a decision (all prices, pay-offs, etc.), to be able to compare all inputs and outcomes on some precise preference scale of values (e.g. price), to be capable of any calculations necessary to determine an optimum decision, to optimize some objective (e.g. maximize income), and to be capable of carrying out the decision. Since real men seldom approach this ideal behaviour pattern, many have questioned the value of a theory based on such assumptions. One answer given in defence of the theory is that its purpose and usefulness are not descriptive—i.e. it does not seek a complete explanation of what land users actually do; but is normative—it predicts what land users should do in order to achieve certain objectives. This argument has some validity, since one observes that the main use of economic theory in agricultural schools or experimental stations has been to help farmers make better decisions. In a partial contradiction of the argument, it can be stated that the traditional theory is not even a particularly good normative theory since the land-use decisions which it indicates may be incompatible with the behaviour of those expected to carry them out. A second defence of traditional theory is that, although it is inadequate due to the behavioural assumptions on which it is based, it represents the first step or approximation of a better theory, either normative or descriptive. It can be argued that the alternative approach to the development of a theory would be the 'ordering' of masses of descriptive data on man's use of the land, which would be so complex and imprecise as to impede the clarification of individual processes or behaviour patterns. One advantage of the traditional economic theory is that it is precise, logically consistent, and, although unrealistic, representative of a careful, conservative approach to model-building. No matter what arguments are used in defence of traditional theoretical developments, however, one must accept on logical grounds that a theory based on assumptions of more realistic human behaviour would provide better models for either descriptive or normative purposes.

Problems regarding the relevance of traditional economic theory are particularly acute for land-use areas with non-market economies. To what extent can the theory apply in areas where no products of land use are sold or traded, and no value yardsticks, such as price, exist? Do 'von Thünen' concepts have any relevance in areas of non-market orientated subsistence agriculture, for example? Can we expect the theory to shed much light on regional variations in land use in countries with 'planned' economies, such as some Communist nations?

It may seem odd that it has taken so long and has been, apparently, so difficult to incorporate life-like conditions, something with which we should all have some familiarity, into land-use models. There are, perhaps, three reasons. First, it is wrong to assume that most researchers have been unfamiliar with aspects of behaviourism. Very old and more recent writings, often by cultural geographers or anthropologists, reveal very genuine intuitive insights into the human decision-making process. But most of these writers have been reluctant to specify or classify recurrent aspects of behaviour, at least in an explicit model format which can be compared by the scientific method with other studies. One of the reasons for this failure may be a basic pessimism about the universal or nomothetic applications of their findings. Whether or not this is true, much valuable research has been wasted because the researchers failed to present the findings in a conceptual format which permitted others to build on the results. A second reason for the difficulty in formulating a behavioural theory relates to the problem of observing human behaviour objectively. It has been stated that more is known about the behaviour of rats than humans, partly because we find it easier to observe rats without becoming involved with them. Human behaviour is also difficult to study because many of the questions that need to be asked cannot be answered adequately by human respondents. Land users can be unaware of the bases for their decisions; they may be influenced unknowingly by factors which the researchers must identify. As a further complicating problem, decision makers are bound to be influenced by any researcher trying to probe their behavioural patterns. Simply asking questions may present new ideas to the subject, whose behaviour will be consequently altered. One of the best examples of this process is in capitalist countries where decision making in commercial agriculture has been strongly affected by economic models—which were originally devised, at least in part, to describe decision making in commercial agriculture. A third reason for difficulty in developing behavioural theory is that human decision making is a very complex process.

Utility, transitivity, and subjective probability

Certain behavioural concepts are quite closely related to normative economic ones, and their development has been achieved by scientists of economic as well as psychological bent. Utility, transitivity, and subjective probability, as well as a basic decision making model based on them, are examples of such concepts. They can be seen as helping form a transition from economic to more purely behavioural theory.

One of the premises on which traditional economic theory is based is that decision makers can evaluate, on a common comparative scale, all inputs and outputs of land use. We have encountered no difficulties associated with this premise in our examples in earlier chapters since market price has been used in all cases as the common yardstick. But how useful would the theory be for the analysis of land use in non-market economies where the land is used solely to feed the family? In a partial attempt to overcome this problem, economists have used the term '*utility*' to describe the most general common denominator for comparative value. It has been argued that if individual utility is used to replace market value or price, then much of the existing theory is generally applicable.

But serious problems arise with the utility concept. In areas of free-enterprise commercial agriculture, utility may be fairly easy to measure. Market value probably approximates closely utility to a business-like operator. Even here, however, the correspondence between price and utility may not be perfect. Some researchers suspect that the utility of $2,000.00 to an individual may be less than two times $1,000.00—in other words, the relationship between personal utility and price may not be linear.[1] Furthermore, the extent of this linearity may vary from person to person. The discrepancy between the two value measures is bound to have an important effect on decision making. Is a farmer earning $2,000.00 as willing to work twice as hard to double his income as a farmer who earns $1,000.00, assuming linear production functions between 'work' and income in both cases?

When prices cannot be determined or when the products of land use are not to be sold, measurement of utility is much more difficult. How, for example, does a farmer compare three oranges with two bananas? Does he consider weight, calorific value, taste, etc? One method which has been used in experiments with non-agricultural products has been to ask subjects to determine pairs of objects between which they are *indifferent* as an indirect way of discovering their utility ratings.[2] A person might be willing to say, for example, that he is just as content to have a pair of brown shoes as a green umbrella. It would be very interesting, and should be equally possible, to 'discover' indifference ratings for products of land use to obtain some measure of utility.

A result from non-agricultural research which probably applies to land-use phenomena as well relates to the problem of intransitivity, which complicates the findings of indifference tests to a considerable degree. It has been found that a person who ranks A over B and B over C may, unexpectedly, rank C over A. The last is said to be an *intransitive choice*.[3] For transitivity to exist, all rankings must be consistent with each other. A further complication arises when it is observed that different persons have different choice rankings or indifferences. Intransitivity has been attributed to more than the unpredictability of human nature. If a crop or object can be evaluated in a number of ways (e.g. weight, taste, durability) intransitive choices can be expected.[4] A peasant may prefer oranges to bananas because oranges can be sold if necessary; and bananas to yams because he prefers the taste of bananas; but he may prefer yams to oranges because he can store or preserve yams more easily.

On farms where non-commercial land users require a mix of land uses to satisfy their diets, minimize risks, or fulfil some other function, a different problem is encountered if the quantities required for the different products vary a great deal. An operator might prefer one coconut to a handful of

[1] S. S. Stevens 1959: Measurement, psychophysics and utility. In C. W. Churchman and P. Ratoosh (Editors), *Measurement: definitions and theories* (New York).
[2] See W. Edwards and A. Tversky 1967: *Decision making* (London) 21–3.
[3] W. Edwards and A. Tversky 1967, 44–7.
[4] K. O. May 1954: Transitivity, utility and aggregation in preference patterns. *Econometrica* **22**, 1–13.

beans, but he would not prefer 1,000 coconuts to 1,000 handfuls of beans since he doesn't 'need' 1,000 coconuts.

The reader can easily envisage the problems in using traditional economic models arising from the problems in measuring utility to land users. But some problems can be partially overcome. With respect to the last example, for instance, one might specify the required quantities of products as constraints, and then determine an optimum land-use pattern using traditional models and some measure of utility, assuming that some objective is to be optimized. But quite important modifications of the original statements of economic theory are required to facilitate the individual characteristics of such decisions.

Subjective probability (also known as imputed risk and personal probability) has been the subject of much experimentation since it lies at the core of much behavioural theory.[1] In the last chapter it was introduced under the topic of 'decision making under imputed risk', but its full theoretical implications were not discussed. All we stated was that, in the absence of known probabilities, individuals might select probabilities on the basis of their psychological characteristics, and apply them to decision making. A number of decision models based on such probabilities were then analysed.

The great importance of subjective probability is derived from a basic behavioural hypothesis that human decisions result from a tendency to *maximize expected utility*, which is seen as the product of the utility of a pay-off and the subjective probability of the pay-off occurring. Subjective probability is defined by Savage as a number that represents the extent to which an individual thinks a given event is likely to occur.[2] A great deal of research has been carried out in attempts to measure the two basic components of this hypothesis—personal utility and personal probability. In situations where individuals are forced to make decisions the results suggest that people attempt to maximize expected utility based on a subjective probability (which experimenters have measured) rather than on *objective* or *real* probability.

We have already related subjective probability to personal characteristics, such as degree of optimism (see Chapter 6). It also depends largely on the prior experience of the decision maker. A person who has observed the outcome of a strategy a number of times comes to have an increasingly better estimate of the objective probability of given pay-offs. Savage has shown that the gradual 'improvement' of estimates of probability occurs in a predictable fashion. Another variable which may affect subjective probability is the utility of pay-offs. It is conceivable, for example, that continued agricultural success in a given area may lead

Edwards and Tversky, 1967, 35–41; 71–4.
2 L. J. Savage 1954: *The foundations of statistics* (New York).

individuals to optimism, whereas those living in areas of marginal agriculture may tend towards conservatism or pessimism.

Recent interest has centred on the extent to which non-market agriculturalists attempt to maximize expected utility. A number of papers have claimed that the supposedly chaotic land-use patterns of subsistent agriculturalists actually represent a careful plan to maximize the use of the environment. Lipton has illustrated that if behavioural theory, particularly of a game theoretic type, is taken into account, peasants can indeed be seen as optimizers.[1] He also indicates that traditional theory without the behavioural modifications offers us little explanation of their land use.

Problem-solving versus routine behaviour

Psychologists have classified decision making into a number of types, ranging from highly deliberate problem solving to automatic, subconscious decision behaviour. It is generally concluded that most decision making tends towards the latter type.[2] But this is quite inconsistent with an unstated assumption behind the decision frameworks we have discussed, which is that land users very deliberately specify management problems, carefully evaluate all alternative solutions, and select the best ones. Since this assumption appears to be wrong in most cases, we must carefully re-evaluate the relevance of theoretical models for which it is a basis.

Why does decision making tend to differ from the deliberate, problem solving type? We can relate the tendency partly to two human traits—the inability to process large amounts of data, and the desire to avoid effort-requiring work. Simon suggests that one way humans compensate for these traits is to greatly simplify the decision process, partly by avoiding conscious decision making.[3] This is an extremely important concept as it modifies, and complicates enormously, our traditional assumption about optimization. We must reword our assumption somewhat like—man attempts to optimize some utility objective *while minimizing his own effort*. This paradox suggests that man somehow determines an equilibrium point between expected utility and effort. An extreme solution would be to go through life accepting minimum utility while following a path of minimum action. As for man's inability to process data, it appears that decision makers often prefer to follow a pattern already established, either by themselves or by somebody else, rather than take on the formidable task of re-evaluating the situation to make new decisions. Furthermore,

[1] M. Lipton 1968: The theory of the optimising peasant. *Journal of Development Studies* **4**, 327–51.
[2] G. Katona 1951, *The psychological analysis of economic behaviour* (New York) 139.
[3] H. A. Simon 1955: A behavioural model of rational choice. *Quarterly Journal of Economics* **69**, 99–118.

man has learned to be aware of his data-processing limitations, and likes to avoid the risk of making poor decisions. The traits of poor data-processing ability and a desire to avoid effort may be major factors helping to explain the commonly-observed phenomena of 'tradition' and 'habit' in agricultural land use.[1] They may also help explain why decision making in given regions is often so uniform from farm to farm. Farmers may prefer to adopt land-use patterns which their neighbours have found successful rather than experiment with new practices. Other factors also appear to contribute to regional uniformity. These include (1) the desire of individuals not to appear to deviate from the area's 'normal' behaviour pattern; and (2) the advantages of using central facilities, such as equipment or market outlets, which can be achieved only if several farmers have similar land uses. Decision making of the type envisaged in traditional models may be much more exceptional than normal.

How relevant, then, can we expect traditional models to be? Strong support for their descriptive utility is still expressed, mainly on the basis of two arguments: (1) although human limitations may not permit the accurate, deliberate decision making necessary to formulate a complete optimum land-use pattern at a given moment in time, gradual adjustments of existing patterns to optimum ones can be achieved over many seasons. Man may be incapable of massive decision making, but he is capable of continual minor adjustments which, after a long trial-and-error process, enable him to achieve optimality. (2) In many areas, particularly industrialized countries, much of the complicated decision-making is done for farmers by either government agencies or corporations (e.g. fertilizer companies); and the decisions are derived directly from traditional normative models. The first argument is a fascinating idea, although it has yet to be conclusively proved. No one has suggested how long the process of adjustment takes or if conditions (e.g. prices, technology) ever remain constant long enough for optimal patterns to develop. The second argument is quite valid, although one doubts whether the 'external' decision making is ever complete enough to develop optimal land-use patterns on given farms. There is also much evidence to suggest that a farmer may prefer to ignore such advice if it conflicts too markedly from ideas currently prevailing in his mind or in the minds of his neighbours. Both arguments in support of traditional models can be accepted to a degree. The important question, however, is whether behaviourist models can add a useful degree of further explanation of real-life decision making. It is logical to expect that models taking into account man's inability and unwillingness to undertake deliberate, large-scale decisions will greatly illuminate our understanding of land-use patterns.

[1] C. L. Hull 1964, *A behaviour system* (New York) 228.

Information and the decision environment

The land-use models considered earlier assume that rational, optimizing, super-computational man has a basic set of information available before making a decision. The set includes knowledge of all possible decisions or strategies; the pay-off or possible pay-offs associated with each strategy; a value scale with which to compare the utility of each pay-off; and the probability (real or imputed) that each pay-off will result from a given strategy. For most of the models discussed (all except those in Chapter 6) no risk or uncertainty is assumed, so that each strategy has only one possible pay-off. The number of strategies in these models is also assumed to be infinite, and is represented by infinitesimally small points joined together to form lines on graphs (e.g. isoproduct lines). Obviously, all of the information specified in these models is seldom available in real life. It is useful to call the information which is available to the decision maker the *decision environment*, and the complete set of information assumed in most traditional models as the *extended* or *real environment*.[1]

The decision and extended environments are seldom the same for two main reasons: (1) man seldom feels the need or the ability to learn about the extended environment. If he does recognize the need to obtain a mass of information, his limited perceptual abilities force him to simplify the real environment into something with which he can cope. (2) Imperfect communication restricts the information with which he can come into contact.

As for the first point, an individual may not consciously wish to consider a decision, as described in the preceding section; so the only decision environment which concerns him may contain only one strategy—the same one used by him or his neighbours in a preceding time period. The idea of alternative strategies may have barely entered his mind. A more deliberate decision maker might consider a number of courses of action, but only a range of possibilities within his comprehensible grasp. As far as pay-offs are concerned, Simon has suggested that people tend to reduce the complex set of ranked outcomes to a manageable number, perhaps classifying pay-offs as good, indifferent or bad. On the other hand, it is not difficult to find farmers who do consider a number of action alternatives and corresponding income pay-offs; but farmers who think consciously of anything as complex as a complete pay-off matrix are most rare. Obviously the cost or effort of obtaining information greatly affect the amount of information in an individual's decision environment. If he, with a very limited background in decision making or computation, must painstakingly search out information, his decision environment is bound to be limited. If, on the other hand, he is highly educated and information is

[1] H. A. Simon 1956: Rational choice and the structure of the environment. *Psychological Review* **63**, 129–38.

readily available—even forced on him by some external agency—the costs of acquiring information are low, and the decision environment begins to approximate the extended environment. In all cases the decision environment is a function of his needs or goals, his perceptual abilities, and the availability of information.

It is useful to examine decision making in terms of two separate parts, the decision environment and the actions of the individual acting within that environment. But we must realize that the two parts are partially interdependent. The decision environment is strongly determined by the nature of the decision maker, since he searches out the types of information which relate to his basic motivation. But his motivation is partially acquired from former experiences within his decision environment.

With respect to the second reason for the difference between decision and real environments, communication plays a vital role in determining the availability of information. A number of models have been developed to recreate the essential aspects of this relationship, some of which will be considered in the next chapter.

As cultural geographers and anthropologists will undoubtedly recognize, all aspects of the decision environment are closely related to *culture* and *technology*. Known strategies, expected pay-offs, utility-value systems and basic motivations are strongly affected by the culture-group within which an individual finds himself. This can be added to the aforementioned list as another reason for the uniformity of land-use patterns within given regions. A conscious tie-in between research by cultural and decision specialists has not occurred to much extent. Collaboration between the two groups should be highly rewarding.

Multiple objectives and Simon's satisficer

Simon has cast the severest doubt on the assumption that man optimizes some objective—even the maximization of expected utility.[1] He argues that it is so far beyond the capabilities and real desires of an individual to examine all the possibilities offered in the extended environment that he probably seizes on the first *satisfactory* decision which he encounters. Man may seek to optimize, but he is willing to *satisfice* to avoid the insurmountable and effort-requiring process of discovering courses of action progressively closer to optimum.

A second part of Simon's argument relates to the concept of multiple objectives. Most theory—even behavioural theory—assumes that man seeks to attain one objective, the maximization of utility. But Simon points out that utility can be obtained from a variety of aspects of life, not necessarily all from the proposed action being considered at one point in time. So an individual must discover short cuts to decision making on one

[1] H. A. Simon 1957: *Models of man* (New York), chapters 14 and 15.

problem to allow for action to be taken on others. This, plus the limited capabilities of humans, forces the individual to simplify his decision by establishing levels of satisfactory outcome. What determines a satisfactory pay-off? Simon's writing suggests that expected utility, information, and the pressures of time and effort required to discover better decisions all relate to levels of satisfaction. Others have conducted research on *levels of aspiration* which, presumably, should bear some relation to satisfaction.

Simon discusses a concept which should be useful for us—subjective rationality. He argues that the traditional or objective rationality referred to in classical models is beyond the capabilities of real men, but that individuals obtain subjective rationality when they make decisions meeting the requirements of their levels of satisfaction.

Stochastic decision making

Individuals vary from each other in their decision-making behaviour for a variety of reasons—differences in decision environment, personality, rationality, etc. But experiments show that a single individual may also make different decisions at different times even though all other conditions are identical.[1] So it appears probable that even the most sophisticated decision theory will be incapable of predicting individual behaviour on all occasions. The conclusion is that a basic feature of human decision making is stochasticism—the tendency towards a degree of randomness.

Models which fail to account for this random element are termed *deterministic models*. All of the models which we have examined are deterministic. A number of stochastic models have now been developed, however, one of which we will discuss in Chapter 8. These models make the explicit assumption that a degree of randomness exists in human action. This can, incidentally, be an explanation for intransitive choices (see section above on intransitivity).

Randomness in human behaviour is not chaotic—i.e. patterns of randomness can normally be determined. The usual assumption is that individuals will not make given choices with 100 per cent certainty, but that the probabilities of their making those choices are known. For example, a person might identify a choice which is highly rational, and make that choice when given the opportunity 98 per cent of the time. A less obvious choice might be made 60 per cent of the time. About each choice we can envisage a statistical distribution of probabilities for selecting it, together with a known variance. As the reader can imagine, several of the stochastic models are highly mathematical and present unique problems of testing.

---

[1] Edwards and Tversky, 1967, 74–5.

Adaptive decision making

The decision models discussed so far are basically static; they consider decisions made at points in time rather than series of interdependent decisions made through time. Edwards points out that static models really don't go far enough since, in real life, decisions at one time are normally related to decisions and their outcomes in preceding time periods.[1] Research on dynamic decision models has been continuing, but has not advanced as far as that concerned with static models.

One can identify a number of dynamic links between decisions made in sequence. The most obvious process is a change in the decision environment. Information is continually obtained about pay-offs, strategies and probabilities. As we mentioned earlier, one might expect subjective probabilities to gradually become better estimates of objective probabilities. The process is easy to envisage and, perhaps, measure if the extended environment remains constant. In real life, however, the real environment constantly changes, which complicates model-building somewhat.

Simon suggests that satisfaction or aspiration levels also change as decisions are made in sequence.[2] An individual unfamiliar with the real environment will start with modest, manageable aspiration levels which he considers satisfactory. If he obtains satisfaction fairly easily he will gradually increase his levels of acceptance. The process should work in reverse as well. We have many documented cases where agricultural settlers moved into frontier lands with hopes high, only to have their aspirations destroyed by crop failure. In many cases they were too optimistic, expecting too much from the environment. Through time they learned to use different land-use patterns, capable of providing low but dependable production.

Group versus individual behaviour

The decision-making behaviour of groups of people is sufficiently different from that of individuals to constitute a separate study focus. It appears to be considerably easier to analyse, since group decisions are often deliberate, explicit and fairly well publicized. Often, however, group decision making tends to be taken for granted or unrecognized, since the constraints which group decisions can place on individual behaviour are sometimes mistaken as constraints established by 'nature'. Such group decisions can be of enormous importance in explaining regional land-use patterns.

The groups most concerned with land-use decisions include governments, marketing boards, and companies producing farm capital inputs.

[1] Edwards and Tversky, 1967, 84.
[2] Simon 1956: Rational choice and the structure of the environment.

Much of the theory relating to individual decision making can be applied to them if suitable modifications are made. For example, group decisions seem to reflect some tendency to maximize expected utility. In this case, however, a question of inevitable concern is 'expected utility for whom?' Decisions depend very much on whether or not maximum utility is to be attained for farmers as a whole, in which case total utility could be maximized even though utility to some individuals could be very small; or whether a higher utility is to be attained for every producer. To achieve the former objective the government could make loans and market contracts available to a selected number of large, efficient farms, at the expense of putting smaller farms out of business. For the latter objective, the government might have to sacrifice overall efficiency to protect the utility of all producers. In most countries governments have adopted plans to achieve both objectives, usually with a strong concern for protecting every individual. It is generally accepted that government planning should attempt to distribute wealth more-or-less evenly among the population. This objective, of course, is counter to that on which traditional economic theory is based, which is to maximize total utility. So traditional models must be modified within constraints set by group behaviour if it is to attempt to account for real-world land-use patterns. North America is an area where governments have characteristically protected the existence of 'small' family farms. If this behavioural tendency was not considered in land-use models of North American areas, such models might well predict that much larger farms with different land-use economies should have developed. Similarly, the government decision to develop large communal farms in the USSR is essential for an understanding of Soviet agriculture.

The role of politics in group land-use decisions, particularly those of the government, has received much attention since the beginning of recorded time. We will not elaborate on the topic here except to point out that, in the final analysis, the large-scale decisions which affect the real and decision environments of every land user are made largely by political groups. Land tenure and reform, rural area planning, artificial price and production controls, and the type of economy (e.g. free market versus strictly controlled) are all determined by such groups. Their decisions may relate to traditional economic models, but they need not. Government decisions can be based on the desire to please the electorate without concern for real economic implications.

In many cases government and marketing-board plans are not aimed at maximizing income for individuals or entire groups. Often security or stabilization of price, income, or land tenure is of prime concern. Another common objective is the maximization of very long-run utility, which may affect future populations more than current ones. Soil conservation plans are usually based on this principle. In contrast, companies producing farm capital inputs, at least in free-enterprise market economies, do wish to maximize their profits. Their decisions which relate to this motivation, such as to develop and advertise a new type of machinery, can have the effect of increasing an individual farmer's income and changing his land-use pattern if he can use the new machinery effectively; or, if he cannot use the new product for reasons such as insolvency, the decision may force a farmer to fall behind technologically, which may eventually destroy his operation.

We have considered very briefly the decision behaviour of groups—a process which often outranks all others in determining types of land use on a large scale. The reader is referred to the many excellent books and articles relating such behaviour to politics, culture and society.[1]

Further reading

The following theoretical references concern various behavioural aspects of individual and group decision making.

ARIETI, S. 1965: Towards a unifying theory of cognition.

BECKER, G. M., DE GROOT, M. H., and MARSCHAK, J. 1963: Stochastic models of choice behaviour.

BLACK, J. D. 1925: The role of public agencies in the internal readjustments of the farm.

BURKHILL, I. H. 1962: Habits of man and the origins of the cultivated plants of the Old World.

CARTER, H. C. 1963: Representative farms—guides for decision making.

CHAYANOV, A. V. 1966: On the theory of non-capitalist economic systems.

CHERNOFF, H., and MOSES, L. E. 1959: *Elementary decision theory.*

CHURCHMAN, C. W. 1964: Decision and value theory.

COOMBS, C. H. 1964: Inconsistency of preferences: a test of unfolding theory.

D'ANDRADE, R. G., and ROMNEY, A. K. 1964: Transcultural studies in cognition.

DUNCAN, O. D., and SCHNORE, L. F. 1959: Cultural, behavioural and ecological perspectives in the study of social organization.

EDWARDS, W., and TVERSKY, A. 1967: *Decision making,* chapters 1 and 2.

FLOYD, M. L. 1954: On game learning theory and some decision making experiments.

FRIED, M. H. 1952: Land tenure, geography and ecology in the contact of cultures.

GILLETTE, J. M. 1949: Crop response as a testing ground for geo-cultural regionalism.

HENDRIX, W. E. 1956: Institutional-tenure approach to 'size-of-farm' research.

HULL, C. L. 1964: *A behavior system,* p. 228.

JOHNSON, G. L. 1956: Institutional considerations relevant in studying resource productivity and size of business.

KARLSSON, G. 1958: *Social mechanisms.*

KATONA, G. 1951: *The psychological analysis of economic behaviour,* p. 139.

KIRK, W. 1951: Historical geography and the concept of the behavioural environment.

KLOPFER, P. H. 1962: *Behavioural aspects of ecology.*

[1] See, e.g., R. J. Hildreth (Editor) 1968: *Readings in agricultural policy* (Lincoln).

MAY, K. O. 1954: Transitivity, utility, and aggregation in preference patterns.
MEGGERS, B. 1954: Environmental limitations on the development of culture.
POND, G. A. 1932: Studying the human factor in farm management.
PORTER, P. W. 1965: Environmental potential and economic opportunities—a background for cultural adaptation.
SAVAGE, L. J. 1954: *The foundations of statistics.*
SHELLY, M. W., and BRYAN, G. L. (Editors) 1964: *Human judgements and optimality.*
SIMON, H. A. 1951: *Models of man.*
    1955: A behavioural model of rational choice.
    1956: Rational choice and the structure of the environment.
SIMON, H. A., and P. A. 1962: Trial and error search in solving difficult problems: evidence from the game of chess.
SMITH, T. L. 1947: *The sociology of rural life.*
STEVENS, S. S. 1959: Measurement, psychophysics, and utility.
STOYLE, J. 1963: Land utilization as a stochastic process.
THOMAS, D. W. 1955: Sociological aspects of the decision making process.
TVERSKY, A. 1967: Additivity, utility and subjective probability.
WILDE, D. J. 1964: *Optimum seeking methods.*

The following are empirical studies concerning various behavioural concepts in land-use settings.

FIELDING, G. J. 1954: The Los Angeles milkshed: a study of the political factor in agriculture.
GOOCH, D. W. 1951: *World land reform, a selected bibliography.*
HILDRETH, R. J. (Editor) 1968: *Readings in agricultural policy.*
ISAAC, E. 1959: The citron in the Mediterranean: a study in religious influences.
KOLARS, J. 1966: Locational aspects of cultural ecology: the case of the goat in non-Western agriculture.
LIPTON, M. 1968a: A game against nature: strategies of security.
    1968b: A game against nature: theories of peasant decision-making.
    1968c: The theory of the optimising peasant.
MILLER, W. G. 1959: Comparative efficiency of farm tenure classes in the combination of resources.
SALTER, L. A. 1943: Farm property and agricultural policy.
SCHICKELE, R. 1937: Tenure problems and research needs in the Middle West.
WILCOX, W. W., and LLOYD, O. G. 1932: *The human factor in the management of Indiana farms.*
WOLPERT, J. 1964: The decision process in a spatial context.

8   INNOVATION, INFORMATION, AND LEARNING

Learning theories—The Relation of information diffusion to the behavioural characteristics of decision makers—The Relation of information diffusion and innovation adoption to expected utility—The relation of information and innovation diffusion to communication patterns—Logistic trends—Hypothetical problem— Further reading

Land-use decisions depend, in part, on the decision environment within which an individual operates. The decision environment can be very different from the real environment if the individual has had insufficient time, ability, motivation or communication to learn about the world which surrounds him. Part of the explanation for the difference between the environments relates to the individual himself, particularly his ability to identify the possible strategies, utilities, and pay-off probabilities facing him. His motivation to obtain new information is also a personal attribute, although it may be strongly affected by the general utility of the environment or by the culture of the group with which he lives. Part of the explanation also lies with factors external to the individual, such as the availability of information, which may reflect the efficiency of communication networks.

Decision environments vary spatially, which is one of the reasons for spatial variations in land use. Part of the explanation is that extended environments also vary spatially. For example, production functions, which form part of the environment, change from location to location due to changes in the natural environment. But variations in the decision environment can also be related to other factors, such as the availability of information and the extent to which decision makers seek, learn, and use it. Obviously, these variations relate to individuals, and reflect their specific personalities and capabilities. Yet broader, regional patterns can also be discerned. Individual behaviour is, within normal limits of variation, strongly related to the behaviour of the group, so that one can define regional 'personalities' or capabilities. Furthermore, information normally becomes available to groups living together in space rather than to isolated individuals since communication is facilitated by proximity.

Much of the literature concerned with spatial variations in land use which relate to information and learning is concerned with (1) cultural and sociological characteristics of the decision makers, and (2) mechanisms by which information about new innovations spreads. The former tends to be somewhat descriptive at this stage, whereas the latter, which deals with a phenomenon which is fairly easy to observe, measure, and separate into components, includes carefully formulated theoretical models which have been tested against empirical evidence. It is with the latter that we will deal primarily in this chapter.

Learning theories

Learning has been a subject of much concern during the past twenty years, and a considerable body of theory has been developed. Psychologists are responsible for most of the developments, although geographers and economists have shown a recent concern with specific aspects. We can not undertake a comprehensive review of the subject in this short section, but will present some of the theoretical concepts of particular significance to land use. Highly mathematical models, which are numerous in the literature, will be avoided.

Learning refers to the process whereby an individual or group develops a behaviour pattern in response to situations through time. It may be a conscious process, as when individuals seek to improve decisions through *problem-solving behaviour*; or it may occur unknown to an individual, who is oblivious to any systematic action or response. It is a highly relevant process since, psychologists tell us, almost all human behaviour is learned. So the deviation between a theoretical behaviour (or land-use) pattern and an actual one can be explained by the degree of learning achieved by the individuals involved, provided that the theoretical prediction has already taken account of behavioural tendencies (e.g. aspiration levels) other than learning.

Learning is closely related to adaptive decision making, which was discussed in the preceding chapter. Adaptive decision making necessarily involves learning and the reverse is true if we define all behaviour, conscious and routine, as the result of the decision-making process. Some argue, however, that learning can occur which does not affect decision making, at least for a very long time.[1]

One of the simplest learning situations to envisage is where an individual enters a new area, is unfamiliar with the real environment, and develops a behaviour pattern to attain some objective. Suppose that the settler has forgotten or succeeds in not preferring any land-use systems learned formerly, that he is isolated from behavioural patterns already existing in the area, and that he wishes to undertake a form of agriculture which will yield him enough produce to feed his family and provide a specified income. Assume also that the real environment (production functions,

[1] C. H. Hanzik and E. C. Tolman 1936: The perception of spatial relations by the rat: a type of response not easily explained by conditioning. *Journal of Comparative Psychology* **22**, 287–318.

weather, prices, technology, etc., normal to the area) remains constant throughout the learning period. It is unrealistic, of course, to assume that he is completely independent of all former behavioural patterns, since the decision to undertake agriculture involves the use of a learned procedure (agriculture). But we can assume behavioural ignorance aside from this basic sort of background.

Will the individual's behaviour in the first instance be conscious or routine? It has been suggested that the degree of conscious behaviour is partially dependent on the demand for obtaining information; so we would expect our individual consciously to set about learning a suitable land-use system since the demand for information is enormous. Initially he will search for alternative courses of action, perhaps fervently. If he is fortunate enough to discover communication links with other farmers or agencies capable of providing useful information, he will try practices recommended to him which seem to be the most rational. If he is unable to find useful communication links, he will have to begin by using a *trial-and-error* procedure, selecting crops randomly in an effort to discover useful ones. Such action represents *hypothesis behaviour* or *first try*. He might consider the probability of success equal for all crops, and, following the equal-likelihood criterion, plant equal amounts of each.

At the conclusion of the first crop year the settler is in a position to have learned, and we expect future decisions to reflect the learning process. If advice obtained from a particular source did not lead to utility, the individual might well avoid following advice from that source in the next time period. The degree to which he will avoid it should depend on the extent to which the advice was bad and the degree to which the settler considers the advice will be consistently bad. He might consider one failure as sufficient to avoid all future advice from that source; or he might generously assume that the advice would normally have been good, but that the rare probability of failure happened to have been realized. Similarly, if some of his randomly chosen crops grew poorly, he might or might not grow them again, depending on his feelings about the future success of growing those crops. These 'feelings' are really subjective probabilities, which are partially dependent on personality. As for advice or randomly-chosen crops which led to utility, we expect the settler to use them again. The extent to which he grows particular crops again (e.g. the relative acreage devoted to each) will reflect the utility derived from them in the first year.

At the conclusion of the second crop year the individual has learned more. Decision responses which occurred in similar fashion both years lead to *reinforced conclusions* about the utility pay-offs of different courses of action. At the same time the intensity of search may be somewhat curtailed if crops which appear to give satisfactory results have been discovered. In the crop years which follow, crop decisions consistently yielding good results are reinforced, and those crops are grown with increasing conviction and confidence. Subjective probabilities become better estimates of objective probabilities, as the sample size (number of years) is increased. This process, referred to as *statistical learning*, may follow carefully formulated statistical laws.[1] Variation in cropping patterns and search procedures diminish each year, as satisfactory land-use practices evolve.

After a long time period a fairly constant land-use pattern, which reflects a stabilized behaviour pattern, is established. We can not say that learning is completed; but much learning has occurred, and conscious information-searching and problem-solving has terminated. The settler's responses to advice, weather and other variables are conditioned and predictable within the bounds of stochastic variation. He has learned gradually by an incremental, year-by-year process; and he now appears to be a creature of *habit*, unconsciously following a *path of least resistance*.

The above description should not be considered the only or, necessarily, the normal learning process. But it does involve many of the concepts currently popular. The reader should be able to realize how the concepts might be modified to account for group behaviour, or to permit varying degrees of communication. He might also realize how theoretical learning processes might be represented rather easily by mathematics.

Our hypothetical example assumed that the real environment was constant, whereas we know that it changes constantly. Changes in price, technology, and other factors present land users with learning situations all of the time. The situation wherein an individual moves to a new area about which he knows nothing is rare. But the changing nature of the environment does provide new information incessantly. The way in which an individual reacts to it is a function of the type of learning process which has come to characterize him. We might hypothesize that in areas where the use of new information has led to utility in past times, individuals will be willing to use new information in the future. In areas where former experience has led individuals to expect disaster from new ideas, we might expect considerable resistance to new ideas in the future.

Information and utility seem to be closely interrelated in some areas, particularly those where new information is associated with utility. One of the sources of new information within an area is innovation, which some have referred to as the highest form of decision making. Whether or not important innovations in the past resulted from necessity or accident, modern man has come to expect much from them, and seeks consciously to develop them. The creation of experimental farms, etc., can be seen as an extremely positive response to the former learning experiences of industrialized society.

Two aspects of learning are of particular concern to us. In order to understand land use in a given area, we must know the learning stage of

[1] L. J. Savage 1954: *The foundations of statistics* (New York).

the decision makers. Is it an area where new arrivals or adventurous farmers are still in a search stage? Or is it an area of complete, routine behaviour? Secondly, we must know something of the conditioned responses to information of the individuals, which reflects their learning experiences. Only then can we predict the potential or past impact of external information.

The relation of information diffusion to the behavioural characteristics of decision makers

Much research relating the diffusion and use of new information to the behavioural characteristics of individuals and groups has been undertaken since approximately 1920, primarily by rural sociologists.[1] It has long been recognized that individuals vary considerably with respect to the extent to which they search for information and use it. Theoretically we expect such variation to relate in part to the personalities and prior learning experiences of decision makers, and there is much evidence to support this hypothesis. In general, farmers with high education seek and use new information to a greater degree than those with less formal education. Consequently, they tend to adopt new innovations sooner than others. One could argue that this tendency reflects an awareness of the positive utilities obtainable from new information—an awareness which developed from their formal education. It might also reflect a learned ability to think in terms of the conscious planning of strategies or of business-like, orderly, decision making. Other research has shown that the time of the adoption of innovations varies among social or cultural groups.[2] The decison environment of an individual and his propensity to change it are strongly dependent on the behavioural patterns of the culture group to which he belongs, so this conclusion is not unexpected. Other social characteristics related to innovation adoption include the 'urbaneness' and age of individuals. Jones suggests that the correlation between 'urbaneness' and early innovation adoption might really reflect superior communication links among urban types, rather than differences in behaviour from farmers from more 'rural' areas.[3] With respect to age, the research shows a tendency for older persons to seek and use new information less than younger people. This may reflect more habitual or routine behaviour patterns among the old. It may also indicate a realization by older persons that the utility of a new innovation may not be as great to them as to a younger person who can remain in farming long enough to enjoy all of the benefits.

[1] See G. E. Jones 1963: The diffusion of agricultural innovations. *Journal of Agricultural Economics* **15**, 387.
[2] B. Benvenuti 1962: *Farming in cultural change* (Assen) 37–73.
[3] Jones (1963).

Person-to-person variation in the diffusion of information has an important effect on farm-to-farm variations in land use. Of equal interest to us, however, are large-scale, interregional variations. It is logical that such variations in information-seeking should occur, partly because of regional concentration of culture groups, and partly because of regional variations in learning experiences. One would expect new innovations to be discovered and adopted more readily by persons living in areas where innovations normally yield high utilities than persons who have had poor or modest success with innovations.

The relation of information diffusion and innovation adoption to expected utility

Since expected utility appears to be one of the main components affecting decisions, we should expect it to have an important effect on the diffusion and use of new ideas. Much research on the diffusion and adoption of agricultural innovations supports this general hypothesis, although several of the relationships have turned out to be much more complicated than originally expected. Most of the literature is concerned with local, almost aspatial diffusions among farms within local areas. Research on broader patterns of diffusion has been less common, but has revealed some intriguing relationships with utility.

A common type of study has examined situations where the information about and the supply of a new innovation are generally available; and the researchers have hypothesized that farms with particular economic characteristics and farmers with specific expected utilities will adopt the innovation towards the beginning, middle, or end of the adoption time period. It has been shown that farms that will benefit most from an innovation tend to adopt it first. For example, if a new type of equipment will replace older, inferior types, farms where the older equipment is worn out will adopt the new type before farms whose older equipment can still provide a few years of service.[1] Other research has examined the relative speed with which a number of innovations are adopted. It has been concluded that innovations offering the greatest expected utilities tend to be adopted first. Innovations which are particularly conspicuous to farmers, which are economically compatible with existing capital, or which are divisible and can be obtained gradually or in small quantities (e.g. fertilizer) all tend to be adopted more quickly than others. Innovations which appear to be complex to understand, use, or obtain are adopted later than others.

It has been hypothesized that expected increase in farm income and the speed of return on investment correlate positively with the speed of

---

[1] J. Robinson 1956: *The accumulation of capital* (London) 85.

adopting innovations; but, at least in one area, this has proved to be untrue.[1] The reasons seem somewhat unclear. They might reflect that the expected utilities of farmers are not always objectively determined; or they might point out the difference between selecting a strategy on the basis of expected utility versus selecting the speed with which to undertake a strategy on the same basis. This is a probe requiring further research, since the initial indications are so completely contrary to what existing theory suggests.

The cost or disutility of adopting an innovation should also affect its adoption rate. Research has indicated that high initial cost does tend to decrease the speed with which innovations are accepted. Furthermore, innovations are liable to be adopted on large farms (where, presumably, the costs can be covered relatively easily) before smaller farms. Farmers with higher incomes also tend to adopt before those with lower incomes.

Since farm size, income, and expected utility from innovations exhibit strong regional variations, we should expect regional patterns of innovation diffusion to occur. A most interesting piece of research examining the diffusion of hybrid corn in the United States does confirm this hypothesis—but somewhat indirectly.[2] In this discussion we have assumed that the timing and rate of innovation adoption are dependent on a *demand* related to the expected utility of farmers. But Griliches shows that the regional diffusion of hybrid corn is really a function of the *supply* of the hybrid seed, which was determined by hybrid seed companies. The motivating mechanism behind the companies' actions was their attempt to maximize expected utility, or profitability. In the first years of hybrid seed use, different varieties had to be developed for different climatic regions of the United States. Companies were faced with selecting the areas for which they would first undertake expensive research to provide hybrid seed. Although the first experimental hybrid was developed in Connecticut, the companies first developed commercial seed for the environment of Iowa—the area where most corn was grown and where they could expect the greatest profits from seed sales. In later years varieties were developed for surrounding areas, primarily for areas with climates similar to that of Iowa, since the cost of developing these seeds was less than for areas with very different climatic conditions. In the last years of 'hybridization', varieties were developed for the states in the South—an area where a relatively small market existed for seed, and where the costs of developing hybrid varieties were high. The geographic diffusion of the use of hybrid seed was a direct function of the date of availability of the seed, which was determined by the expected profitability to the seed companies. It is

[1] F. C. Fliegel and J. E. Kivlin 1962: Farm practice attributes and adoption rates. *Social Forces* **40**, 364–70.
[2] Z. Griliches 1960: Hybrid corn and the economics of innovation. *Science* **132**, 275–80.

interesting to note that the diffusion occurred more quickly along an east–west axis than north–south, because of the lower costs and expected returns of developing seeds for the east–west states, which are rather similar climatically.

One can relate this diffusion process to the expected utilities of farmers, although this provides a less direct explanation of the spatio-temporal process. Expected profits for the seed companies depend entirely on the purchase of hybrid seed by farmers. But this demand depends on individual farmers' expected utilities from using the seed and on the total number of farmers who grow corn. So the diffusion process is an indirect function of the expected profits of regional groups of decision makers.

The relation of information and innovation diffusion to communication patterns

Many theoretical models relating spatial diffusion to communication networks and habits have been developed recently by geographers.[1] They show promise of leading to a much better understanding of this dynamic process, which leads to regional variation in information availability and decision environments. Their application in analysing spatial variation in land-use practices has already been proved. Some of the models have gone beyond the process of information diffusion to incorporate concepts of learning, which should improve their usefulness in explaining real-world land-use variation.

Information diffuses at many scales, from the international to the inter-person; and by many media, from electronic devices to word-of-mouth. Obviously, the spatial processes and models used to describe them vary with scale and medium; and the overall process by which information travels from its original source to an individual land user normally involves a combination of communication channels. The problem of analysing the diffusion of information by these processes might be fairly simple except for one fact: the important thing about information is the extent to which individuals and groups search for and learn to use it; and this varies considerably according to the scale and medium through which the information is obtained. A related complication is that it seems to be impossible to communicate information completely objectively. Individuals or groups passing on facts distort them somewhat, either consciously or subconsciously. And part of a receiver's learning experience concerns the extent to which he considers the information communicated to him to be objective.

Much early research, largely by rural sociologists, was concerned with the channels through which farmers sought, learned, and used land-use information. The motivation for the research was practical, as government

[1] See P. R. Gould 1969: *Spatial diffusion* (Washington).

extension agencies wanted to discover the most effective ways of communicating new information to farmers. Results of the research were remarkably uniform in many areas.[1] It was discovered that, in a given area, a few farmers tend to actively seek new information by reading farm journals or newspapers, listening to radio or television, and contacting representatives of companies or government agencies. These people tend to be early adopters of innovations. Most farmers tend to be more conservative, and range from those who are oblivious to information provided by the mass media to those who are mildly interested. They only adopt innovations after coming into contact with some other farmer or farmers who have used them successfully. As time passes, then, inter-farmer contacts become much more important than the mass media in persuading individuals to adopt new innovations. One result of the research has been a wide-spread adoption by extension agencies of the practice of 'reaching' farmers through the early innovators in their community. Agencies often expend little effort in trying to introduce innovations to the majority, but do contact the early innovators, since they expect others to eventually follow their example.

Due to the importance of inter-farmer communication in the diffusion and learning process, it is not surprising that spatial diffusion models based on this communicative link have been quite successful in 'explaining' real-world patterns. The diffusions of the acceptance of government subsidies to improve pastures (Sweden), of tuberculin-tested dairy herds (Sweden), and of the decision to irrigate (USA) are three of the processes for which useful theoretical models have been developed. Many of the models are modifications of an early one developed by Hägerstrand, which deserves special discussion because it illustrates a number of features common to several behavioural models, spatial and otherwise.[2]

The Hägerstrand-type model is a simulation model—i.e. it attempts to recreate or simulate a process through time by following rigid mathematical rules which relate to assumptions about the real-world diffusion pattern. The output of the model is a series of maps which show, at sequential time periods, the spatial distribution of the adoption of an innovation. Simulation is used not only because maps are required for several points in time, but also because it is impossible to predict with one calculation the final diffusion pattern. The pattern at each point in time is dependent on the pattern generated for the preceding time period. This reflects the fact that persons cannot learn about an innovation except from individuals who have already adopted it.

In the simplest type of Hägerstrand model we assume uniform population density in the study area. The area is divided into a matrix of square

[1] E. M. Rogers 1962: *Diffusion of innovations* (New York).
[2] T. Hägerstrand 1965: A Monte Carlo approach to diffusion. *Archives Europeanes de Sociologie* 6, 43–67.

cells, each containing equal numbers of people. Suppose that Fig. 8.1 represents the study area divided into cells, each one containing one square mile and five farmers. The cell containing the first adopter of the innovation is indicated, and Fig. 8.1 represents the study area at time 1.

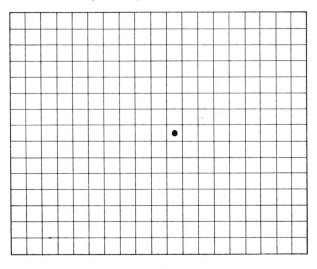

0 1 2 3 4 5 6 7
Scale (miles)
Fig. 8.1 : Study area at time 1

The mechanism by which information about the innovation is spread is person-to-person contact, so we need some measure of the extent to which people come in contact with others at varying distances. Häger-strand used a variety of sources for this data, such as records of telephone calls and marriages. The records, of course, must refer to the time period of our simulated diffusion, since individuals' personal-communication habits change with time and technology. Suppose in this case that the population is somewhat reclusive, and an average person in a given time period comes in contact with 8 people who live within his own cell, 6 people each in the cells located one mile away, 4 people each in the cells two miles away, and so on. This distance–contact relationship is illustrated graphically in Fig. 8.2. From the graph we can interpolate the number of contacts expected in cells any distance from the individual.

The problem remaining is to make use of the distance–contact relation-ship, known as the *neighbourhood effect*, to simulate the diffusion process. To allow for the stochastic nature of human behaviour Hägerstrand adapted a *Monte Carlo* technique in his model. By using this technique, we repre-sent the random or unpredictable nature of human behaviour, which

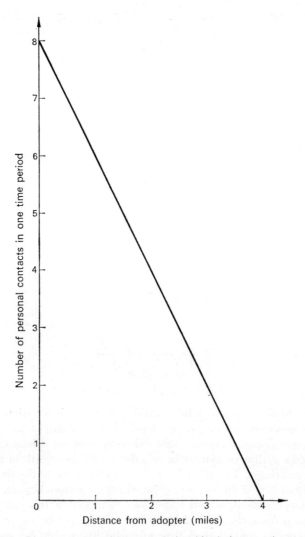

Fig. 8.2 : Distance–personal contact relationship during one time period

makes it possible for the model to predict different patterns on different 'runs'. We begin by constructing a *floating grid* (Fig. 8.3), a five-cell by five-cell matrix whose cells are the same size as those in Fig. 8.1. We assume that our initial adopter is located in the middle cell and place the number 8 there (the number of persons with whom he comes in contact in the given time period). Correspondingly, we put the number 6 in the cells one 'mile' away, and so on (see Fig. 8.2). The completed grid is called the *number-of-cases* or *contact frequency grid*. Next, we calculate the sum of the

2·31	3·57	4·00	3·57	2·31
3·57	5·16	6·00	5·16	3·57
4·00	6·00	8·00	6·00	4·00
3·57	5·16	6·00	5·16	3·57
2·31	3·57	4·00	3·57	2·31

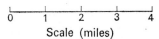

Scale (miles)

Fig. 8.3: Floating grid, indicating number of personal contacts in one time period

numbers in all of the cells in the grid (106·44) and divide the number in each cell to produce the *mean information field* (MIF) (Fig. 8.4). Finally the *accumulative information field* (AIF) is calculated (Fig. 8.5). The upper left-hand cell is assigned a range of values from zero to the number in the corresponding cell of the MIF. The cell to the right includes a range beginning just above the upper limit in the first cell and going to an upper

0·0217	0·0335	0·0376	0·0335	0·0217
0·0335	0·0485	0·0564	0·0485	0·0335
0·0376	0·0564	0·0752	0·0564	0·0367
0·0335	0·0485	0·0564	0·0485	0·0335
0·0217	0·0335	0·0376	0·0335	0·0217

0·0217	0·0552	0·0928	0·1263	0·1480
0·1815	0·2300	0·2864	0·3349	0·3684
0·4060	0·4624	0·5376	0·5940	0·6316
0·6651	0·7136	0·7700	0·8125	0·8520
0·8737	0·9072	0·9448	0·9783	1·0000

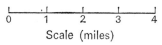

Scale (miles)

Fig. 8.4: Mean information field   Fig. 8.5: Accumulative information field

limit equal to the sum of the numbers in the first two cells of the MIF. The third cell's lower range is just above this value, and goes to the sum of the first three cells in the MIF; and so on. Note that the upper limit of the lower right-hand corner cell is 1·000.

The AIF has a very special property. The size of the number ranges in the cells is directly proportional to the corresponding numbers in the contact frequency grid. Suppose that random numbers ranging from 0 to 1·000 are chosen and assigned to the cells of the AIF whose number ranges include them. There will be a tendency for the assignments to cluster towards the centre of the AIF, to the same extent as a tendency existed for an individual to contact persons living close to him. By choosing random numbers we introduce a stochastic element similar to the stochastic contact behaviour of our individual. But, by using the AIF which is 'weighted' towards the centre, we still impose a tendency for orderly space-behaviour.

Now we are prepared to begin the simulation of the diffusion process. Suppose that in each time period each individual contacts two others, both of whom immediately adopt the innovation if they have not done so already. We centre the AIF on our first adopter, select two random numbers between 0 and 1·000, and assign them to the appropriate cells. These represent the two persons, contacted by our first individual, who now adopt the innovation. Suppose that the two random numbers are 0·219 and 0·643. The cells they fall in are indicated in Fig. 8.6, which represents the diffusion map at time 2. In the next time period the AIF

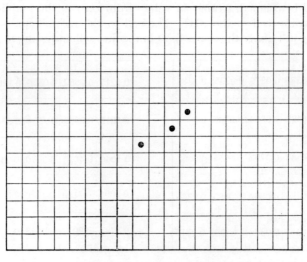

0 1 2 3 4 5 6 7
Scale (miles)
Fig. 8.6: Diffusion map at time 2

is placed on top of each of the three adopters, and two more 'individuals' are 'contacted' by each. The process continues for as many time periods as desired.

We have described a very simple type of Hägerstrand model, although the reader will realize it can become very cumbersome to run as the number of time periods increases. Hägerstrand's own models were run on a computer, and they were more complex in order to approach more closely real-life conditions. Population density was allowed to vary, for example, to allow for different hypothesized learning and communication processes. The number of persons contacted in each time period and the number of times a person had to be contacted before he adopted an innovation were varied. Barriers to communication were also introduced. The distance-decay functions describing the neighbourhood effect were somewhat more complicated than the linear one used in our example. By including adjustments of this type, Hägerstrand's models proved to be quite representative of real-life.

Much research has been stimulated by Hägerstrand's original work. More recent models represent attempts to consider different types of learning behaviour and communication, and to develop mathematical formulations which can be tested more readily against reality. An important probe which has not received too much attention concerns the attempt to include personal-contact diffusion models within larger-scale models which allow for communication with mass media or diffusion in response to expected utility.

Logistic trends

Many writers have noted that if the total number of individuals having adopted an innovation is plotted against time during a diffusion process in a given area, a logistic curve is formed.[1] It is 'S-shaped' (Fig. 8.7) and is described by the equation $P = \dfrac{U}{1 + e^{(a-b.T)}}$, where P is the proportion of individuals already having adopted, T is the time in the diffusion process, U is the upper limit of P, e is 2·7183 (the natural log base), and a and b are parameters which vary with the diffusion process, a determines the height above the time axis where the curve begins, and b determines the slope of the curve.

The S-shape is attributed to the tendency for only a few persons to adopt initially, for the majority to adopt during a short time period during the middle of the process, and for a few 'laggards' to adopt towards the end of the process. The curve can also be seen to reflect the fact that in the initial stages, the probability of coming in contact with a person who

[1] P. R. Gould, 1969, 19–21.

has adopted is slight, whereas the probability is great after more people have obtained the information. Towards the end of the process the probability of communicating with an individual who has not adopted the innovation is greatly decreased.

Griliches related the slope of the curve to the relative profitability or expected utility of the adopters.[1] He notes, for example, that hybrid corn

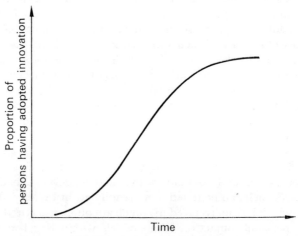

Fig. 8.7: S-shaped logistic curve

was adopted much more rapidly, once it became available, in areas of intensive and widespread corn cultivation than in areas where corn-growing was of marginal importance. One might also relate the steepness of the slope (rate of acceptance) to some features of communication. Frequent contact, which could reflect high population density, should lead to faster rates than low-frequency contact.

Hypothetical problem

A farmer living in the middle of a 225-square-mile area has just developed a new potato variety which is superior to any other known, and which will have a profound effect on the land-use economy of anyone who finds out about and uses it. The area in which the farmer lives has a uniform population density, with one farm per square mile. Communication is by direct word-of-mouth only.

Questions

Assuming that a Hägerstrand-type of diffusion model is in operation,

[1] Griliches 1960.

predict the spatial pattern of diffusion of the use of the new potato variety for eight time periods under the following assumptions:

(*a*) the supply of the new potato variety is unlimited;

(*b*) individual farms adopt the use of the new variety as soon as they hear about it. Make the predictions assuming that, in each time period, each adopter tells (i) one, and (ii) three other persons. Also, make the predictions on the basis of three different linear distance-decay functions: (i) $C = 5 - D$ (C = no. of contacts, D = distance from adopter's farm in miles), (ii) $C = 5 - 1 \cdot 75D$, and (iii) $C = 5 - 2 \cdot 5D$. In each case plot the accumulated number of adoptions against time.

Solutions

The simulated diffusion patterns were calculated and mapped using a computer program which simulated a process almost identical to that described in the second-last section.[1] The only difference is that the process used in the program is not restricted to a five-by-five-cell AIF. The AIF size is adjusted for every problem so that the zero-contact distance coincides with the outer edge of the AIF. The maps, which are direct computer print-outs, are indicated for every second time period in Figs. 8.8 to 8.13. The graphs relating the accumulated number of adopters to time are indicated in the same figures. Graphs of the three distance-decay functions (neighbourhood effects) are illustrated in Fig. 8.14.

Note that the diffusion process is highly dependent on the number of persons told in a time period and the 'steepness' of the neighbourhood effect. The distance-decay function reflecting little long-distance contact $(C = 5 - 2 \cdot 5D)$ produces a highly nucleated diffusion pattern compared with the function reflecting a weak neighbourhood effect $(C = 5 - D)$. The function $C = 5 - 1 \cdot 75D$ gives rise to a diffusion pattern intermediary between the two extremes. The total number of adopters at the end of the eight time periods varies greatly, from 224 (for $C = 5 - D$ and three persons contacted per time period) to 25 (for $C = 5 - 2 \cdot 5D$ and one person contacted).

It is interesting to note that all of the accumulative-adopter graphs tend to be S-shaped, except where small numbers of adopters suggest that the declining portions of the graphs have not yet been reached. This result supports the hypothesis that logistic trends reflect the communication process, and not necessarily the selective behaviour of early adopters or laggards.

[1] An APL program (HAGER) was written and used on the York University Terminal System (IBM 360–50 computer).

154

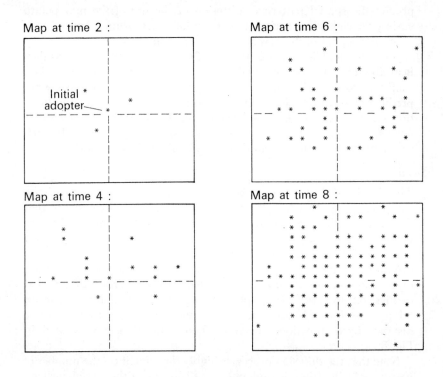

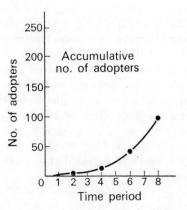

Fig. 8.8: Diffusion with $C = 5 - D$ decay function, each adopter contacting 1 person per time period

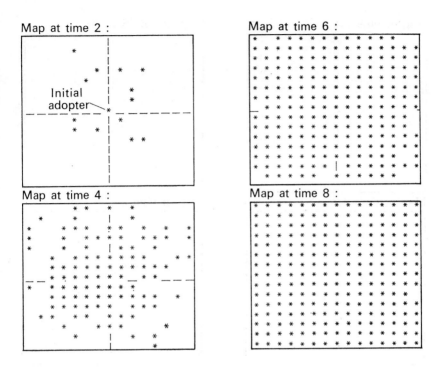

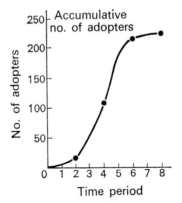

Fig. 8.9: Diffusion with $C = 5 - D$ decay function, each adopter contacting 3 persons per time period

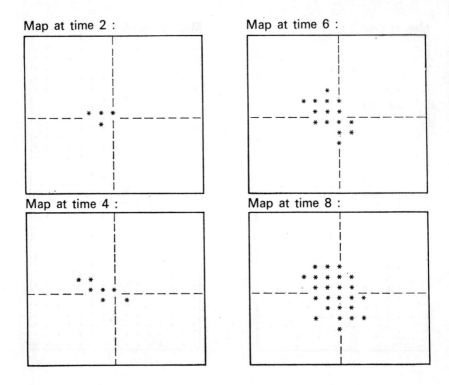

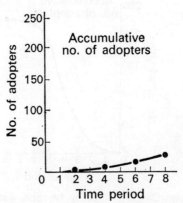

Fig. 8.10: Diffusion with $C = 5 - 1.75D$ decay function, each adopter contacting 1 person per time period

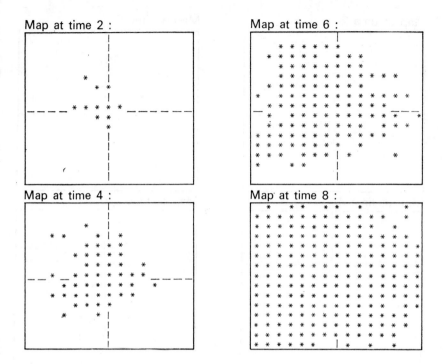

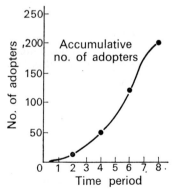

Fig. 8.11: Diffusion with $C = 5 - 1.75D$ decay function, each adopter contacting 3 persons per time period

158

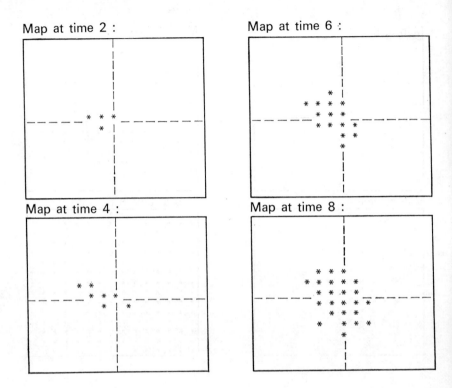

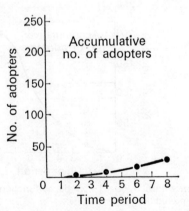

Fig. 8.12: Diffusion with $C = 5 - 2 \cdot 5D$ decay function, each adopter contacting 1 person per time period

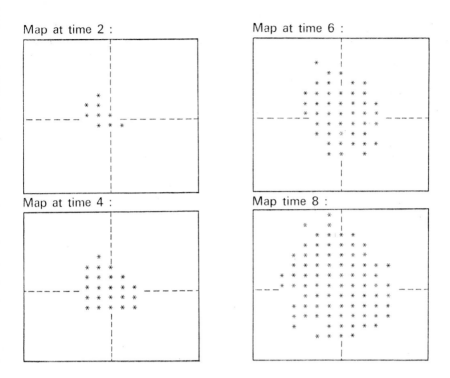

Map at time 2 :

Map at time 6 :

Map at time 4 :

Map time 8 :

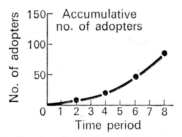

Fig. 8.13 : Diffusion with $C = 5 - 2.5D$ decay function, each adopter contacting 3 persons per time period

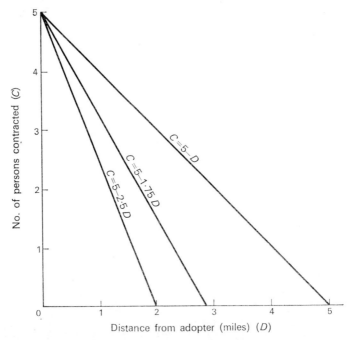

Fig. 8.14 : Distance decay functions used in hypothetical problem

Further reading

The following theoretical references concern learning and the diffusion of information.

BENVENUTI, B. 1962: *Farming in cultural change*, pp. 37–73.
BIRCH, H. G. 1945: The relation of previous experience to insightful problem-solving.
BRANDNER, L., and KEARL, B. 1964: Evaluation for congruence as a factor in the adoption rate of innovations.
BROWN, L. 1965: *A bibliography on spatial diffusion*.
    1968: *Diffusion processes and location: a conceptual framework and bibliography*.
BUSH, R. R., and MOSTELLER, F. 1955: *Stochastic models for learning*.
CASSETTI, E. 1969: Why do diffusion processes conform to logistic trends?
COPP, J. H., SILL, M. L., and BROWN, E. J. 1958: The function of information sources in the farm practice adoption process.
COUGHENOUR, C. M. 1960: The functioning of farmer's characteristics in relation to contact with media and practice adoption.
DILLON, J. L., and HEADY, E. O. 1958: Decision criteria for innovation.
ESTES, W. K. 1950: Towards a statistical theory of learning.
FLIEGEL, F. C., and KIVLIN, J. E. 1962: Farm practice attributes and adoption rates.
FLOYOD, M. M. 1960: Sequential decisioning.
GOLLEDGE, R. G. 1968: *The geographical relevance of some learning theories*.
GOULD, P. R. 1969: *Spatial diffusion*.

HÄGERSTRAND, T. 1966: Aspects of the spatial structure of social communication and the diffusion of information.

HILL, W. F. 1963: *Learning, a survey of psychological interpretations.*

JONES, G. E. 1963: The diffusion of agricultural innovations.

KATZ, B., LEVIN, M. L., and HAMILTON, H. 1963: Traditions of research on the diffusion of innovations.

LANZETTA, J. T., and KANAREFF, V. T. 1962: Information cost, amount of payoff, and level of aspiration as determinants of information seeking in decision making.

LIONBERGER, H. E. 1952: The diffusion of farm and home information as an area of sociological research.

MACHOL, R. E. (Editor) 1960: *Information and decision processes.*

MARGALEF, R. 1958: Information theory in ecology.

MARSH, C. P., and COLEMAN, A. L. 1955: The relation of farmer characteristics to the adoption of recommended farm practices.

MASON, R. G. 1964: The use of information sources in the process of adoption.

PEDERSON, H. 1957: Cultural differences in the acceptance of recommended practices.

PHOTIADIS, J. D. 1962: Motivation, contacts and technical change.

PITTS, F. R. 1963: Problems in computer simulation of diffusion.

RAMSEY, C. E., POLSON, R. A., and SPENCER, G. E. 1959: Values and the adoption of practices.

ROGERS, E. M. 1962: *Diffusion of innovations.*

SAVAGE, L. J. 1954: *The foundations of statistics.*

SPENCE, K. W., (Editor) 1960: *Behaviour theory and learning.*

WILKENING, E. A. 1950: A sociopsychological approach to the study of the acceptance of innovations in farming.

WILLEM VAN DEN BAN, ANNE 1960: Locality group differences in the adoption of new farm practices.

The following are empirical analyses of diffusion and learning processes in agriculture.

BOWDEN, L. W. 1965: *The diffusion of the decision to irrigate.*

COLEMAN, A. L., and MARSH, C. P. 1955: Differential communication among farmers in a Kentucky county.

EIDMAN, V. R. *et al.* 1967: An application of statistical decision theory to commercial turkey production.

FATHI, A. 1965: Leadership and resistance to change: a case from an underdeveloped area.

FLIEGEL, F. G. 1966: Literacy and exposure to instrumental information among farmers in southern Brazil.

GRILICHES, Z. 1960: Hybrid corn and the economics of innovation.

HÄGERSTRAND, T. 1965: A Monte Carlo approach to diffusion.

HOFFER, C. R., and STRANGLAND, D. 1958: Farmers' attitudes and values in relation to adoption of approved practices in corn growing.

LIONBERGER, H. E., and HASSINGER, E. 1954: Neighbourhoods as a factor in the diffusion of farm information in a northeast Missouri farming community.

9 PERCEPTION, IMAGE, AND LAND USE

Perception, learning, and decision making—Summary and conclusions—Further reading

Perception is a highly complex concept, as Saarinen has recently pointed out.[1] One result has been a considerable variation in the use of the term by social scientists. To some, a person's *perception* of reality refers to his subjective assessment or conception of it. Most would agree that this is an improper use of the term, and that the individual's personal assessment or 'picture' of reality is his *image*.[2] To others, particularly some psychologists, perception refers to the process by which individuals evaluate or become aware of reality. Perception studies related to this concept tend to emphasize the physiological processes by which persons become aware.[3] A third meaning of the term, the one which seems to be most common and the one assumed in most studies relating to land use, is that perception refers to an individual's immediate evaluation of or reaction to reality when confronted with it. Such a short-term reaction is bound to be conditioned by prior experience and personality, but may involve an assessment of reality which is quite different from the 'image' which the individual would hold after a long, 'rational' deliberation. Perception may or may not relate to actual decision making, as will be discussed below.

Perception, learning, and decision making

We have indicated previously the importance of the decision (or behavioural) environment in the making of land-use decisions. An important part of the decision environment is the collection of images of reality which relate to land use. Perception is important in the decision-making process to the extent that it influences the learning process whereby the images of the decision environment are determined. No clear agreement regarding this relationship has been reached, but the following conceptual framework appears to be emerging.[4]

Learning in a land-use setting occurs in response to two types of

[1] T. F. Saarinen 1969: *Perception of environment* (Washington) 5.
[2] See K. E. Boulding 1956: *The image* (Ann Arbor).
[3] M. D. Vernon 1962: *The psychology of perception* (London).
[4] See, e.g., Saarinen's (1969) discussion of the perceptual and behavioural environments, pp. 5 and 6.

information: (1) knowledge gained through the experience of the individual himself, and (2) knowledge obtained from exogenous sources through communication with others. Learning related to the first source of information can be seen as a function of man's perception of the real environment, since such learning would be accompanied and, perhaps, affected by a number—perhaps a continuous series—of perceptions of the real world. One would expect an individual's image of some element of the environment to have been modified somewhat by past perceptions. The following example serves to illustrate this possibility.

Suppose that a number of farmers with varying backgrounds inhabit a valley which is subject to occasional flooding. Following a particular flood, individuals' perceptions of the event could vary greatly. Highly rational persons familiar with floods could perceive the occurrence in a highly objective fashion. They should be able to compare accurately the destructiveness of the flood with that of other floods; they should appreciate the scientific causes of the flood; and they should maintain an objective measure of the probability of such a flood occurring again. Given human limitations of rationality, information, and experience, however, it would be normal to expect distortion of the event in the perceptions of some individuals. The distortions could result from a natural tendency to oversimplify reality. For example, some might classify the flood as 'destructive' or 'non-destructive', without allowing for intermediary degrees of destructiveness. Some might see the cause as 'an act of God'. Others might immediately conclude that such floods occur very often, or, taking the opposite extreme, that such a flood will never occur again. Personal experience could also cause variations in personal perception. Persons never having experienced a flood before might over- or underestimate its destructiveness. Those without scientific backgrounds could reach many alternative conclusions regarding the cause. And those having migrated from areas subject to much flooding could overestimate the frequency of flood occurrence.

As more floods occur through time, we would expect the perceptions of an individual to change. With a new flood an individual might remember the last flood and his prior immediate estimation of destructiveness, which was too pessimistic. His new perception may be more cautious or optimistic. Eventually, past perceptions may combine to encourage more objective perceptions. The learning process is related to other factors as well, however. Normally the individual would exchange relevant information with other persons between floods, so changing perceptions would be a *result of* as well as a possible *influence on* the learning process.

In our example, decision making would be directly affected by perception only if an individual made a land-use decision (e.g. to construct drainage ditches) as part of a direct response to a flood. He might order construction of the ditches before the water subsided. Such hasty decisions are probably rare, however. Most would be made without immediate reference to the individual's perception of a particular flood. Rather, he would refer to his normal image of the reality of floods. Perceptions could affect decisions indirectly, though, since they seem to have some influence on the long-run learning process whereby images of the environment are determined.

Knowledge about farmers' perceptions is not entirely speculative or theoretical. A number of empirical studies on human perceptions of natural hazards (e.g. floods or droughts) have been undertaken in the past few years.[1] Variations in human perceptions of the probability of the occurrence of hazards have been revealed. As expected, technical experts concerned with hazard control tend to have much better estimates of the probabilities, although it is recognized that even these people are limited by a lack of data and theoretical knowledge in making such predictions.[2] Non-technical individuals generalize and simplify reality in their perceptions. Non-existent time cycles of floods occur in some men's minds. People in certain areas tend to regard natural catastrophes (e.g. floods) as one-occurrence phenomena which will not recur. Where hazards are perceived as a continual possibility man tends to overestimate the ability of technical combatants (such as dykes) to protect him from harm; and is unwilling to recognise that part of the adjustment to the hazard should involve a change in his habits (e.g. location or land use). The degree to which individuals have accurate perceptions of hazards is positively correlated with the extent to which the hazards affect their dominant type of resource use and with the frequency of the hazards. Both factors, of course, affect the farmers' utility, so one might conclude that the extent to which hazards are accurately perceived is a function of their impact on farmers' utility from land use. Saarinen also concludes that perception improves with experience over the years, which follows normal notions of learning.[3]

Studies have shown that human perception of hazards is a function of personality and culture (prior learning experiences therefore). Some people view nature as a neutral agent which undergoes normal variations in 'providing' catastrophes. Others see nature as a benevolent agent or an opponent, helping or frustrating man's actions. Some groups perceive man as totally subject to the whims of nature; others see that man can work with or control nature to suit his needs.[4]

Other research on perception has been more closely related to land-use

[1] See, e.g. I. Burton and R. W. Kates 1964: The perception of natural hazards in resource management. *Natural Resources Journal* **3**, 412–41, and T. F. Saarinen 1966: *Perception of the drought hazard on the Great Plains* (Chicago).
[2] Burton and Kates, 1964.
[3] Saarinen, 1969.
[4] M. M. Malya 1964: Nature of risk associated with rainfall and its effect on farming. *Indian Journal of Agricultural Economics* **19**, 76–81.

decision making. Fonaroff has shown that one particular culture group (Navaho Indian) is unaware of the cause-effect relationship between over-grazing and soil erosion.[1] Blaut has reached similar conclusions among cultivators in the Blue Mountains of Jamaica.[2] Tuan has shown that man's image of the environment and his philosophical response to it vary with culture, which has very great implications for land-use decision making.[3] For example, the extent to which individuals or groups decide to set aside land for recreational pleasure should relate partly to their response to land of varying qualities.

Summary and conclusions

We have discussed a great many theoretical concepts in a very short space. Based on the assumption that land-use patterns can only be understood by understanding the relevant processes of human decision making, we have examined most of the current set of decision models which refer to

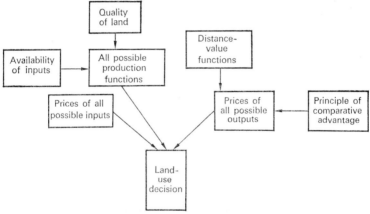

Fig. 9.1 : Decision framework for *economic man* at a particular location operating under pure competition (greatly simplified)

man's use of the land. These range from the classical models of normative economics to the more recent formulations which attempt to build in realistic assumptions regarding human behaviour. Fig. 9.1 is a diagram illustrating in greatly simplified fashion the forces which we have seen influencing land-use decisions for *homo economicus* seeking to optimize net

[1] L. S. Fonaroff 1963: Conservation and stock reduction on the Navaho tribal range. *Geographical Review* **53**, 200–23.
[2] J. Blaut 1959: A study of the cultural determinants of soil erosion and conserva-tion in the Blue Mountains of Jamaica. *Social and Economic Studies* **7**, 402–20.
[3] Yi-Fu Tuan 1967: Attitudes towards environment: themes and approaches. In D. Lowenthal (Editor), *Environmental perception and behaviour* (Chicago) 4–17.

income in a purely competitive system. No attempt has been made to indicate two-way relationships among the variables or to present much of the complexity of the framework. It represents one extreme in our discussion—the decision framework for a man possessing perfect information and capabilities. In comparision, Fig. 9.2 illustrates a simplified view of the much more general decision-making framework which we have sought to explore in the last four chapters. Again, it is highly abstracted, with a number of interlinking variables, such as communication, omitted for the sake of simplicity.

It is essential that decision-making models of the traditional economic and the behavioural types be viewed in perspective, and that one not

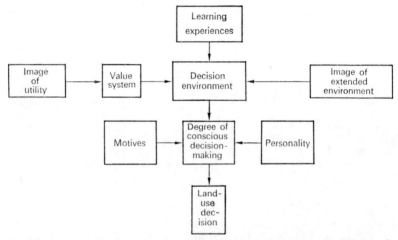

Fig. 9.2 : Simplified view of an individual's general decision-making framework

underestimate the importance of either type. One must also appreciate the interrelationships between the two. Together, traditional economic and behavioural concepts cover the complete range of a continuum of decision-making possibilities. For some situations, such as an analysis of inter-regional trade of agricultural products in an area with pure competition in a free enterprise economy, the rigid economic models may provide the most useful key to an understanding of reality. Understanding which farmers in an area of subsistence agriculture first undertake new practices obviously requires the use of behavioural concepts. It is doubtful if one could understand any land-use situation well without drawing on concepts of both the economic and the behavioural traditions. For example, any study of commercial agriculture must include an analysis of or assume the operation of group behaviour, which lies behind the decisions to maintain a price system and a particular type of market economy. In addition to providing valuable insights into land use in areas with free market economies or in situations where individuals behave like optimizers, traditional economic theory presents a fairly complete, integrated model which is logical within the behavioural assumptions on which it is based, and against which one can measure observed behaviour. It also involves the use of standard principles, such as marginal analysis, which can be applied in a variety of settings. On the other hand, behavioural theory attempts to deal with real-life human behaviour, although elegant, integrated models have yet to be developed.

An important conclusion stemming from an overview of preceding chapters concerns the relevance of 'man–land' studies. In Chapter 2 we discussed traditional man–land studies, indicating how they could be interpreted in terms of normative economic theory. It was practically inferred that man–land relationships involve no process other than the relationships between regional variations in land use and production functions. It was also suggested that ecological studies are superficial unless traditional economic concepts are considered. It should be clear by now that the traditional economic view of man–land studies is not the only view, and that certain direct natural environment/land-use concepts can be quite valid.

In explaining real-life land-use variations, economic decision models are valid only if we can assume that real men behave according to the assumptions on which the models are based. We have used four chapters to illustrate that this assumption is rarely upheld. In Chapter 2 we spoke of the over-simplified relationship between land use and land quality which is often proposed in man–land studies. But we have noted that man himself tends to abstract from reality to create a simple decision environment. So is it not possible that the simple land-quality/land-use relationship could be expected if man views the real environment in a simple manner? We noted that insufficient allowance for variations in land-use intensity is given if we try to relate land-use type and intensity to soil type without considering marginal analysis (e.g. the equation of marginal cost with marginal revenue). But do farmers have the precision to think in terms of marginal analysis; or do they consider only one general level of intensity for land use on land of a given type? If the price of fertilizer increases by 50 cents per bag do farmers reduce the application rates by 0·6 bags per acre; or are they not more likely to adjust application rates only if very major changes in price occur? Obviously the answers to these questions vary from place to place. One can find areas where farmers are highly responsive to changes in the economic environment, and adjust to them. But one also finds vast areas where operators are not trained in economic thinking and, envisaging a direct land-quality/land-use relationship, base their decisions on it.

It is still unfortunate that so few researchers concerned with man–land studies have stated their findings in such a theoretical manner. Too often the decision-makers' evaluation of the environment is not specified or compared with alternative evaluations. Consequently, the most relevant conclusions from the standpoint of land-use theory are not stated.

Perception research also relates to man–land concepts. Geographers, anthropologists, sociologists, philosophers and others have long been concerned with man's image of his natural environment. More recently, psychologists have begun to undertake experimental research on the topic, with a particular concern for man's response to his environment.[1] With greater emphasis on theoretical approaches, more specific conclusions about variations in human perception of environment are being reached. It has been illustrated that, in many cases, man perceives a direct inter-action between himself and the environment. The physical world is not just an entity to be manipulated according to economic rules to yield income from land use. It can be seen as giving man a direct satisfaction from contact with nature. The full implications of this man–land concept for understanding land-use decision making are unknown, and require study.

The final conclusion is an acknowledgement of the work that remains to be done in developing theoretical concepts which help us to understand rural land-use patterns. Important theorizing remains to be done, particu-larly in the behavioural field. But an essential step in the process is the testing of conceptual hypotheses in the real world. In many cases, theo-retical models have been well developed, yet little empirical testing has occurred. Models of comparative advantage, of general spatial equilib-rium, and almost all behavioural formulations are examples. Numerous references are available on game theory, learning, decision environments, and related concepts; but practically no testing of these concepts in the real world has occurred. Until such testing occurs our theoretical formu-lations and understanding of land-use decision making will be greatly impeded.

Further reading

The following concern various aspects of the role of perception in rural land use.

ALLPORT, F. H. 1964: *Theories of perception and the concept of structure.*
BEVAN, W. 1958: Perception: evolution of a concept.
BLAUT, J. 1959: A study of cultural determinants of soil erosion and conservation in the Blue Mountains of Jamaica.
BOULDING, K. E. 1956: *The image.*
BURTON, I., and KATES, R. W. 1964: The perception of natural hazards in Resource management.

[1] See, e.g., R. W. Kates and J. F. Wohlwill (Editors) 1966: Man's response to the physical environment. Special issue of *Journal of Social Issues* **22**(2).

CURRY, L. 1966: Seasonal programming and Bayesian assessment of atmospheric resources.

DENNIS, W. 1951: Cultural and developmental factors in perception.

FIERY, W. 1960: *Man, mind and land.*

FLIEGEL, F. F., and KIVLIN, J. E. 1966: Farmers' perceptions and farm practice attributes.

FONAROFF, L. S. 1963: Conservation and stock reduction on the Navaho tribal range.

HARVEY, D. 1969: *Explanation in geography,* pp. 249–59.

KATES, R. W. 1962: *Hazard and choice perception in flood plain management.*

1963: Perceptual regions and regional perception in flood plain management.

KATES, R. W., and WOHLWILL, J. F. (Editors) 1966: Man's response to the physical environment.

LOWENTHAL, D. 1961: Geography, experience, and imagination; towards a geographical epistemology.

(Editor) 1966: *Environmental perception and behavior.*

MALYA, M. M., and RAJAGOPALAN, R. 1964: The nature of risk associated with rainfall and its effect on farming.

SAARINEN, T. F. 1966: *Perception of the drought hazard on the Great Plains.*

1969: *Perception of environment.*

SAVAGE, L. J. 1954: *The foundations of statistics.*

SEWELL, W. R. D., KATES, R. W., and PHILLIPS, L. E. 1968: Human response to weather and climate: geographical contributions.

SIMMONDS, I. 1966: Ecology and land use.

TUAN, Y. 1967: Attitudes towards environment: themes and approaches.

1968: Discrepancies between environmental attitude and behaviour: examples from Europe and China.

VERNON, M. D. 1962: *The psychology of perception.*

BIBLIOGRAPHY

AGRAWAL, G. D., and FOREMAN, W. J. 1959: Farm resource productivity in west Uttar Pradesh. *Indian Journal of Agricultural Economics* **14**, 115-33.

ALLEN, C. W. 1954: *Substitution relationships between forage and grain in milk production.* Unpublished Ph.D. Thesis, Iowa State University.

ALLPORT, F. H. 1964: *Theories of perception and the concept of structure.* New York: John Wiley and Sons, Inc.

ANDERSON, R. L. 1956: A comparison of discrete and continuous models in agricultural production analysis. In Baum, E. L., Heady, E. O., and Blackmore, J. (Editors), *Methodological procedures in the economic Analysis of fertilizer use data,* Ames: Iowa State University Press.

1968: A simulation program to establish optimum crop patterns on irrigated farms based on preseason estimates of water supply. *American Journal of Agricultural Economics* **50**, 1586-90.

ANTILL, A. G. 1955: Towards a production function for dairy farms. *The Farm Economist* **8**, 1-11.

ARIETI, S. 1965: Towards a unifying theory of cognition. *General Systems Yearbook.* **10**, 190-15.

AUDREY, R. 1965: *African genesis.* New York: Atheneum.

BAKER, O. E. 1921: The increasing importance of the physical conditions in determining the utilization of land for agricultural and forest production in the U.S. *Annals of Association of American Geographers* **11**, 17-46.

1926: Agricultural regions of north America. *Economic Geography* **2**, 459-93.

BARLOWE, R. 1958: *Land resource economics.* Englewood Cliffs: Prentice-Hall, Inc.

BARNES, C. P. 1935: Economics of the long-lot farm. *Geographical Review* **25**, 298-301.

BAUM, E. L., HEADY, E. O., PESEK, J. T., and HILDRETH, C. G. (Editors) 1957: *Economic and technical analysis of fertilizer innovations and resource use.* Ames: Iowa State University Press.

BAUM, E. L., HEADY, E. O., and BLACKMORE, J. (Editors) 1956: *Methodological procedures in the economic analysis of fertilizer use data.* Ames: Iowa State University Press.

BAUM, E. L., and WALKUP, H. G. 1953: Some economic implications of input–output relationships in fryer production. *Journal of Farm Economics* **35**, 223-36.

BAUMOL, W. J. 1965: *Economic theory and operations analysis* (second edition). Englewood Cliffs: Prentice-Hall, Inc.

BECKER, G. M., DE GROOT, M. H., and MARSCHAK, J. Stochastic models of choice behaviour. *Behavioral Science* **8**, 41-55.

BELLMAN, R. 1954: Decision making in the face of uncertainty. *Naval Research Logistics Quarterly* **1**, 327-32.

1957: *Dynamic programming.* Princeton: Princeton University Press.

BELLMAN, R., and DREYFUS, S. F. 1962: *Applied dynamic programming.* Princeton: Princeton University Press.

BENEDICT, E. T. (Editor) 1935: *Theodor Brinkmann's economics of the farm business.* Berkeley: University of California Press.

BENVENUTI, B. 1962: *Farming in cultural change.* Assen: Van Gorcum and Co.

BERKMAN, H. G. 1965: The game theory of land use determination. *Land Economics* **41**, 11-19.

BEVAN, W. 1958: Perception: evolution of a concept. *Psychological Review* **65**, 34-55.

BHATTACHARJEE, J. P. 1955: Resource use and productivity in world agriculture. *Journal of Farm Economics* **37**, 57-72.

BIRCH, H. G. 1945: The relation of previous experience to insightful problem-solving. *Journal of Comparative Psychology* **33**, 367–82.

BIRCH, J. W. 1963: Rural land use and location theory: a review. *Economic Geography* **39**, 273–6.

BISHOP, C. E., and TOUSSAINT, W. D. 1958: *Introduction to agricultural economic analysis.* New York: John Wiley and Sons, Inc.

BLACK, J. D. 1924: Elasticity of supply of farm products. *Journal of Farm Economics* **6**, 145–55.

  1925: The role of public agencies in the internal readjustments of the farm. *Journal of Farm Economics* **7**, 153–75.

  1931: Statistical measurements of the operation of the law of diminishing returns by Mordecai Ezekiel and others. In Rice, S. W. (Editor) *Methods in social science: a case book.* Chicago: University of Chicago Press.

  1957: A formal proof of the concavity of the production possibility function. *Economic Journal* **67**, 133–5.

BLACK, J. D., and MIGHELL, R. L. 1951: *Interregional competition in agriculture with special reference to dairy farming in the Lake States and New England.* Cambridge: Harvard University Press.

BLAUT, J. 1959: A study of cultural determinants of soil erosion and conservation in the Blue Mountains of Jamaica. *Social and Economic Studies* **8**, 402–20.

BOLES, J. N. 1955: Linear programming and farm management. *Journal of Farm Economics* **37**, 1–24.

BOULDING, K. E. 1956: *The image.* Ann Arbor: University of Michigan Press.

BOUSSARD, J. M., and PETIT, M. 1967: Representation of farmers' behaviour under uncertainty with a focus on loss constraint. *Journal of Farm Economics* **49**, 869–80.

BOWDEN, L. W. 1965: *The diffusion of the decision to irrigate.* Department of Geography, University of Chicago, Research Paper **97** (Chicago).

BOWLEN, B., and HEADY, E. O. 1955: Optimum combinations of competitive crops at particular locations. Iowa State A.E.S. Bulletin **426** (Ames).

BOX, G. E. P. 1954: The exploration and exploitation of response surfaces: some general considerations and examples. *Biometrics* **10**, 16–60.

BRANDNER, L., and KEARL, B. 1964: Evaluation for congruence as a factor in the adoption rate of innovations. *Rural Sociology* **29**, 288–303.

BRANDOW, G. E. 1968: A framework for the farm problem. In Hildreth, R. J. (Editor), *Readings in Agricultural Policy.* Lincoln: University of Nebraska Press.

BREDO, W., and ROJKO, A. S. 1952: *Prices and milksheds of northeastern markets.* Northeast Regional Publication **9**, Massachusetts A.E.S. Bulletin **47** (Amherst).

BRONFENBRENNER, M. 1944: Production functions: Cobb-Douglas, interfirm, intrafirm. *Econometrica* **12**, 35–44.

BROWN, E. H. P. 1957: The meaning of the fitted Cobb-Douglas function. *Quarterly Journal of Economics* **71**, 546–60.

BROWN, L. 1965: *A bibliography on spatial diffusion.* Department of Geography, Northwestern University, Discussion Paper **5** (Evanston).

  1968: *Diffusion processes and location: a conceptual framework and bibliography.* Philadelphia: Regional Science Research Institute.

BROWN, R. C. 1968: The use and mis-use of distance variables in landuse analysis. *Professional Geographer* **20**, 337–41.

BROWN, W. G., and ARSCOTT, G. H. 1958: A method for dealing with time in determining optimum factor inputs. *Journal of Farm Economics* **40**, 666–73.

BROWN, W. G., and OVESON, M. M. 1958: Production functions from data over a series of years. *Journal of Farm Economics* **40**, 451–57.

BURKHILL, I. H. 1962: Habits of man and the origins of the cultivated plants of the Old World, in Wagner and Mikesell, *Readings in cultural geography.* Chicago: University of Chicago Press, 248–81.

BURTON, I., and KATES, R. W. 1964: The perception of natural hazards in resource management. *Natural Resources Journal* **3**, 412–41.
BUSH, R. R., and MOSTELLER, F. 1955: *Stochastic models for learning*. New York: John Wiley and Sons, Inc.
CALDWELL, H. W. 1956: An application of linear programming to farm planning. *Canadian Journal of Agricultural Economics* **4**, 51–61.
CANDLER, W. 1960: Reflections on dynamic programming models. *Journal of Farm Economics* **42**, 920–6.
CARTER, H. A., and HEADY, E. O. 1959: *An input–output analysis emphasizing regional and commodity sectors of agriculture*. Iowa State A.E.S. Bulletin **469** (Ames).
CARTER, H. C. 1963: Representative farms—guides for decision making. *Journal of Farm Economics* **45**, 1149–55.
CASSELS, J. M. 1933: History of research in prices. *Research in Prices of Farm Products*, Social Science Research Council Bulletin **9** (New York).
1937: *A study of fluid milk prices*. Cambridge: Harvard University Press.
CASSETTI, E. 1969: Why do diffusion processes conform to logistic trends? *Geographical Analysis* **1**, 101–5.
CHANG, J. 1968a: Agricultural potential of the humid tropics. *Geographical Review* **58**, 333–61.
1968b: Progress in agricultural climatology. *Professional Geographer* **20**, 317–20.
CHAYANOV, A. V. 1966: On the theory of non-Capitalist economic systems. Translated by Christel Lane, in Chayanov, A. V. Thorner, D., Kerblay, B., and Smith, R. E. F. (Editors), *The theory of peasant economy*. Homewood, Illinois: Richard D. Irwin, Inc.
CHEIN, I. 1954: The environment as a detriment of behaviour. *Journal of Social Psychology* **39**, 115–27.
CHERNOFF, H., and MOSES, L. E. 1959: *Elementary decision theory*. New York: John Wiley and Sons, Inc.
CHISHOLM, M. 1962: *Rural settlement and land use*. London: Hutchinson University Library.
CHURCHMAN, C. W. 1964: Decision and value theory. In Ackoff, R. L. (Editor), *Progress in Operations Research*. New York: John Wiley and Sons, Inc, 35–64.
CLARKE, J. W. 1950: *An analysis of the application of the production function to a sample of farms in southern Saskatchewan*. Unpublished M.S. thesis, University of Saskatchewan.
CLAWSON, M. 1934: Relationship between farmer's return from an enterprise and changes in the size of the enterprise. *Journal of Farm Economics* **16**, 526–33.
1963: Introduction to economics of land use. In Cavin, J. P. (Editor), *Economics for Agriculture*. Cambridge: Harvard University Press, 91–106.
COCHRANE, W. W. 1955: Conceptualizing the supply relation in agriculture. *Journal of Farm Economics* **37**, 1161–76.
COLEMAN, A. L., and MARSH, C. P. 1955: Differential communication among farmers in a Kentucky county. *Rural Sociology* **20**, 93–101.
1964: Inconsistency of preferences: a test of unfolding theory. From Coombs, C. H. (Editor), *A theory of data*. New York: John Wiley and Sons, Inc., 106–18.
COPP, J. H., SILL, M. L., and BROWN, E. J. 1958: The function of information sources in the farm practice adoption process. *Rural Sociology* **23**, 146–57.
COUGHENOUR, C. M. 1960: The functioning of farmers' characteristics in relation to contact with media and practice adoption. *Rural Sociology* **25**, 283–297.
CRADDOCK, W. J. 1970: *Interregional competition in Canadian cereal production*. Economic Council of Canada Special Study **12** (Ottawa: Government Printer).
CURRY, L. 1966: Seasonal programming and Bayesian assessment of atmospheric

resources. In Sewell, W. R. D. (Editor), *Human Dimensions of Weather Modification*, University of Chicago, Department of Geography, Research Report **105** (Chicago), 127–38.

D'ANDRADE, R. G., and ROMNEY, A. K. 1964: Transcultural studies in cognition. *American Anthropologist* **66**(3), Part 2.

DARCOVICH, W. 1958: The use of production functions in the study of resource productivity in some beef producing areas of Alberta. *Economic Annalist* **28**, 85–93.

DAY, R. H. 1962: An approach to production response. *Agricultural Economic Research* **14**, 134–48.

1963a: On aggregating linear programming models of production. *Journal of Farm Economics* **45**, 797–813.

1963b: *Recursive programming and production response*. Amsterdam: North-Holland.

DAY, R. H., and KENNEDY, P. E. 1970: On a dynamic location model of production. *Journal of Regional Science* **10**, 191–8.

DAY, R. H., and TINNEY, E. H. 1969: A dynamic von Thünen model. Geographical Analysis **1**, 138–51.

DENNIS, W. 1951: Cultural and developmental factors in perception. In Blake, R. R., and Ramsey, G. V. (Editors), *Perception, an approach to personality*, New York: Ronald Press Co., 148–69.

DENT, J. B. 1964: Optimal rations for livestock with special reference to bacon pigs. *Journal of Agricultural Economics* **16**, 68–87.

DILLON, J. L., and HEADY, E. O. 1958: Decision criteria for innovation. *Australian Journal of Agricultural Economics* **2**, 113–20.

1960: *Theories of choice in relation to farmer decisions*. Iowa State A.E.S. Bulletin, **485** (Ames).

DUNCAN, O. D., and SCHNORE, L. F. 1959: Cultural, behavioral and ecological perspectives in the study of social organization. *American Journal of Sociology* **65**, 132–46.

DUNN, E. S. 1954: *The location of agricultural production*. Gainesville: University of Florida Press.

1955: The equilibrium of land-use patterns in agriculture. *Southern Economic Journal* **21**, 173–87.

EDWARDS, D. 1961: *An economic study of small farming in Jamaica*. Kingston: Institute of Social and Economic Research.

EDWARDS, W., and TVERSKY, A. 1967: *Decision making*. Baltimore: Penguin Books.

EGBERT, A. C., and HEADY, E. O. 1961: *Regional adjustments in grain production: a linear programming analysis*. United States Department of Agriculture Technical Bulletin **1241** (Washington: Government Printing Office).

EGBERT, A. C., HEADY, E. O., and BROKKEN, R. F. 1964: *Regional changes in grain production*. Iowa State A.E.S. Bulletin **521** (Ames).

EGBERT, A. C., and RENTLINGER, S. 1965: A dynamic model of the livestock feed sector. *Journal of Farm Economics* **47**, 1288–305.

EIDMAN, V. R. *et al.* 1967: An application of statistical decision theory to commercial turkey production. *Journal of Farm Economics* **49**, 852–68.

ELLIOTT, F. F. 1927: *Adjusting hog production to market demand*. Illinois A.E.S. Bulletin **293** (Urbana).

ELY, R. T., and WEHRWEIN, G. S. 1940: *Land economics*. New York: The Macmillan Co.

ENGLUND, E. 1923: Fallacies of a plan to fix prices of farm products by government control of the exportable surplus. *Journal of Farm Economics* **5**, 86–7.

ENKE, S. 1951: Equilibrium among spatially separated markets: solution by electric analogue. *Econometrica* **19**, 40–7.

ESTES, W. K. 1950: Towards a statistical theory of learning. *Psychological Review* **57**, 94–107.

FATHI, A. 1965: Leadership and resistance to change: a case from an under-developed area. *Rural Sociology* **30**, 204–12.

FELLOWS, I. F. 1949: Developing and applying production functions in farm management. *Journal of Farm Economics* **31**, 1058–64.

1955: Production functions in farm management. In Halcrow, H. G. (Editor), *Contemporary readings in agricultural economics*, New York: Prentice-Hall, Inc.

FIELDING, G. J. 1964: The Los Angeles milkshed: a study of the political factor in agriculture. *Geographical Review* **54**, 1–13.

FIREY, W. 1960: *Man, mind and land*. Glencoe, The Free Press.

FLIEGEL, F. C. 1966: Literacy and exposure to instrumental information among farmers in southern Brazil. *Rural Sociology* **31**, 15.

FLIEGEL, F. C., and KIVLIN, J. E. 1962: Farm practice attributes and adoption rates. *Social Forces* **40**, 364–70.

1966: Farmers' perceptions and farm practice attributes. *Rural Sociology* **31**, 197.

FLOOD, M. M. 1960: Sequential decisioning. In Machol, R. E. (Editor), *Information and decision processes*, New York: McGraw-Hill Book Co. Inc., 34–52.

FLOYD, M. L. 1954: On game learning theory and some decision making experiments. In Thrall, R. M., Coombs, C. H., and Davis, R. L. (Editors), *Decision processes*, New York: John Wiley and Sons, Inc., 139–58.

FONAROFF, L. S. 1965: Conservation and stock reduction on the Navaho tribal range. *Geographical Review* **53**, 200–23.

FOUND, W. C. 1965: The relation of the distribution of citrus to soil type and winter temperature in Orange County, Florida. *Canadian Geographer* **9**, 64–73.

1970: Towards a general theory relating distance between farm and home to agricultural production. *Geographical Analysis* **2**, 165–76.

FOX, K. A. 1951a: Factors affecting farm income, farm prices, and food consumption. *Agricultural Economics Research* **3**, 65–82.

1951b: Relations between price, consumption and production. *Journal of American Statistical Association* **46**, 323–33.

1953: A spatial equilibrium model of the livestock-feed economy in the United States. *Econometrica* **21**, 547–66.

FOX, K. A., and TAEBER, R. 1955: Spatial equilibrium models of the livestock-feed economy. *American Economic Review* **45**, 584–608.

FRENCH, B. L. 1956: Functional relationships for irrigated corn response to nitrogen. *Journal of Farm Economics* **38**, 736–47.

FRIED, M. H. 1952: Land tenure, geography and ecology in the contact of culture. *American Journal of Sociology* **11**, 391–412.

FRIEDMAN, M. 1949: The Marshallian demand curve. *Journal of Political Economy* **57**, 463–95.

GALBRAITH, J. D. 1963: John D. Black: a portrait. In Cavin, J. P. (Editor), *Economics for agriculture*, Cambridge: Harvard University Press, 1–20.

GARRISON, W. L. 1959: The spatial structure of the economy. *Annals of Association of American Geographers* **49**, 234.

GARRISON, W. L., and MARBLE, D. F. 1957: The spatial structure of agricultural activities. *Annals of Association of American Geographers* **47**, 137–44.

GIAEVER, H., and SEAGRAVES, J. 1960: Linear programming and economies of size. *Journal of Farm Economics* **42**, 103–17.

GILLETTE, J. M. 1949: Crop response as a testing ground for geo-cultural regionalism. *Rural Sociology* **14**, 51–8.

GILSON, J. C., and BJARNARSON, V. W. 1958: Effects of fertilizer use on barley in northern Manitoba. *Journal of Farm Economics* **40**, 932–41.

GOLLEDGE, R. G. 1968: *The geographical relevance of some learning theories*. Paper read at annual meeting, Association of American Geographers, St. Louis. (Mimeo.)

GOOCH, D. W. 1957: *World land reform, a selected bibliography*. United States Department of Agriculture Library List **55** (Washington).

GOULD, P. R. 1963: Man against his environment: a game theoretic framework. *Annals of Association of American Geographers* **53**, 290–7.

1965: Wheat on Kilimanjaro: the perception of choice within game and learning model frameworks. *General Systems Yearbook* **10**, 157–66.

1969: *Spatial diffusion*. Commission on College Geography Resource Paper **4**, (Washington: Association of American Geographers).

GRILICHES, Z. 1957: Specification bias in estimates of production functions. *Journal of Farm Economics* **39**, 8–20.

1960: Hybrid corn and the economics of innovation. *Science* **132**, 275–80.

GROTEWALD, A. 1959: Von Thünen in retrospect. *Economic Geography* **35**, 346–55.

GROVES, H. M. 1969: Richard T. Ely: an appreciation. *Land Economics* **45**, 1–9.

HADLEY, G. 1964: *Nonlinear and dynamic programming*. Reading, Massachusetts: Addison-Wesley.

HÄGERSTRAND, T. 1965: A Monte Carlo approach to diffusion. *Archives Europeanes de Sociologie* **6**, 43–67.

1966: Aspects of the spatial structure of social communication and the diffusion of information. *Papers and Proceedings of the Regional Science Association* (European Session) **16**, 27–42.

HALL, H. H., HEADY, E. O., and PLESSNER, Y. 1968: Quadratic programming solution of competitive equilibrium for U.S. agriculture. *American Journal of Agricultural Economics* **50**, 536–55.

HALL, P. (Editor) 1966: *Von Thünen's isolated state*. New York and London: Pergamon Press.

HAMMERBERG, D. O. 1940: Allocation of milk supplies among contiguous markets. *Journal of Farm Economics* **22**, 215–19.

HANSEN, P. L. 1949: Input–output relationships in egg production. *Journal of Farm Economics* **31**, 687–97.

HANSEN, W. G. 1959: How accessibility shapes land use. *Journal of the American Institute of Planners* **25**, 73–7.

HANZIK, C. H., and TOLMAN, E. C. 1936: The perception of spatial relations by the rat: a type of response not easily explained by conditioning. *Journal of Comparative Psychology* **22**, 287–318.

HARRIS, H. 1947: The development and use of production functions for firms in agriculture. *Scientific Agriculture* **27**, 487–95.

HARVEY, D. W. 1963: Locational change in the Kentish hop industry and the analysis of land use patterns. *Transactions of Institute of British Geographers* **33**, 123–44.

1966: Theoretical concepts and the analysis of agricultural land-use patterns in geography. *Annals of the Association of American Geographers* **56**, 361–74.

1969: *Explanation in geography*. London: Edward Arnold; New York: St. Martin's Press.

HARVEY, R. O., and CLARKE, W. A. V. 1965: The nature and economics of urban sprawl. *Land Economics* **41**, 1–9.

HASSLER, J. B. 1959: Interregional competition in agriculture: principal forces, normative models and reality. *Journal of Farm Economics* **41**, 959–68.

HEADY, E. O. 1946: Production functions from a random sample of farms. *Journal of Farm Economics* **28**, 989–1004.

1951: A production function and marginal rates of substitution in the utilization of feed resources for dairy cows. *Journal of Farm Economics* **33**, 485–95.

1952: *Economics of agricultural production and resource use*. Englewood Cliffs: Prentice-Hall, Inc.

1954a: Simplified presentation and logical aspects of linear programming technique. *Journal of Farm Economics* **36**, 1035–48.

1954b: Use and estimation of input–output relationships or productivity coefficients. *Journal of Farm Economics* **34**, 36–52.

1956a: Budgeting and linear programming in estimating resource productivity and cost relationships. Chapter 7 in Heady, E. O., Johnson, G. L., and Hardin, L. S. (Editors), *Resource productivity, returns to scale, and farm size.* Ames: Iowa State University Press, 67–81.

1956b: Integration of physical sciences and agricultural economics. *Canadian Journal of Agricultural Economics* 4, 1–15.

1956c: Technical considerations in estimating production functions, Chapter 1 in Heady, E. O., Johnson, G. L., and Hardin, L. S. (Editors), *Resource productivity, returns to scale, and farm size.* Ames: Iowa State University Press, 3–15.

1957: An economic investigation of the technology of agricultural production functions. *Econometrica* 25, 49–68.

1958a: Application of game theory in agricultural economics. *Canadian Journal of Agricultural Economics* 6, 1–15.

1958b: Output in relation to input for the agricultural industry. *Journal of Farm Economics* 40, 393–406.

(Editor) 1961: *Agricultural supply functions.* Ames: Iowa State University Press.

HEADY, E. O., BALLOUN, S., and DEAN, G. W. 1956: *Least-cost rations and optimum marketing weights for turkeys.* Iowa A.E.S. Bulletin 443 (Ames).

HEADY, E. O., and BROWN, W. G. 1954: *Crop response surfaces and economic optima in fertilizer use.* Iowa A.E.S. Bulletin 424 (Ames).

HEADY, E. O., and CANDLER, W. 1958: *Linear programming methods.* Ames: Iowa State University Press.

HEADY, E. O., and DILLON, J. L. 1961: *Agricultural production functions.* Ames: Iowa State University Press.

HEADY, E. O., DOLL, J. P., and PESEK, J. T. 1958: *Fertilizer production functions for corn and oats: including analysis of irrigated and residual return.* Iowa A.E.S. Bulletin 463 (Ames).

HEADY, E. O., and EGBERT, A. C. 1964: Regional programming of efficient agricultural production patterns. *Econometrica* 32, 374–86.

HEADY, E. O., and HALL, H. H. 1968: Linear and non-linear spatial models in agricultural competition, land use and production potential. *American Journal of Agricultural Economics* 50, 1539–48.

HEADY, E. O., JACOBSON, N. L., and BLOOM, S. 1956: *Milk production functions, hay/grain substitution rates and economic optima in dairy cow rations.* Iowa A.E.S. Bulletin 444 (Ames).

HEADY, E. O., and JENSEN, H. R. 1951: *The economics of crop rotations and land use.* Iowa State College A.E.S. Bulletin 383 (Ames).

HEADY, E. O., MADDEN, J. P., JACOBSON, M. L., and FREEMAN, A. E. 1964: Milk production functions incorporating variables for cow characteristics and environment. *Journal of Farm Economics* 46, 1–19.

HEADY, E. O., and ALEXANDER, R. 1956: *Least-cost rations and optimum marketing weights for broilers.* Iowa A.E.S. Bulletin 442 (Ames).

HEADY, E. O., and OLSON, R. O. 1951: Marginal rates of substitution and uncertainty in the utilization of feed resources with particular emphasis on forage crops. *Iowa State Journal of Science* 26, 49–71.

HEADY, E. O., and OLSON, R. O. 1952: *Substitution relationships, resource requirements, and income variability in the utilization of forage crops.* Iowa State A.E.S. Bulletin 390 (Ames).

HEADY, E. O., and PESEK, J. 1954: A fertilizer production surface with specification of economic optima for corn grown on calcareous Ida Silt loam. *Journal of Farm Economics* 36, 466–82.

HEADY, E. O., and SHRADER, W. D. 1953: The interrelationships of agronomy and economics in research and recommendations to farmers. *Agron. Journal* 45, 496–501.

HEADY, E. O., and SKOLD, M. 1965: *Projections of U.S. agricultural capacity and interregional adjustments in production and land use with spatial programming models.* Iowa State A.E.S. Bulletin 539 (Ames).

HEADY, E. O., and WHITTLESEY, N. K. 1965: *A programming analysis of inter-regional competition and surplus capacity of American agriculture.* Iowa State A.E.S. Bulletin **538** (Ames).

HENDRIX, W. E. 1956: Institutional-tenure approach to 'size-of-farm' research. Chapter 22 in Heady, E. O., Johnson, G. L., and Hardin, L. S. (Editors), *Resource Productivity, Returns to Scale, and Size of Farm.* Ames: Iowa State University Press, 185–95.

HENSHALL, JANET D. 1967: Models of agricultural activity. In *Models in Geography*, Chorley, R. J., and Haggett, P. (Editors). London: Methuen and Co. Ltd., 425–60.

HERRMANN, L. F. 1943: Diminishing returns in feeding commercial dairy herds. *Journal of Farm Economics* **25**, 397–409.

HERTSGAARD, T. A. 1962: *Interregional analysis of the corn sector.* Department of Agricultural Economics, University of Illinois, Rept. AERR–**55** (Urbana).

    1963: *Interregional analysis of the soybean sector.* Department of Agricultural Economics, University of Illinois, Rept. AERR–**67** (Urbana).

    1964: *Optimum patterns of production and distribution of livestock and poultry products.* Upper Midwest Economic Study, Technical Paper **10**. Minneapolis: University of Minnesota Press.

HILDRETH, R. J. 1957: Influence of rainfall on fertilizer profits. *Journal of Farm Economics* **39**, 522–4.

    (Editor) 1968: *Readings in agricultural policy.* Lincoln: University of Nebraska Press.

HILL, L. D. 1965: *Agricultural market planning in resource development.* Special Publication **9**, University of Illinois College of Agriculture (Urbana), 96–7.

HILL, W. F. 1963: *Learning, a survey of psychological interpretations.* San Francisco: Chandler Publishing Company.

HJELM, L. 1953: *Utbylesrelationer i mjolkproduktionen* (with English summary: input–output relationships in milk production). Stockholm: Institutionem for Lantbrukets Driftsekonomi.

HOFFER, C. R., and STRANGLAND, D. 1958: Farmers' attitudes and values in relation to adoption of approved practices in corn growing. *Rural Sociology* **23**, 112–20.

HOOVER, E. M. 1948: *The location of economic activity.* New York: McGraw-Hill Book Co. Inc.

HOOVER, L. M. *et al.* 1967: Economic relationships of hay and concentrate consumption to milk production. *Journal of Farm Economics* **49**, 64–78.

HORVATH, R. J., and SPENCER, J. E. 1963: How does an agricultural region originate. *Annals of Association of American Geographers* **53**, 60–74.

HOWES, R. 1967: A test of a linear programming model of agriculture. *Journal of Regional Science* **19**, 123.

HULL, C. L. 1964: *A behavior system.* New York: John Wiley and Sons, Inc.

HURWICZ, L. 1950: *Optimality criteria for decision making under risk.* Cowles Commission Discussion Paper, Statistics, **350**. (Mimeo.)

HUTTON, L. F. 1957: Determining least cost combinations. *Journal of Farm Economics* **39**, 936–41.

ISAAC, E. 1959: The citron in the Mediterranean: a study in religious influences. *Economic Geography* **35**, 71–8.

ISARD, W. 1956: *Location and space economy.* Cambridge: Technology Press of Massachusetts Institute of Technology.

JAMES, P. E., JONES, C. F., and WRIGHT, J. K. (Editors) 1954: *American geography: inventory and prospect.* Syracuse: Syracuse University Press.

JARRETT, F. G. 1959: Estimation of resource productivities as illustrated by a survey of the lower Murray Valley dairying area. *Australian Journal of Statistics* **1**, 3–11.

JAWETZ, M. B. 1957: *Farm size, farming intensity and the input–output relationships of some Welsh and West of England dairy farms.* Aberystwyth: University College of Wales.

JENSEN, E., and SUNDQUIST, W. B. 1955: *Resource productivity, and income for a sample of West Kentucky farms.* Kentucky A.E.S. Bulletin **630** (Lexington).

JOHNSON, G. L. 1956: Institutional considerations relevant in studying resource productivity and size of business. Chapter 3 in Heady, E. O., Johnson, G. L., and Hardin, L. S. (Editors), *Resource productivity, returns to scale, and farm size.* Ames: Iowa State University Press, 24–5.

JOHNSON, H. B. 1962: A note on Thünen's circles. *Annals of Association of American Geographers* **52**, 213–20.

JOHNSON, P. R. 1953: Alternative functions for analysing a fertilizer-yield relationship. *Journal of Farm Economics* **35**, 519–29.

JOHNSON, S. E. 1933: The theory of combination of enterprises on individual farms. *Journal of Farm Economics* **15**, 656–67.

1937: Interregional competition and comparative advantage in agriculture. *Journal of Farm Economics* **19**, 224–38.

JOHNSON, S. E., and BACHMAN, K. L. 1963: Introduction to development of production economics in agriculture. In Cavin, J. P. (Editor), *Economics for Agriculture,* Cambridge: Harvard University Press, 21–47.

JONASSON, O. 1925, 1926: Agricultural regions of Europe. *Economic Geography* **1**, 277–314, and **2**, 19–48.

JONES, G. E. 1963: The diffusion of agricultural innovations. *Journal of Agricultural Economics* **15**, 387.

JUDGE, G. T., and WALLACE, T. D. 1958: Estimation of spatial price equilibrium models. *Journal of Farm Economics* **50**, 801–20.

KARLSSON, G. 1958: *Social mechanisms.* Uppsala: Almkvist and Wicksell.

KATES, R. W. 1962: *Hazard and choice perception in flood plain management.* Department of Geography, University of Chicago, Research Paper **78**.

1963: Perceptual regions and regional perception in flood plain management. *Papers and Proceedings of the Regional Science Association* **11**, 217–27.

KATES, R. W., and WOHLWILL, J. F. (Editors) 1966: Man's response to the physical environment. Special issue of *Journal of Social Issues* **22**.

KATONA, G. 1951: *The psychological analysis of economic behaviour.* New York: McGraw-Hill Book Co.

KATZ, B., LEVIN, M. L., and HAMILTON, H. 1963: Traditions of research on the diffusion of innovations. *American Sociological Review* **28**, 237–52.

KAUFMANN, A. 1968: *The science of decision making.* New York: McGraw-Hill Book Co.

KIRK, W. 1951: Historical geography and the concept of the behavioural environment. *Indian Geographical Journal:* Silver Jubilee Edition, 152–60.

KLOPFER, P. H. 1962: *Behavioral aspects of ecology.* Englewood Cliffs: Prentice-Hall.

KNETSCH, J. L., ROBERTSON, L. S. JNR., and SUNDQUIST, W. G. 1956: *Economic considerations in soil fertility research.* Michigan A.E.S. Quarterly Bulletin **39** (East Lansing).

KOLARS, J. 1966: Locational aspects of cultural ecology: the case of the goat in non-Western agriculture. *Geographical Review* **56**, 577–84.

KONIJN, H. S. 1959: Estimation of an average production function from surveys. *Economic Record* **35**, 118–25.

KOTTKE, M. 1970: Spatial, temporal and product-use allocation of milk in an imperfectly competitive dairy industry. *American Journal of Agricultural Economics* **52**, 33–40.

KOTZMAN, I. 1956: Solving feed problems through linear programming. *Journal of Farm Economics* **38**, 420–9.

KRYMOWSKI, R. 1928: Graphical presentation of Thünen's theory of Intensity. *Journal of Farm Economics* **10**, 461–82.

LANGHAM, M. R. 1963: Game theory applied to a policy problem of rice farmers. *Journal of Farm Economics* **45**, 151–62.

LANZETTA, J. T., and KANAREFF, V. T. 1962: Information cost, amount of payoff, and level of aspiration as determinants of information seeking in decision making. *Behavioural Science* **7**, 459–73.

LEFTWICH, R. H. 1963: *The price system and resource allocation* (revised edition). New York: Holt, Rinehart and Winston.

LESER, C. E. V. 1958: Statistical production functions and economic development. *Scottish Journal of Political Economy* **5**, 40–9.

LEWTHWAITE, G. R. 1964: Wisconsin cheese and farm type; a locational hypothesis. *Economic Geography* **40**, 95–112.

LIONBERGER, H. E. 1952: The diffusion of farm and home information as an area of sociological research. *Rural Sociology* **17**, 132–43.

LIONBERGER, H. E., and HASSINGER, E. 1954: Neighbourhoods as a factor in the diffusion of farm information in a northeast Missouri farming community. *Rural Sociology* **19**, 377–84.

LIPTON, M. 1968a: A game against nature: theories of peasant decision-making. *The Listener*, March 28, 1968 401–3 (London).

    1968b: A game against nature: strategies of security. *The Listener*, April 4, 1968, 437–9 (London).

    1968c: The theory of the optimising peasant. *Journal of Development Studies* **4**.

LOFTSGARD, L. D. and HEADY, E. O. 1959: Application of dynamic programming models for optimum farm and home plans. *Journal of Farm Economics* **41**, 51–62.

LOMAX, K. S. 1949: *An agricultural production function for the United Kingdom. 1924 to 1947*. Manchester School of Economic and Social Studies **17**, 146–60.

LÖSCH, A. 1954: *The economics of location*. Translated by Woglom, W. H., and Stolper, W. F., New Haven: Yale University Press.

LOWENTHAL, D. 1961: Geography, experience, and imagination. Towards a geographical epistemology. *Annals of Association of American Geographers* **51**, 241–60.

    1966: *Environmental perception and behavior*. Department of Geography, University of Chicago, Research Paper **109** (Chicago).

LUCE, R. D., and RAIFFA, H. 1957: *Games and decisions*. New York: John Wiley and Sons, Inc.

MACHOL, R. E. (Editor) 1960: *Information and decision processes*. New York: McGraw-Hill Book Co. Inc.

MACLEOD, A. 1937: *The milksheds of New Hampshire*. New Hampshire A.E.S. Bulletin **295** (Durham).

MALYA, M. M., and RAJAGOPALAN, R. 1964: Nature of risk associated with rainfall and its effect on farming—a case study of Kumool District, Andbra Pradesh. *Indian Journal of Agricultural Economics* **19**, 76–81.

MARGALEF, R. 1958: Information theory in ecology. *General Systems* **2**, 36–71.

MARSH, C. P., and COLEMAN, A. L. 1955: The relation of farmer characteristics to the adoption of recommended farm practices. *Rural Sociology* **20**, 289–296.

MASON, R. G. 1964: The use of information sources in the process of adoption. *Rural Sociology* **29**, 40–52.

MAY, K. O. 1954: Transitivity, utility, and aggregation in preference patterns. *Econometrica* **22**, 1–13.

MCCARTY, H. H. 1946: The theoretical nature of land use regions. *Annals of Association of American Geographers* **36**, 97–8.

    1954: Agricultural geography. In James P. E., and Jones, C. F. (Editors), *American geography: inventory and prospect*, Syracuse: University of Syracuse Press, 258–77.

MCDONALD, G. T. 1970: *Background to constructing a synthetic predictive model of agricultural land use in Ontario.* Centre for Urban and Community Studies, University of Toronto, Research Paper **37** (Toronto).

MCFARQUHAR, A. M. M. 1961: Rational decision making and risk in farm planning. *Journal of Agricultural Economics* **14**, 552.

MCFARQUHAR, M. M., and EVANS, A. 1957: Linear programming and the combination of enterprises in tropical agriculture. *Journal of Agricultural Economics* **12**, 474.

MCINERNEY, J. P. 1967: Maximin programming—an approach to farm planning under uncertainty. *Journal of Agricultural Economics* **18**, 279–89.

MCLOUGHLIN, P. F. M. 1966: Development policy-making and the geographers' regions: comments by an economist. *Land Economics* **42**, 75–84.

MEGGERS, B. 1954: Environmental limitations on the development of culture. *American Anthropologist* **56**, 801–24.

MERRILL, W. C. 1965: Alternative programming models involving uncertainty. *Journal of Farm Economics* **47**, 595–610.

MEYER, C. F., and NEWETT, R. J. 1970: Dynamic programming for feedlot optimization. *Management Science* **16**, B410–26.

MIGHELL, R. L., and ALLEN, R. H. 1940: Supply schedules—'long-time' and 'short-time'. *Journal of Farm Economics* **22**, 544–57.

MIGHELL, R. L., and BLACK, J. D. 1951: *Interregional competition in agriculture.* Cambridge: Harvard University Press.

MILLER, W. G. 1959: Comparative efficiency of farm tenure classes in the combination of resources. *Agricultural Economic Research* **11**, 6–16.

MINDEN, A. J. 1968: Dynamic programming: a tool for farm firm growth research. *Canadian Journal of Agricultural Economics* **16**, 38–45.

MORRILL, R. L., and GARRISON, W. L. 1960: Projections of interregional patterns of trade in wheat and flour. *Economic Geography* **36**, 116–26.

MOSER, C. O. 1927: The surplus in cooperative cotton marketing. *American Cooperation* **1**.

NERLOVE, M. 1956: Estimates of the elasticities of supply of selected agricultural commodites. *Journal of Farm Economics* **38**, 496–509.

1958: *The dynamics of supply.* Baltimore: Johns Hopkins University Press.

NERLOVE, M., and ADDISON, W. W. 1958: Statistical estimation of long run elasticities of supply and demand. *Journal of Farm Economics* **40**, 861–80.

NERLOVE, M., and BACHMAN, K. L. 1960: The analysis of changes in agricultural supply: problems and approaches. *Journal of Farm Economics* **42**, 531–54.

NEWSHAUSER, G. L. 1966: *Introduction to dynamic programming.* New York: John Wiley and Sons, Inc.

OFFICER, R. R., and ANDERSON, J. R. 1968: Risk, uncertainty and farm management decisions. *Review of Marketing and Agricultural Economics* **36**, 3–19.

PARISH, R. M., and DILLON, J. L. 1955: Recent applications of the production function in farm management research. *Review of Marketing and Agricultural Economics* **23**, 215–36.

PARKS, W. L., and KNETSCH, J. L. 1959: Corn yields as influenced by nitrogen level and drouth intensity. *Agron. Journal* **51**, 363–4.

PAULSON, W. E. 1950: Cooperatives, competition and free enterprize. *American Cooperation* **22**, 226.

PEDERSON, H. 1951: Cultural differences in the acceptance of recommended practices. *Rural Sociology* **16**, 37–49.

PENN, R. J. 1956: Theoretical concepts relevant to studies in resource productivity and size of business. Chapter 21 in Heady, E. O., Johnson, G. L., and Hardin, L. S. (Editors), *Resource productivity, returns to scale, and farm size,* Ames: Iowa State University Press, 182–4.

PETERSON, G. A. 1955: Selection of maximum profit combinations of livestock enterprises and crop rotations. *Journal of Farm Economics* **37**, 1298–301.

PHOTIADIS, J. D. 1962: Motivation, contacts and technical change. *Rural Sociology* **27**, 316–26.

PITTS, F. R. 1963: Problems in computer simulation of diffusion. *Papers of the Regional Science Association* **11**, 111–19.

POND, G. A. 1932: Studying the human factor in farm management. *Journal of Farm Economics* **14**, 470–9.

PORTER, P. W. 1965: Environmental potential and economic opportunities—a background for cultural adaptation. *American Anthropologist* **67**, 409–20.

RAEBURN, J. R. 1958: Economies of scale in farming. *Journal of Agricultural Economics* **13**, 72–9.

RAMSEY, C. E., POLSON, R. A., and SPENCER, G. E. 1959: Values and the adoption of practices. *Rural Sociology* **24**, 35–47.

RANDHAWA, N. S., and HEADY, E. O. 1964: An interregional programming model for agricultural planning in India. *Journal of Farm Economics* **46**, 137–149.

REDMAN, J. C., and ALLEN, S. Q. 1954: Some interrelationships of economic and agronomic concepts. *Journal of Farm Economics* **36**, 453–65.

REEDS, L. G. 1964: Agricultural geography: progress and prospects. *Canadian Geographer* **8**, 51–63.

RICARDO, D. 1817: *The principles of political economy and taxation.* London: Everyman Edition, Dent.

ROBINSON, JOAN 1955: The production function. *Economic Journal* **65**, 67–71.
1956: *The accumulation of capital.* London: Macmillan.

ROGERS, E. M. 1962: *Diffusion of innovations.* New York: Free Press of Glencoe.

RUSHTON, G. 1969: A computer model for the study of agricultural land use patterns. *Computer assisted instruction in geography,* Commission on College Geography Technical Paper **2** (Washington: Association of American Geographers), 141–50.

SAARINEN, T. F. 1966: *Perception of the drought hazard in the Great Plains.* Department of Geography, University of Chicago, Research Paper **106** (Chicago).
1969: *Perception of environment.* Commission on College Geography Resource Paper **5** (Washing: Association of American Geographers).

SALTER, L. A. 1943: Farm property and agricultural policy. *Journal of Political Economy* **51**, 13–22.

SALTER, L. A. JNR. 1948: *A critical review of research in land economics.* Minneapolis: University of Minnesota Press.

SAVAGE, L. J. 1951: The theory of statistical decision. *Journal of the American Statistical Association* **46**, 55–67.
1954: *The foundations of statistics.* New York: John Wiley and Sons, Inc.

SCHALLER, W. N., and DEAN, G. W. 1965: *Predicting regional crop production: an application of recursive programming.* United States Department of Agriculture Bulletin **1329** (Washington).

SCHAPPER, H. P., and MAULDON, R. G. 1957: A production function for farms in the wholemilk region of Western Australia. *Economic Record* **33**, 52–9.

SCHICKELE, R. 1937: Tenure problems and research needs in the Middle West. *Journal of Farm Economics* **19**, 112–27.

SCHLAIFER, R. 1970: *Analysis of decisions under uncertainty.* New York: McGraw-Hill.

SCHMITZ, A. 1967: Production function analysis as a guide to policy in low-income farm areas. *Canadian Journal of Agricultural Economics* **15**, 100–11.

SCHNITTKAR, J. A., and HEADY, E. O. 1958: *Application of input–output analysis to a regional model stressing agriculture.* Iowa State A.E.S. Bulletin **454** (Ames).

SCHULTZ, H. 1928: *Statistical laws of demand and supply.* Chicago: University of Chicago Press.
1925: The statistical law of demand as illustrated by the demand for sugar. *Journal of Political Economy* **33**, 577–637.

SCHULTZ, T. W. 1951: A framework for land economics—the long view. In *Journal of Farm Economics* 33, 204–15.

SEWELL, W. R. D., KATES, R. W., and PHILLIPS, L. E. 1968: Human response to weather and climate: geographical contributions. *Geographical Review* 58, 262–80.

SHELLY, M. W., and BRYAN, G. L. (Editors) 1964: *Human judgements and optimality*. New York: John Wiley and Sons, Inc.

SHEPHARD, R. W. 1953: *Cost and production functions*. Princeton: Princeton University Press.

SIMKIN, C. G. F. 1955: Aggregate production functions. *Economic Record* 30, 50–60.

SIMMONS, I. 1966: Ecology and land use. *Transactions of Institute of British Geographers* 38, 59–72.

SIMON, H. A. 1955: A behavioural model of rational choice. *Quarterly Journal of Economics* 69, 99–118.

1956: Rational choice and the structure of the environment. *Psychological Review* 63, 129–38.

1957: *Models of man*. New York: John Wiley and Sons, Inc.

SIMON, H. A., and P. A. 1962: Trial and error search in solving difficult problems: evidence from the game of chess. *Behavioural Science* 7, 425–9.

SINCLAIR, R. 1967: Von Thünen and urban sprawl. *Annals of Association of American Geographers* 57, 72–87.

SMITH, T. L. 1947: *The sociology of rural life*. New York: Harper and Brothers.

SNODGRASS, M. M. 1956: Linear programming—a new approach to interregional competition in dairying. *Journal of Farm Economics* 38, 1501–10.

SPENCE, K. W. (Editor) 1960: *Behavior theory and learning*. Englewood Cliffs: Prentice-Hall.

SPILLMAN, W. J. 1923: Application of the law of diminishing returns to some fertilizer and feed data. *Journal of Farm Economics* 5, 36–52.

1924: Law of the diminishing increment in the fattening of steers and hogs. *Journal of Farm Economics* 6, 179–91.

STARR, M. K. 1963: *Product design and decision theory*. Englewood Cliffs: Prentice-Hall, Inc.

ST. CLAIR, O. 1965: *A key to Ricardo*. New York: Reprints of Economic Classics.

STEVENS, S. S. 1959: Measurement, psychophysics, and utility. In Churchman, C. W., and Ratoosh, P. (Editors), *Measurement: definitions and theories*, New York: John Wiley and Sons, Inc., 18–63.

STEWART, C. L. 1936: Land values as affected by roads and distance. *Journal of Farm Economics* 18, 724–35.

STOYLE, J. 1963: Land utilization as a stochastic process. *Canadian Journal of Agricultural Economics* 11, 52–64.

SURYANARAYANA, K. S. 1958: Resource returns in Telegana farms—a production function study. *Indian Journal of Agricultural Economics* 13, 20–6.

SWANSON, E. R. 1955: Solving minimum-cost feed mix problems. *Journal of Farm Economics* 37, 135–9.

1956: Application of programming analysis to cornbelt farms. *Journal of Farm Economics* 38, 408–19.

TAYLOR, H. C., and ANNE D. 1952: *The story of agricultural economics in the United States*. Iowa City: University of Iowa Press.

THOMAS, D. W. 1955: Sociological aspects of the decision making process. *Journal of Farm Economics* 37, 1115–21.

THROSBY, C. D. 1964: Some dynamic programming models for farm management research. *Journal of Agricultural Economics* 16, 98–110.

TINTNER, G. 1939: The theory and measurement of demand. *Journal of Farm Economics* 21, 606–13.

TOLLEY, H. R., and EZEKIEL, M. J. B. 1924: *Input as related to output in farm organization and cost-of-production studies*. United States Department of Agriculture Bulletin 1277 (Washington).

TRAMEL, T. E. 1957: Alternative methods for using production functions for making recommendations. *Journal of Farm Economics* **39**, 790–4.

TSUCHIYA, K. 1955: Production functions of agriculture in Japan. *Quarterly Journal of Agricultural Economy* **9**.

TUAN, Y. 1967: Attitudes towards environment: themes and approaches. In Lowenthal, D. (Editor), *Environmental perception and behaviour*. Department of Geography, University of Chicago, Research Paper **109** (Chicago), 4–17.
    1968: Discrepencies between environmental attitude and behaviour: examples from Europe and China. *Canadian Geographer* **12**, 176–91.

TUCK, R. H. 1961: *An introduction to the principles of agricultural economics*. London: Longman.

TVERSKY, A. 1967: Additivity, utility and subjective probability. *Journal of Mathematical Psychology* **4**, 175–202.

VERNON, M. D. 1962: *The psychology of perception*. London: University of London Press.

VON BOVENTER, E. 1967: Land values and spatial structure: a comparative presentation of agricultural, urban and tourist location theory. *Journal of Regional Science* **18**, 231.

VON NEUMANN, J., and MORGENSTERN, O. 1944: *Theory of games and economic behaviour*. Princeton: Princeton University Press.

VON THÜNEN, J. H. 1826: *Der Isolierte Staat in Beziehung auf Landwirtschaft und Nationalokonomic*. Rostock.

WAITE, W. C., and TRELOGAN, H. C. 1951: *Agricultural market prices*. New York.

WALD, A. 1950: *Statistical decision functions*. New York: John Wiley and Sons, Inc.

WALKER, O. L., HEADY, E. O., TWEETEN, L. G., and PESEK, J. T. 1960: *Application of game theory models to decisions on farm practices and resource use*. Iowa State A.E.S. Bulletin **488** (Ames).

WANG, Y. 1959: *Resource returns and productivity coefficients for selected crop systems in Tainan area*. Proceedings of Agricultural Economics Seminars, National Taiwan University, Taipei, Taiwan, Formosa, 16–20 September, 1958, 90–8.

WARREN, G. E., and PEARSON, F. A. *Interrelationships of supply and price*. Cornell University A.E.S. Bulletin **466** (Ithaca).

WATANABE, T. 1945: Theory of production function. *Journal of Rural Economy* **21**.

WEHRWEIN, G. S. 1942: The rural urban fringe. *Economic Geography* **18**, 217–28.

WEINSCHENK, G., HENRICHSMEYER, W., and ALDINGER, F. 1969: The theory of spatial equilibrium and optimal location in agriculture: a survey. In New South Wales State Department of Agriculture, *Review of marketing and agricultural economics*, Sydney.

WHITTLESEY, D. 1936: Major agricultural regions of the Earth. *Annals of the Association of American Geographers* **26**, 199–240.

WIECKING, E. H. 1950: Land economics in retrospect and prospect. *Journal of Farm Economics* **32**, 1064–75.

WILCOX, W. W., and LLOYD, O. G. 1932: *The human factor in the management of Indiana farms*. Indiana A.E.S. Bulletin **360** (Indianapolis).

WILDE, D. J. 1964: *Optimum seeking methods*. Englewood Cliffs: Prentice-Hall.

WILKENING, E. A. 1950: A sociopsychological approach to the study of the acceptance of innovations in farming. *Rural Sociology* **15**, 252–64.

WILLEM VAN DEN BAN, ANNE, 1960: Locality group differences in the adoption of new farm practices. *Rural Sociology* **25**, 308–20.

WILSON, R. R., and THOMPSON, R. G. 1967: Demand, supply and price relationships for the dairy sector, post-World War II period. *Journal of Farm Economics* **49**, 360–71.

WOLD, H. 1953: *Demand analysis*. New York: John Wiley and Sons, Inc.

WOLPERT, J. 1964: The decision process in a spatial context. *Annals of Association of American Geographers* **54**, 537–58.

WOOD, A. W. 1965: The implications of interregional competition in Canadian agriculture for government programs aimed at direct support for farm incomes. *Canadian Journal of Agricultural Economics* **13**, 1–19.

WOOD, H. A. 1961: Physical influences on peasant agriculture in northern Haiti. *Canadian Geographer* **5**, 10–18.

WORKING, E. J. 1927: What do 'statistical demand' curves show? *Quarterly Journal of Economics* **41**, 212–35.

WRAGG, S. R., and GODSELL, T. E. 1956: Production functions for dairy farming and their application. *The Farm Economist* **8**, 1–6.

YANKOROSKY, Z. 1968: Agricultural demand and supply projections for 1980. *Canadian Farm Economics* **3**, 11–18.

YARON, D., PLESSNER, Y., and HEADY, E. O. 1965: Competitive equilibrium. *Canadian Journal of Agricultural Economics* **13**, 65–79.

YUWATA, Y. 1953: Production functions for rice and barley. *Quarterly Journal of Agricultural Economy* **7**.

INDEX

187